LAWYERS AND THIEVES

Roy Grutman
and
Bill Thomas

SIMON AND SCHUSTER

New York   London   Toronto   Sydney   Tokyo   Singapore

Simon and Schuster
Simon & Schuster Building
Rockefeller Center
1230 Avenue of the Americas
New York, New York 10020

SIMON AND SCHUSTER and colophon are registered trademarks
of Simon & Schuster Inc.

Designed by Carla Weise/Levavi & Levavi
Manufactured in the United States of America

1 3 5 7 9 10 8 6 4 2

Library of Congress Cataloging in Publication Data

Grutman, Roy.
Lawyers and thieves /Roy Grutman, Bill Thomas.
p.   cm.
1. Law—United States—Anecdotes.   2. Practice of law—United
States—Corrupt practices.   3. Lawyers—United States.   I. Thomas,
Bill, 1943– .   II. Title.
K184.78   1990
349.73′0207—dc20
[347.300207]   90-32163
                                                        CIP

ISBN 0-671-66960-5

CONTENTS

For Bijou: The best and
brightest Jewel of all

OTHER PEOPLE'S MONEY

My mother has sued everyone in our family but me. I used to take that as a compliment, in view of her high principles and low tolerance for losing, but something tells me she must be busy building a case. Like anyone addicted to litigation, her long list of opponents proves that familiarity breeds contempt. Most people who know her have heard from her lawyers, usually for some minor annoyance. Yet where lawyers are concerned, no annoyance is minor, which means my mother never has far to look for legal advice.

Statistics show she has lots of company. Relatives, next-door neighbors and business partners are dragging each other to court in record numbers. From personal slights to company takeovers, lawsuits have become the latest form of unfriendly communication, and lawyers are the messengers who bring the bad news.

If you are like most Americans, you have probably thought more than once about suing someone as a way to get even, or better yet, get rich. Maybe you felt like hiring an attorney to go after your boss for discrimination, or your doctor for malpractice, or your spouse for sheer revenge. If you did more than just think about it, you know there is no shortage of licensed professionals eager to take your case. What you may *not* have noticed is that while you were looking for a lawyer, lawyers were also looking for you.

For attorneys these days, the law is not a search for truth, it's a search for clients, and the tricks used to find and keep them are the most closely guarded secrets in the trade.

Lawyers and Thieves is an insider's view of how those tricks work. Its subject is not the law as it is venerated in speeches, but the law as it is practiced every day by predatory attorneys determined to defeat their adversaries and fleece the people they represent. It examines how lawyers have become cutthroat salesmen and law firms have turned into high-volume retail outlets. You will be shown how the legal game is rigged and won by some of the biggest names in the business. And you will also meet some of the most amazing and amusing crooks who were ever disbarred.

This is not a book about shopping for attorneys; but it is about how much they cost, in money, time and trouble. It is not about forgotten ethics; rather, it's about the constant competition for cases that keeps the courts clogged and makes sure lawyers are always on the prowl.

Of course, not all lawyers are thieves. There are many who would never think of cheating anybody. Still, as you will see, cunning and deception are talents useful in every legal action, and these very same qualities perfectly equip a lawyer to become a thief.

Even St. Yves, a fourteenth-century French lawyer who became the patron saint of attorneys, seemed too good to be true. According to one account, St. Yves, who wore a hair shirt to law school, "always strove if possible to reconcile people who were at enmity, and to induce them to settle their quarrels out of court. In this manner he prevented many of those who came to him from embarking on costly and unnecessary lawsuits."

Then as now, a law degree was regarded by many as a license to steal, and St. Yves, by *not* taking his clients for all they were worth, gained fame far and wide.

If that seems improbable in an era of junk bond deals and buyouts, it was just as hard to believe in the Middle Ages, as this Latin rhyme about the holy litigator indicates:

Sanctus Ivo era Brito	St. Yves was a Breton,
advocatus et non latro	a lawyer not a thief,
res mirando populo	which astonished everybody.

An attorney who treats his clients fairly and uses his skills to save their money instead of fill his own pockets is still rare enough to cause instant disbelief.

The judicial system in this country is an institutionalized form of give-and-take. Too often, though, clients are the ones who give while lawyers take. In 1974, former Supreme Court Chief Justice Warren Burger claimed that "75 to 90 percent of all American trial lawyers are incompetent, dishonest or both." At that rate, justice for all is more like justice for some, and with the population of lawyers in this country growing by 40,000 new ones annually, that "some" keeps getting smaller.

Many people today who hire lawyers come away from the experience shaking their heads in disbelief at how they have been bilked, mistreated and ill served. The premise of *Lawyers and Thieves* is simple: Attorneys are not good samaritans. Some may take pleasure in helping their fellow man, but not many even pretend to do it for free. Enter any courtroom in America and you enter a theater where money talks, where fact and fiction are interchangeable and winning or losing depends on which side hires the best actor.

I know divorce attorneys who are so skilled at instilling panic that all it takes is a phone call to start their victims begging—and paying—for mercy. One New York merger-and-acquisitions expert strikes such fear in the hearts of big corporations that they keep him on retainer just to avoid having to face him in a takeover attempt. If that sounds like a protection racket, it is. The only way to be safe from lawyers is to hire them. Americans spend billions of dollars every year on legal protection, and most consider themselves ahead of the game if their attorneys can temporarily delay an attack by someone else's.

What drives all this legal activity is something lawyers like to call "other people's money," or OPM for short. Whether it's Wall Street or Walla Walla, wherever earning potential exists there is OPM, and wherever you find OPM there are lawyers.

In principle, every U.S. citizen is entitled to an attorney. But people forget that lawyers are paid to perform, and very few come cheap. Claiming the biggest share of the take are the "front loaders," huge law firms that attach themselves to every major business and jack up the consumer price index whenever they submit a bill. Next are the "back loaders," contingent-fee lawyers who roll personal-injury clients into court like dice, hoping the right numbers come up and they hit the jackpot. Under them are the "unloaders," government prosecutors and defense lawyers who sift through crimes and complaints at the low end of the system. At each level, OPM is what separates clients with promise from clients with problems, and the first thing a smart lawyer learns is how to tell the difference.

After graduating from Yale and Columbia Law School, I began my legal career at the venerable New York firm of Wellman & Smyth. Francis L. Wellman had written the greatest American classic on courtroom technique, *The Art of Cross-Examination*, a book that had become my bible, and I was thrilled to be employed by the firm he and Smyth had built. Under their guidance, I imagined, I would be transformed into a brilliant litigator. I soon learned for that to happen I would need exposure to more than a steady stream of corporate bumps and bruises. I would need real life, real people and real problems. If I was to become the kind of lawyer I wanted to be, I would have to quit Wellman & Smyth and go someplace where I could be tested under fire. So I moved my practice to the Bronx.

For a time, I thought I knew something about law, but the graft and corruption I encountered in the Bronx courts—not to mention the con artists who practiced there—were a far cry from the lofty principles I had studied in school. Looking back, almost thirty-five years later, even those experiences seem tame compared to what goes on today.

I have argued before the United States Supreme Court, where each case is treated like a rare antique, and in courts where cases are handled like crates on a loading dock. I have known lawyers who would not think twice about bribing witnesses, and investigators whose specialty is moving the site of a car wreck blocks from where it really took place. I have seen divorce lawyers, with their meters running full tilt, destroy people's lives, and judges who use secrecy orders to keep life-saving information from ever reaching the public.

After thousands of cases, taking on foes from the Mafia to the Mayo Clinic and Henry Kissinger to Jim and Tammy Bakker, I have learned how the system works—and does not work—and in the chapters ahead you will too.

Although it draws heavily on my own experience in the law as a trial attorney, this book is an investigation of the legal profession itself, of lawyers and judges as well as the network of services that keeps them supplied with customers. Its focus is not just on knock-down-drag-out court battles; it also exposes the behind-the-scenes maneuvers that precede them and almost always dictate their outcome: how scare tactics are used to speed up lucrative settlements, how delays are devised to exhaust the opposition's resources, how lawyers set traps to disqualify each other and leave their opponents' clients defenseless.

In less civilized times going to court meant being subjected to an ordeal. The preferred method was grilling the accused party over hot coals. If death resulted, it was considered a sign that justice was done; if not, it meant the authorities had cooked the wrong person. With improvements in the system, defendants were allowed to pay stand-ins, known as champions, to take their place in tests of strength. As proficient in fighting as they were in arguing, champions were the closest thing to medieval life insurance. They were also the first "lawyers," and their talent for manipulating the truth—and emptying purses—is part of every attorney's heritage.

So is putting on a good show. A trial lawyer's work is equal parts business and show business. I learned that lesson very early. The first case I ever tried alone was in a courtroom in Brooklyn. My clients were two brothers whose car had collided with a bus. I arrived for the trial wearing a three-piece suit and a gold watch chain, and while I declaimed on the brothers' behalf, my opponent just smiled at the judge. I was on his turf and it was obvious to everyone but me that I did not blend in.

After the case was settled for much less than it was worth, an elderly Jewish man came over to me and asked, "Counselor, are you, by chancest, Ivy League?"

"Yes," I proudly replied. "Yale."

"Vell, dat don't vork aroun' here," he warned.

The lawyer I should copy, he told me, was a man named Izzy Halpern, a respected courthouse fixture who wore alligator shoes, monogrammed silk shirts and smoked a cigar the size of a baseball bat.

Izzy Halpern, I later discovered, not only dressed like a Brooklyn lawyer, he advertised himself every chance he got. Even his chauffeur, who drove him around town in a Rolls-Royce, had his boss's name sewn in gold letters on the front of his hat. Everything Izzy said and did told people that he was one of them—with more money and better connections.

"Dat's vat vorks," the old man said. And he was right.

I know something now that I failed to understand then—that justice is not democratic, it's local. Laws change from state to state and city to city. The way laws are enforced can change from one neighborhood to the next. A courthouse reflects the values and expectations of the community around it. If a community is honest, its legal system usually is. If a community is corrupt, so are its courts.

Like Izzy Halpern, all good lawyers adapt to their environment, taking on the coloration of their immediate surroundings like chameleons. Their stock-in-trade is their ability to champion anyone or any cause with equal conviction. If I only represented people I agreed with, I would never be in court. I have defended pornographers against preachers and preachers against pornographers, not because I changed my mind between cases, but because clients hire me to win on the basis of certain principles. And, in a courtroom, winning is what counts.

For lawyers, however, winning isn't everything—getting paid is. Regardless of the prospect for victory, if a case comes with a hefty retainer and the promise of dragging on for months, even years, at a profitable pace, almost any attorney will take it.

But selecting the right lawyer requires a complete reversal of most, if not all, of your normal human impulses. Qualities like kindness, patience and sensitivity, the first things you look for in a friend, are the last traits you want in an attorney, particularly one whose main function will be to ward off a ruthless enemy or take your archrival to the cleaners. Good lawyers tend to be just the opposite of good companions. And it helps to remember when you hire one that you are paying for self-preservation, not a warm relationship.

Given the nature of most legal difficulties, and the people who handle them for a living, it is important to make sure that your lawyer's killer instinct works for rather than against you. This can be done by smart shopping to start with, and by keeping a clear head throughout the process.

Attorneys profit from people's problems. Practicing law is a form of venture capitalism, and schemes for generating revenue exist everywhere lawyers do. Not long ago a man strolled into my New York office actually *selling* accident victims. For a price, assuming I bought one of his cases, he would supply me with everything I needed: a client, friendly witnesses and a completely fake medical history.

The offer was illegal, but not that unusual. Lawyers and law firms have always made money by making shady deals, some of epic proportions. At the turn of the century, the Wall Street firm of Sullivan & Cromwell earned a fortune by using political connections to have the Panama Canal moved hundreds of miles to its present location. In today's high-risk, high-yield legal market, business as usual can mean anything from stock manipulation to loan fraud, one of the scams used by the firm of Finley, Kumble, which, just before folding, swindled several banks out of more than $80 million, then used the entire amount to pay its partners' salaries. Even when the money is stolen, lawyers get their cut.

In New York, partners of six law firms earn over $1 million a year. Cravath, Swaine & Moore leads the competition with incomes averaging $1.6 million. Paychecks like that dwarf the mere $370,000 earned by partners at the Washington firm of Arnold & Porter. It just goes to show you how the value of money loses its meaning once lawyers get their hands on it. It also shows how much individuals and corporations are willing to spend for protection from one another— and from one another's lawyers, who generally profit no matter who pays the bills.

Shortly before his death in 1961, Learned Hand, one of the most respected judges of the twentieth century, was asked what had been the greatest satisfaction of his many years on the bench. "As far as I'm concerned," he ruefully replied, "I've spent my life shoveling smoke." With the current caseload, Judge Hand would need a bulldozer to keep pace.

In New York, "spiritual advisers" advertise their services by putting business cards under the windshield wipers of parked cars. I found one staring me in the face recently and realized that lawyers and fortune-tellers have a lot in common.

"Let Sister Tanya make your wishes come true," it read. "Defeat your Enemies and Rivals. If you have any problem concerning the Past, Present and Future, Marriage, Business, Finance and Health, Sister Tanya will help you. If you are in Trouble or Sick, there is no Burden too great for her to lift. She succeeds where others fail."

Attorneys promise their clients exactly the same thing, usually in mumbo jumbo far less specific. But lawyers do not always lift burdens; some of the time they add to them. And unlike Sister Tanya, the voodoo they do is real and can be very expensive.

Everything that exists is a potential source of legal employment.

Think about that for a while and you're thinking like a lawyer. Each year, armies of eager young attorneys are released into the world. Their mission, in theory, is to uphold the rule of law. The secret ambition of most is to find new gray areas, those unexplained gaps between legal precedents where shoveling smoke equals earning potential. Palimony and alimony, malpractice and malfeasance. At one time these were all gray areas. Now each is an income-producing gold mine of its own.

A large part of the credit for this expansion must go to law schools, which train the lawyers who keep the system running smoothly and profitably.

Over a hundred years ago the dean of Harvard's law school, Christopher Columbus Langdell, taught students that by studying judicial opinions of the past they would learn the unchanging principles that determined all court decisions. Know the precedents, Langdell said, and you know the law.

A century later Langdell's case-history theory still forms the basis of every law-school curriculum. Guided by professors, students study arguments and rebuttals until they mumble the last names of litigants in their sleep. In Langdell's day lawyers were logicians who saw the law as a scientific tool for organizing society. Now lawyers are more like magicians who see law as a sleight-of-hand game for rearranging wealth.

Law schools have become incubators for the production of legal entrepreneurs. Not satisfied with running the justice system, attorneys have spread into other fields with predictable results. From New York to Washington to Hollywood, a law degree has become *the* primary qualification for wheeling and dealing in the 1990s. There are lawyer-stockbrokers, lawyer-lobbyists and lawyer–movie producers. Attorneys increase according to the amount of available work, and since they are constantly creating jobs for one another, their population is always growing. A single car wreck can generate enough income to support a dozen legal minds; a billion-dollar corporate merger can employ thousands. At a time when everyone's greatest fear is being wrong—and being sued—no problem is too large or too small not to be litigated, mediated or negotiated by a lawyer.

There is good reason why public opinion polls usually rank lawyers right beside used car salesmen for honesty and integrity. Both are dealmakers, and dealmakers can never be trusted. Just the same, people show no signs of giving up trying to use the law to their advantage.

Some books written by lawyers have suggested ways to beat the system; others have proposed ways to reform it. This one begins with the assumption that neither is possible, that we are stuck with the system we have, and the only way to deal with it is to hire a lawyer who can keep you out of court, or, failing that, can protect you if you're ever required to be there.

The advice I always give anyone considering legal action is to be prepared for the worst. The following pages are filled with reasons why.

CHAPTER 1

THE PICK-UP ARTIST

The Grand Concourse was the Champs-Elysées of the Bronx. The name alone made it sound like something out of a French novel. In the late 1950s, it was the place to see and be seen. Women dressed up just to walk down the sidewalk, and that was just fine with Burton Pugach, who went cruising two or three times a day in his red Lincoln convertible. Pugach's libido operated like radar, and whenever a blip appeared on the screen, he pulled over to the curb and got right to the point: "Hey, precious, hop in."

Nine times out of ten the answer was no. But unfazed by rejection, Pugach would try the same approach over again until he got lucky. Volume, he believed, was the key to success at work and play.

"If I don't get laid at least once a day," he used to say, "I can't function."

In his day, Burton Pugach was the richest personal-injury lawyer in the Bronx. Each morning the tiny reception area of his law office was packed with potential clients: people in neck braces, people on crutches, people with their arms in slings, the lame, the mangled and maimed. By nine-thirty, there were so many cripples waiting to see him that late arrivals had to stand in line outside. And no wonder. Pugach could turn a dislocated knuckle into a six-month paid vacation.

He didn't do it by trying cases. That took too long and involved too many financial risks. It also required skills that Pugach knew he didn't have. What he did was settle cases out of court, and those he couldn't settle he passed along to other law firms for a piece of the take if they won.

Pugach collected lawsuits. He had hundreds at various stages of completion, and every day he added a few more to his inventory. One by one, a secretary with pointed breasts and five-inch heels would lead prospective clients into his office for appraisals. The only furniture was a desk beside a bank of cabinets crammed with the records of human misery, a sofa and two chairs, one for Pugach, the other for victims. Next to the door was an aquarium bathed in red light, and inside was Iggy, a dead iguana that looked like a truck had run over it. Pugach loved all kinds of accident victims, and frequently introduced Iggy to visitors as his brother.

For the entire morning, people spilled out their woes in details Pugach had heard a thousand times before. He decided if a case was worth taking in a minute or two. If it was, his secretary typed up the necessary paperwork. If it was not, he sent it to Kreisell & Powell across the street.

In those days, lawyers divided up the Bronx like Fuller Brush salesmen. Given the constant occurrence of natural and unnatural disasters, there was plenty of work for everybody. Attorneys were technically in competition, but they usually cooperated with one another if it meant bettering their business or defeating their common enemy: the powerful and devious insurance companies.

Under a special nonaggression treaty, the territory was gerrymandered so that Pugach got all the injury and accident victims he could handle. His real aim in life, though, was not picking up clients, which he did better than anybody. It was picking up women. And in both cases his technique was the same. He seduced them with money.

Pugach knew almost nothing about the finer points of law; however, like all shrewd lawyers he did know about greed, which he identified as the chief motivation behind every legal action.

I first met Pugach in 1957. I had litigated some of his hard-to-settle cases when I worked for a negligence firm, and he offered to double my income if I went to work principally for him. He promised to make me rich beyond my wildest dreams. Fifteen thousand . . . twenty thousand dollars a year wasn't out of the question. The offer sounded too good to be true.

Fresh from the firm of Wellman & Smyth, where the pay was meager and partners frowned over the tops of their bifocals at the slightest hint of impropriety, I was completely unprepared for Pugach and his personal-injury conglomerate. Here was a master hustler with half the Bronx in his back pocket. Pugach needed a good trial lawyer. I needed the experience, and in less than an hour we had worked out a deal that allowed me to try cases for him and any one of his friendly competitors willing to pay my fee.

People pretend they are in charge of their fate. Pugach knew better. His view was that an accident is a tragedy only to those who don't see its financial possibilities, and that basic truth had made him a very wealthy man. Where money was concerned Burton Pugach had unlimited vision.

The Bronx was not totally unfamiliar terrain. I was born there. But the world I grew up in was a far cry from the one Pugach and his buddies inhabited. I was the only son in a very successful real estate family, and had all the advantages money could buy—the Horace Mann School for boys, Yale, Columbia Law School, French lessons, piano lessons, trips abroad and winters in Florida.

From the time I was four or five years old, I had wanted to be an attorney. Other kids in the neighborhood looked up to Lefty Gomez and Douglas MacArthur. I did too. But my real heroes were lawyers like Sir Edward Coke, the lord chief justice of England. Reading his closing argument in the treason trial of Sir Walter Raleigh made a lasting impression on me. Who else but an attorney would have the courage to point an accusing finger at the most famous explorer in British history and roar, "Thou art the very spider of Hell"?

That's what lawyers did, I thought. They were soldiers in the war between good and evil. If the law is what makes us civilized, to be an attorney was life's highest calling. What other profession afforded the opportunity to play Hamlet and save the world at the same time? That's why I wanted to be a lawyer, and that's why I studied the dictionary from the time I was seven, to master every lawyer's chief tool and weapon—words.

Little did I realize that Pugach had the same ambition for entirely different reasons. But it didn't take long to find out.

The law firm of Weitz and Pugach was located on 149th Street in the Busher Building, a hangout for private eyes, process servers and other assorted characters who all loved to play cops and robbers. One of the detectives called himself "the Falcon." I would be known as "the Fat Man." If there was something sinister in the air, I was too naive to know what it was, although I did notice that the Falcon was packing a silver revolver. Firepower, he explained, was essential in his line of work.

Bob Janoff, sole proprietor of the Pyramid Detective Agency, also had an office in the Busher Building. Janoff specialized in divorce cases, a staple for most private eyes at the time. This was long before no-fault made spying on unfaithful spouses obsolete, and Janoff's job put him in contact with a lot of very emotional husbands and wives.

"You can't predict human nature," he said the day we met. And to prove it he told me about one of his favorite cases.

A few years earlier, Janoff was hired by a man who suspected his wife of cheating. It didn't take long to confirm his client's suspicions. His wife was sleeping with her boyfriend every other night in a motel. Instead of hitting the roof when he found out, the husband insisted on coming along to see for himself.

The plan was to enter the motel room, take a few pictures for evidence and leave. The husband assured Janoff he could handle it. But when the door opened, that's not what happened. He looked at the other man, looked at his wife, then started smacking her in the head.

"See," she sobbed to her boyfriend. "That's why I'm leaving him. . . . He's a beast."

"Human nature," said Janoff, nonchalantly reaffirming his previous warning. "Who can predict?"

Befitting my new status as Pugach's personal litigator, my office was situated right next to his, but my windowless accommodations looked more like a police interrogation room than the junior-executive suite I was expecting. A naked light bulb hung down from the ceiling, and vats of chemicals for the Verifax, a stone-age photocopy machine, were stored in the corner. The one hopeful sign was a fresh blotter on my Army-surplus desk, courtesy of Pugach's well-built secretary.

As I sat there my first day on the job waiting for Pugach to show up, Herbert Weitz, his partner, stopped by. The two had known one another since Brooklyn Law School. Pugach was a born go-getter.

Weitz, who was always lifting weights, did so little in the way of legal work I assumed Pugach kept him around as a bodyguard.

"Howareya?" Weitz inquired in a heavy Brooklyn accent. "Wadaya-say?"

Before I could tell him, in walked Pugach with a smartly-dressed black man, the victim in a very promising hit-and-run case. Standing in the doorway of the supply closet he had given me for an office, Pugach, who was short and thin with a scraggly Charlie Chan goatee, shook my hand and bragged how lucky he was to have me working for him.

"Best lawyer in New York," Pugach added. "This kid's goin' places."

The black man scrutinized my quarters and with half-closed eyes said, "Well, I can see you ain't exactly the vice president of luxury around here."

"Don't worry," Pugach assured me on the way out. "I'll take care of everything."

Within a week, workmen had installed a used kitchen exhaust fan. By mistake, they put it in backwards. Instead of drawing air into my room, it did just the opposite. The effect was like being inside a vacuum cleaner, which was actually an appropriate sensation, considering the way Weitz and Pugach sucked in clients.

The first business Pugach gave me was a collision case. He represented six people who were injured when the car they were riding in was rear-ended at an intersection. The medical bills and lost wages came to over $6,000, and Pugach was anxious for me to settle as soon as I could. After dickering with the insurance company over the phone, I made an appointment to discuss the particulars in person. The next day I went to the company's office with a briefcase full of supporting evidence. If they wanted to play hardball, the Fat Man was ready.

The claims adjuster flipped through my thickest file, without showing much interest in it or me.

"So, how much do you want?" he said.

I was speechless. Here I was all prepared for a major argument, but before I opened my mouth the other side was ready to settle.

"How much do you want?" the claims adjuster repeated. This time with a little more urgency.

Without waiting for a reply, he pulled the cover off his adding machine and started punching in numbers. When he finished, he jerked the handle and tore off the tally.

"Twelve thousand, two hundred and seventy dollars," he read. The figure was almost twice what our claim asked for. This man must be crazy, I thought, but that was his problem.

"We'll take it."

Fifteen minutes later I left the building with the agreement in my pocket and my ego inflated to full capacity. I was working on a 20 percent fee, which meant that $2,500 of the settlement was mine. I felt like the smartest lawyer in the city, and soon to be one of the richest. Do this nineteen more times, I figured, heading back to the Bronx on the subway, and I could make . . . $50,000 a year!

I walked triumphantly into Pugach's office to report the good news.

"You settled it, didn't you?" he smirked, sounding as if my great accomplishment was business as usual. Which, I soon learned, it was.

The whole case was rigged from beginning to end and I was nothing more than a delivery boy sent to pick up the money. A car wreck had occurred. That much was true. But five of the six people supposedly riding inside when it happened were nowhere near the accident. The medical expenses, missed paychecks, pain and suffering, everything was a "build-up," as they say in the trade, though one of the bogus occupants, a television personality Pugach knew, really had gotten a nose job.

As for the claims adjuster? He was probably the happy recipient of a generous kickback for his part in the plot.

This was the way Pugach operated, and when I returned to my closet cubbyhole to reflect on the events of the day, I realized I might well be working for a crook.

Pugach was not alone. Every attorney in the Bronx seemed to be doing the same thing. The names of people on the take were passed around from lawyer to lawyer like hot tips at the races. Most of the attorneys I dealt with were ambulance chasers—a colorful term that refers to soliciting clients illegally at or near the scene of an accident. They were also paying off gas station mechanics, hospital attendants, undertakers, anybody who could steer business their way. When skid marks had to be shortened, they bribed cops. When medical records needed enhancement, they bribed doctors. Playing by the rules was not a local tradition, and when I protested, Pugach shook his head in disbelief. Where did I think I was, back in law school?

Half of Pugach's clients came by word of mouth. The rest he got via insurance brokers in exchange for payoffs from settlements, which, by the time he and his gang were finished tacking on extras, could grow to immense proportions.

Pugach was a genius at bilking insurance companies. He could easily settle a $500 fender bender and earn half that amount as his fee. But why bother? For him, the original case was just the beginning, a handy excuse for a whole series of fictional problems designed to increase the final bill by thousands of dollars. He sent perfectly healthy clients to see X-ray specialists, physical therapists and psychiatrists, each of whom attached his fee to the claim, then got in line for a cut from the final settlement. After a few months of work, a case originally worth next to nothing could represent a potential killing, with Pugach and his accomplices getting the biggest share.

The front for all this was a company Pugach started called the Merit Medical Association. Posing as a collection agency for doctors' bills, Merit Medical was really a vehicle for inflating doctors' bills to help increase the value of Pugach's accident cases. And that wasn't all it did.

Merit Medical, also conveniently headquartered in the Busher Building, was Pugach's private laboratory for inventing fake injuries. He coached clients on how to describe nonexistent orthopedic problems. He taught them how to limp, hobble and moan. His trainees were so convincing, he used to boast, that Dr. Albert Schweitzer couldn't have told who was actually hurt from who wasn't.

Other attorneys in the vicinity also dabbled in deceit. One friend of Pugach's learned, after considerable experimenting, that when a person holds a fifty-pound weight in his hand, an X-ray of his upper arm shows all the visible symptoms of a separated shoulder. That little discovery made him thousands of dollars before he was caught and disbarred.

Lawyers thrive on deception. It's one of the ways they build up their client's case and make their opponent's disappear. Considering what little material Pugach usually had to work with, he qualified as a consummate trickster.

Yet Pugach never let business interfere with pleasure. Whenever he came across an attractive female client, he always took a personal interest in the case. If there were injuries involved that might require a visit to a real physician, he always administered a preliminary physical examination of his own, complete with a hands-on damage assessment and Polaroid shots for his private album.

"Mr. Pugach cannot be disturbed," his secretary would tell callers. "He's preparing a client for her doctor's exam."

Besides Merit Medical, another thriving Burton Pugach enterprise was a tow-truck fleet that doubled as a client referral service. Drivers were paid a reward for every case they brought in. Pugach also booked seats on the trucks for other lawyers. One of the regulars, a Neanderthal-looking attorney named Marvin Bietterman, routinely went out trying to pick up arm-off and leg-off cases. Some people go fishing in Florida; Bietterman got the same thrill trolling for accident victims from Pugach's tow trucks.

Lawyers weren't the only hustlers in the Bronx. The streets were full of con artists. One of the best was a man known as "the Deacon," who made his living by outsmarting taxicab companies. Then as now, most of the companies were self-insured, meaning they paid their own accident claims, an arrangement that suited the Deacon just fine.

His favorite ploy was throwing himself against the front seat whenever the cab he was in stopped short. The company investigator, with cash in hand, would arrive on the scene, listen to him groan for a while about whiplash, then generally offer to settle right on the spot.

Any time the Deacon wanted more money, he just picked another cab company and got hurt in one of its taxis. He would rip open seats and jab himself with springs; he would cut his hands on loose molding. Unassisted by counsel, the Deacon became the most successful "independent" accident victim in New York.

But nobody had more scams in progress than Pugach. He owned real estate in the Bronx and a Hawaiian nightclub on Long Island. He was heavily invested in a film company too. When I went to work for him, he was making a low-budget love movie in Queens, a vehicle he used for luring would-be starlets into bed. With so much going on, it was easy to see why Pugach only stayed at the office a few hours every morning. But the biggest reason for his absence was not outside business. It was Linda Riss, the girl of his dreams, and the eventual cause of his downfall.

It all started in the fall of 1957. Pugach was cruising down the Grand Concourse when suddenly he caught a glimpse of Linda out of the corner of his eye and slammed on the brakes so hard he nearly went through the windshield. His convertible fishtailed to a stop beside the most beautiful woman he had ever seen in his life. Her flaming red hair matched the color of his car, and her gigantic breasts were pointing right at him.

At the time, Linda was twenty years old and single. Pugach was thirty, which he told her, and married, which he did not.

Pugach's wife, Francine, was a bleached blonde from Brooklyn. He made no attempt to hide the fact that they were not getting along. Francine refused to give him a divorce, and in retaliation, every time she came by the office to collect her monthly allowance, he would throw a handful of money on the floor and tell her to pick it up.

By his own estimate, Pugach spent roughly half of his $100,000-a-year income on women. Linda quickly commanded the biggest share, but he continued to juggle other girlfriends the same way he juggled accident cases. Linda, however, was different. She had class, Pugach declared, maybe more than he anticipated, because when she found out he was married, she stopped sleeping with him.

Pugach kept promising to get divorced. But Linda would not give in until she had proof, which he produced in the form of a doctored separation agreement. Reality, for Pugach, was clearly no obstacle. In legal and personal affairs the only thing that mattered to him was getting what he wanted. He met his match in Linda—she was as stubborn as he was. He had never had a client or a girlfriend who put him through this kind of grief.

Once Linda started asking questions, she soon figured out what Pugach had done and told him they were through.

He could hardly believe it. No one had ever dumped him like that. He still took nude pictures of female clients under the pretext of gathering evidence for their cases. But his heart wasn't in it. He wanted Linda.

Finally, Pugach got a real divorce in Alabama in desperation and called Linda, begging her for one more date. Dinner at the Copacabana. If she didn't want to see him after that, he would go away and never bother her again. The expert at settling cases knew he could persuade her to take him back if he could only get his foot in the door.

At first she agreed. Then, when she changed her mind, Pugach embarked on a reign of terror that was frightening to behold. Linda became his prey. Everywhere she went, he was lurking in the shadows.

One night he cornered her on the street, and she sued him for assault. Pugach countersued her for harassing *him*. The idea was not to take her to court. Acting as his own lawyer, Pugach would have been lost when he got there. He only wanted to see Linda again.

The day for giving her deposition came, and she arrived at the Busher Building with her lawyer. Pugach stared at her for a minute and broke into sobs. "I need you, Linda," he moaned, sounding the same way he did training clients at Merit Medical. "Please don't leave me."

It seemed like one of his typical con jobs, though it was hard to tell for sure. Pugach was a man acutely aware of his own deficiencies, and he had many ways of masking them. This was apparently a crisis beyond his control, and it was starting to affect his business. Cases he should have had first crack at were going to Kreisell & Powell. His Tiki lounge was losing customers. His movie venture was tied up in court over the nonpayment of thousands of dollars in debts. The worst news, however, was yet to come.

Linda announced she was getting engaged.

That afternoon Pugach called a psychiatrist and wanted to know if he could commit himself to a mental hospital.

"Certainly," the psychiatrist said.

"Can I bring girls into my room?" he asked.

Hearing that the rules did not allow female companionship, he dropped the idea of seeking professional help.

A day later I saw Pugach sitting in his office facing the wall. The light above Iggy's aquarium cast everything in a devilish red glow. I was handling his movie case, and in the middle of asking him a question about it, he spun around and glared at me.

"She dies!" he snarled.

I knew exactly who he was talking about, but I never thought he was serious.

The following morning the radio carried an alarming story. A young woman from the Bronx had been blinded by a man who threw acid in her face. Her name was Linda Riss.

"I don't care what you think," Pugach told me when I got to the office. "I didn't do it."

Technically, he was right. He didn't do it. The friend of a client handled the job for $2,000. The day after Linda got engaged, a man came to her house saying he had a delivery, and when she opened the door, he let her have it.

There was no shortage of lawyers eager to take Pugach's case. For days after his arrest, attorneys with whom he did business would show up at his office so Pugach, out of jail on bail, could audition them for the job of defending him. One said he would claim that his constitutional right to free speech had been violated. Another one said he could get the whole case thrown out of court the next day for $1,000.

With his kind of money Pugach could have afforded the best jury fixer in the business. But he wanted me. The reason was fairly obvious. If I were his lawyer, the attorney-client privilege would prevent me from testifying against him for threatening Linda.

In spite of the warm feelings lawyers express about "everybody's right to counsel," accepting a client is ultimately a moral decision. Every malefactor may be entitled to an attorney, but I had decided even before he got into trouble to have nothing more to do with Burton Pugach.

When he realized I was not going to help him, he was very upset. "Your days are numbered," he said. "You're finished, Fat Man."

Shortly afterward, I started to receive threatening phone calls late at night. They ended when the police caught someone who may have been another of Pugach's operatives lurking around my apartment.

Rival attorneys began taking apart his practice as if it were an abandoned car. Kreisell & Powell grabbed the biggest chunk; other firms took what was left. Pugach's tow-truck drivers started sending clients elsewhere, and before long the once-teeming headquarters of Weitz and Pugach was an empty floor in the Busher Building. Even Iggy disappeared.

Like all lawyers who prey on clients, Pugach saw other people as victims, the value-added by-products of crimes and accidents. Linda dropped him, so he simply turned her into an accident case. If he could never have her, he would make sure no one else would want her, or if they did, they would have to accept damaged goods. That is how you deal with somebody who refuses to settle.

Linda was an obsession Pugach never got over, even after she testified against him in court. On the second anniversary of the crime, while his trial was still going on, he tried to kill himself by slitting his wrists.

The papers covered every detail of the story. New Yorkers love trials.

High-density living has made them connoisseurs of what makes people snap, and this was a saga of sex and revenge they could get their teeth into. Pugach became one of those headline villains that entire cities love to hate. The fact that he was a lawyer added another level of evil to his crime and gave everybody one more reason to loathe him. He wasn't just greedy, like most attorneys, he was greedy, rich and life-threatening.

Pugach was found guilty of masterminding the assault and sent to prison for thirty years. The judge did not look kindly on the fact that he was carrying a concealed weapon at the time of his arrest. He was also disbarred because of the felonious nature of his offense.

A year into his sentence, his parents paid me a visit to collect the money I had made for their son on the last of his cases. Pugach, they reported, had become a model convict. He was much in demand as a jailhouse lawyer, and true to form was picking up clients in the slammer as fast as he did in the Bronx. Once again he was doing a volume business, only the payoff this time was in cigarettes.

After several years behind bars, he fell into another old habit. He began writing Linda, pleading with her to forgive him. For a long time she refused, then during the early part of Pugach's second decade in jail she changed her mind.

What he had done to her, he said, was a fantasy, just like one of his insurance settlements.

"You have a feeling that the crime really isn't taking place because you're not doing it," he said. "I was just a person creating something out of his own imagination, telling myself it isn't happening because I can't see it."

That's what he told Linda, and not only did she believe him, she helped get him out of prison. In 1975, she sent a letter to Governor Hugh Carey of New York, a lawyer himself and perhaps sympathetic to the plight of a brother behind bars.

"I'm the victim," Linda wrote. "I pardoned him. I see no reason why you shouldn't too."

When he was released after fourteen years, Pugach said he had two ambitions: to practice law again and to marry Linda. If she rejected his marriage offer, he told the newspapers, he still wanted to take care of her. "But one of the things you don't know" after being locked up for so long, he said, is whether you can "function with a female again."

The court, in its wisdom, declined to restore his lawyer's license. On the other hand, Linda, permanently blind in one eye, did agree to get married. Forgiveness, she explained, had something to do with it, although Pugach's persistence was certainly a factor too.

The Bronx had changed while he was away, but Burton Pugach was exactly the same. Although he eventually got a job as a paralegal, he was still the most complete hustler who ever passed the bar. Every day he practiced law he devised some new scheme for making money. If nothing else, you had to admire his creativity.

I began to appreciate how inventive lawyers were during the ten months I spent with Pugach and his ambulance-chasing cronies. To them, the law was not a collection of precedents for resolving conflicts, it was a tool for producing unearned income. Attorneys cannot control events, but they can direct the results, and Pugach was a master at making misfortune pay off.

The profit motive guarantees that there will always be lawyers like him, maybe not as violence prone, but just as tenacious. When Pugach wanted something, nothing could stop him until he got it. Few attorneys are much different. Those in the Pugach tradition do not even pretend to be. Clients are their hostages, their victims and their sources of revenue. That is as true in a Bronx courthouse as it is in the Supreme Court.

While he was practicing law, Pugach operated like a thief; later, when he got out of jail, he wanted to be a lawyer again. At the time I can recall thinking he had a lot of nerve. Now, after what I have seen of the legal profession, it seems like a perfectly natural transition.

CHAPTER 2

MUDSLINGING

Cass Gilbert always gave his customers what they wanted, and in this case what they had in mind was something along the lines of Mount Olympus. Gilbert, the architect specially chosen for the job, knew everything had to be perfect. Create "a building of dignity and importance suitable for use as the permanent home of the Supreme Court of the United States," said Chief Justice William Howard Taft, who pried $10 million from Congress to pay the bill. Even in 1929, with the Great Depression under way, the portly former president was not a man to cut corners. Neither was Gilbert, known as "the father of skyscrapers" for designing the sixty-story Woolworth Building in New York.

But plans for an eighty-by-ninety-foot courtroom on Capitol Hill, the inner sanctum of his greatest work ever, had hit a serious snag. Gilbert wanted the room decorated with the finest bronze, the richest wood and twenty-four of the best marble columns money could buy. And that was the problem.

The marble he was talking about, a rare cream-colored variety, was only available in Siena, Italy. In the eyes of some members of Congress, using Italian marble in the U.S. Supreme Court building would be un-American. This development had Gilbert worried. If his opponents prevailed, he would be forced to use domestic marble for the Court chamber, and the whole project would be ruined. Already famous for designing *three* state capitols, in Minnesota, Arkansas and West Virginia—never once compromising on aesthetics—he was not about to let amateurs order his building materials for something this big. For months he held his ground, backed up by the nine justices, who saw the entire dispute as a landlord-tenant case. Since 1819, they had been holding court in the U.S. Capitol basement, and as far as they were concerned, it was time to break the lease and move to a better location. Finally the senators gave in. Art triumphed over politics. However, just to be sure there were no more delays, Gilbert decided to make a personal trip to Italy.

In Rome, Italian dictator Benito Mussolini, a lover of buildings himself, welcomed him with open arms. Gilbert wrote to a friend that he showed Il Duce his designs for the Court and recounted all the difficulties he had had with the senators.

"*Italian* senators?" Mussolini demanded.

"No," Gilbert replied, "American."

After being assured that all problems had been resolved, Mussolini "put his hands together with a gesture of applause and said, '*Italian* marble! I'm very much pleased. It is an honor to Italy to have it selected for that purpose.' "

"We shook hands," wrote Gilbert, "and I walked rapidly to the door . . . turned around and [we gave] the Roman salute. . . . I shall always think of him standing there . . . with his hand up in that most impressive of gestures. . . . May his regime long endure."

Gilbert got his marble.

At the exit end of a metal detector, Gilbert's Supreme Court room today looks like a maximum-security mausoleum. There are heavy oak doors, Grecian urns and marble walls topped with friezes depicting the great lawgivers of old: Hammurabi, Moses, Confucius and Mohammed, all wearing the same menacing state-trooper scowls. Behind the bench where the justices sit, and tastefully hidden from public view by a twenty-five-foot red velvet curtain, is the most important closet in America. Inside, there's a mahogany filing cabinet, and inside that . . .

"Well, you name it," said Frank Lorson, chief deputy clerk of the Court, as he opened the door to the evidence room. "Dildos, whips, dirty movies—everything that goes with a case ends up in here."

He forgot the last time the nine justices analyzed the contents of a porno film, but when the next one comes in, he will be the one who runs the projector.

Besides keeping track of items received, the impeccably tailored Lorson also keeps track of incoming lawyers. The Court, when it's in session, convenes promptly at 10 A.M., Monday through Wednesday, and Lorson insists that attorneys of record report to his desk a full hour beforehand so he can fill them in on three basic rules: (1) Be on time when your case is called, (2) Refrain from telling jokes, and (3) Stop talking when your time is up.

Over 150 years ago, Daniel Webster spent six days arguing a single case before the Court, but that was when America only had a few million people—not a half-million lawyers. Today, thirty minutes is the limit, and when a little red light on the attorney's table starts blinking, your turn is over.

A hearing in the Supreme Court is not like an ordinary trial where lawyers ask questions and the judge listens. Here, the attorney is a solicitor in the door-to-door sense of the word, asking the Court to buy his version of the law. But there's a catch. The justices, sitting in their state-of-the-art black leather swivel chairs, can take his argument anywhere they feel inclined. The format is designed to cut through the usual sales pitch to get at the precedents, and whenever a justice thinks a precedent is being mistreated, he springs into action.

With precious minutes ticking off the clock, one of the justices may grab the steering wheel of a case that took years to prepare and drive it down some highway the lawyer never knew existed. As more justices get into the act, the whole courtroom can take off on a joy ride through Law Land, with right turns, left turns and landmarks flying by in every direction. Then suddenly the red light goes on. Your thirty minutes are up and everything comes to a screeching halt. At which point, the nine justices rock back in their La-Z-Boys and start flashing looks that say, "Step out of the *vee*-hicle, please, sir."

Unlike lower-court judges, Supreme Court justices are not particularly interested in deciding who wins in A v. B. Instead, A v. B is an instrument for affirming a principle of law. Any dispute that makes it this far, no matter how insignificant or outrageous its facts may seem, contains some essential legal issue that the justices feel demands their attention. The act of a circus performer can raise an important question of constitutional law, or the removal of a prisoner's art supplies might cast in doubt a complicated criminal procedure. The nine justices pick and choose the cases they want to hear and announce their opinions in written form. That people actually obey them is generally regarded as one of the miracles of self-government.

Just for a case to reach the Supreme Court means making it through a complicated legal obstacle course. Over 5,000 petitions for hearings are received every year, and only slightly more than a hundred are accepted. Most lawyers never get there. I have appeared before the justices on two occasions, both times in cases involving Larry Flynt.

The first item of business on the Court's calendar for December 2, 1987, was *Falwell v. Flynt*. The opposing parties—Flynt, the publisher of *Hustler* magazine, and the Reverend Jerry Falwell, founder of the Moral Majority and host of "The Old-Time Gospel Hour"—were both expected to attend. Falwell was my client. But it was Flynt's name that started Lorson's eyes rolling backwards. The last time he had been seen, in 1983, Flynt, then a Republican candidate for the presidency, was charged with contempt and carted out of the chamber in his gold-plated wheelchair yelling "Fuck this Court!" Chief justice Warren Burger, who used to lecture women attorneys for wearing pants suits in his presence, was incensed. So was Sandra Day O'Connor, the lone female justice, who was indirectly responsible for Flynt's history-making tantrum.

As part of a promotional stunt in the early 1980s, O'Connor, the other eight justices and all 535 members of Congress each month received a complimentary copy of *Hustler* directly from Flynt. O'Connor always trashed it along with the rest of her junk mail, but the idea that a skin magazine was being sent to her office infuriated her. She wrote *Hustler* headquarters in Los Angeles asking to have her name removed from the mailing list, and got back a poison-pen letter from Flynt himself calling her every name in the book. When word of this reached Lea Brilmayer, a Yale Law School professor who had written a brief on behalf of *Hustler* in another case then before the Court, she resigned from the case immediately.

Flynt was not happy. Argument had been scheduled for the following month and he needed Brilmayer's help. That case grew out of a lawsuit against him by my client at the time, *Penthouse* vice president Kathy Keeton. Several years earlier a cartoon had appeared in *Hustler* implying that *Penthouse* publisher Bob Guccione—Flynt's arch-enemy—had given Keeton a venereal disease. The question was jurisdictional, whether Keeton could sue the magazine in New Hampshire, the state with the longest statute of limitations for libel. Left defenseless, Flynt asked permission to represent himself. Having been to the Supreme Court more times than most attorneys, it's easy to see why he felt qualified. But the answer, in strict accordance with the Court's rules, was no, and a lawyer was assigned.

On the day of the hearing, with an angelic smile on his apple-shaped face and a King James Bible in his lap, Flynt was wheeled into the back of the Court, and when his case was called, the tirade began.

"You shoulda seen Sandra Day O'Connor's face," Flynt told a reporter the next day, reciting his version of what took place. "I didn't wanna be sexist, you know. I started to jus' call 'em eight assholes an' one cunt, but I thought that would be a sexist remark, so I jus' said, 'You goddam fuckin' assholes, all nine of you, and you token cunt, you.' And she went, 'Who, me?' I said, 'Yeah you, you bitch. All of you are denyin' me my constitutional right to counsel of my choice, namely myself, an' when I get to 1600 Pennsylvania Avenue, I'm sendin' the FBI over to lock every one of you motherfuckers up. I'm gonna charge you with obstructin' justice.' "

"Remove that man! . . . Take him into custody!" roared Burger from under a flying mane of silver hair. In a building that still has SILENCE signs in the hallways, the episode has not been forgotten. Flynt, as they say in the legal profession, is known to the Court.

The Falwell case had to do with a fake Campari liqueur ad in a 1983 issue of *Hustler* that portrayed Falwell as a drunk who had sex with his mother. (The only actual ads *Hustler* carries are for Flynt's house-brand marital aids.) The full-page spread looked exactly like the real thing, with the exception of a minuscule disclaimer at the bottom that said, "Ad parody—not to be taken seriously." When Falwell saw it, he hit the roof.

The headline read: JERRY FALWELL TALKS ABOUT HIS FIRST TIME.

Falwell: My first time was in an outhouse outside Lynchburg, Virginia.
Interviewer: Wasn't it a little cramped?
Falwell: Not after I kicked the goat out.
Interviewer: I see, you must tell me about it.
Falwell: I never really expected to make it with Mom, but then after

she showed all the other guys in town such a good time, I figured, "What the hell!"

Interviewer: But your Mom? Isn't that a little odd?

Falwell: I don't think so. Looks don't mean that much in a woman.

Interviewer: Go on.

Falwell: Well, we were drunk off our God-fearing asses on Campari . . . and Mom looked better than a Baptist whore with a $100 donation.

Interviewer: Campari in the crapper with Mom . . . how interesting. Well how was it?

Falwell: The Campari was great, but Mom passed out. . . .

Inteviewer: Did you ever try it again?

Falwell: Sure . . . lots of times. But not in the outhouse. Between Mom and the shit, the flies were too much to bear.

Interviewer: We meant the Campari.

Falwell: Oh, yeah. I always get sloshed before I go out to the pulpit. You don't think I could lay down all that bullshit sober, do you?

Larry Flynt is fond of portraying people he dislikes this way, and Falwell is one of his favorite targets. Despite Flynt's admission that he wanted to "assassinate" Falwell's character, the lower courts had ruled that no libel had been committed; twice, though, Flynt was ordered to pay $200,000 in damages for inflicting emotional distress. The Supreme Court was being asked to make the payment stick. Needless to say, reporters and lawyers were watching the case with interest. Not only was a libel fight between a TV evangelist and a porno king great entertainment, but a victory by Falwell could mean a whole new interpretation of free speech, and along with it a mother lode of business for attorneys.

For centuries under common law, insulting remarks did not have to be proven false to be libelous; any personal attack might qualify. All the victim had to do to make a case was (1) to show that a derogatory statement had been made, and (2) to claim that it was untrue. Today, with damage claims approaching the billion-dollar level, libel suits can be lucrative business, but winning, under the law developed by the Supreme Court, especially in cases involving public figures, means proving falsity and a complicated series of motives, known as actual malice or reckless disregard for the truth.

In 1964, the Supreme Court ruled in *New York Times v. Sullivan* that "some degree" of exaggeration and misrepresentation by the media had to be tolerated in order to preserve rights guaranteed by the First Amendment. Since then, the license to exaggerate and misrepresent has been expanded to the point where television, magazines and newspapers now have almost no limits on what they can say. Falwell believed this sinfulness had to be stopped. Every day, he preached, the same TV sets that show "The Old-Time Gospel Hour" also receive programs that distort family values and extol permissive attitudes toward sex and immorality. Of course, Falwell was not alone in going after those responsible. Movie stars, businessmen and politicians were all suing the media for libel, suing mammoths like CBS and *Time* magazine as well as mutants like Flynt.

In every defamation case, the question being put to the courts was as basic to civilized society as a stop sign: Can people trust the institutions that inform them? If Larry Flynt could lie about someone having sex with his mother and get away with it, who would be required to tell the truth?

Then there was another question that any case against *Hustler* automatically raised: Was there an attorney anywhere in America who could put a stop to Flynt?

I had met Jerry Falwell for the first time on a witness stand in 1981, when I was *Penthouse*'s lawyer and he was trying to halt publication of an issue of the magazine that contained an interview he had given to two freelance writers, who, he claimed, had tricked him. If he had known his conversation would end up sandwiched between nude "pictorials," Falwell testified, he would never have agreed to talk. *Penthouse* was "exploiting me financially and hurting me spiritually," he said.

During cross-examination, I made a point of calling him Reverend "Foul-well." The hearing was in Lynchburg, where Falwell had the home-court advantage, so my game plan was to make him look as silly as possible.

"Ye shall know the truth," I said, mimicking his TV delivery, which I had been practicing for days.

"But God will get the last laugh," he shot back, mimicking me.

The exchange, complete with appropriate Bible references, lasted forty-five minutes before the judge threw the case out of court. That was not surprising, but what happened next *was.* I was asked to hold a press conference on the courthouse steps, after which Falwell came over and congratulated me, saying if he ever needed a good lawyer he would be in touch.

Two years later I was talking to Falwell again.

"Help me get Flynt," he said.

Like anyone wise in the ways of the courts, Falwell is a realist when it comes to choosing a lawyer. "It wouldn't bother me a bit to use Bob Guccione's doctor," he explained. "Why shouldn't I use his attorney?"

Clearly he understood the most essential truth about the legal profession. A lawyer is a utensil, like a knife or fork. It makes no difference who ate with it last, only that it was sufficiently sanitized between meals.

I knew this was a man I could work with.

I also knew this was a job I would enjoy. Larry Flynt has always excited my hunting instinct because there has never been anyone in the history of libel law as tricky or elusive. I was hired for the chase by Guccione (when Flynt called him a homosexual), by sex novelist Jackie Collins (when he called her a hooker), and now it was Falwell on the line, whetting my appetite for another try. I have faced Flynt a total of five times in court. I have always won with a jury, but for some strange reason appellate courts have come to his rescue, and have left me with only one big victory. What I wanted to do was finish him off once and for all.

The Falwell–Flynt case was a classic matchup of good against evil, right against wrong. There was also an element of danger involved. Rumors had been circulating for years that Flynt had offered a hit man $1 million to murder Guccione. If that was true, it was not hard to imagine that he entertained the same thoughts about other people he hated, one of whom was surely me. Indeed, he honored me as only he can by designating me "Asshole of the Month" in his magazine. This case had everything. How could I say no?

Jerry Falwell and Larry Flynt were perfectly matched opponents: Both grew up in the Appalachian South, both had huge businesses— Flynt's starting with a string of nude go-go bars; Falwell's when he turned an abandoned soft-drink plant into a church—and both were determined to win.

Similar to most people who end up in court, Falwell and Flynt were also well acquainted. Falwell uses Flynt's attacks on him to raise money, and Flynt uses his regular denunciations of Falwell to advertise *Hustler*. One sells sin, the other salvation, and each claims 25 million satisfied customers.

For a while at least, the two men were alike on the spiritual level too. Each had experienced a life-changing religious awakening: Falwell's coming after two years in college, and Flynt's in 1977 as he flew over Ohio in his pink Lear jet accompanied by the late faith healer Ruth Carter Stapleton, former president Jimmy Carter's sister.

The feeling, Flynt said in an interview shortly afterward, began as a warm tingling sensation. Then he saw two men with him in the plane, one named Paul, the other, he assumed, Jesus. Before his conversion, Flynt was having sex with as many as six different women a day, each interviewed and personally approved by his wife, Althea. If, as Jerry Falwell teaches, a wife's duty is to serve her husband, few women have taken the idea as far as Althea, who died, reportedly of AIDS, in 1987.

"Larry was so promiscuous it was incredible," she once said. "But I never found sex anything to be jealous over."

After Flynt saw Christ, he and Althea became celibate.

"I promised to give up my wife for Him," Flynt remembered, describing his midair vision. "I promised to see myself castrated, to look down and see myself with no sex organs and . . . say, 'Yes, God, it's okay, if it's your will, that's fine.' I spoke in tongues. There were animals eating at my neck, like baboons and monkeys, gnawing at me. He told me my calling was to bring peace to earth. And He told me there had been a distortion of His Word, which confirmed my thing on religion: there are a lot of religions but only one God."

Was Flynt's born-again experience a self-serving prophecy? Writer Paul Krassner, then the editor of *Hustler*, never thought it was anything else. Krassner prepared for his first meeting with Flynt, he said, by fasting for four days. "I wanted to be clearheaded so I could see whether Larry was a con artist or not. And he *was*—a good one. After I told him that, he said, 'I'm the best!' "

Flynt's spiritual rebirth, aside from its mystical implications, presented him with a serious business dilemma. As a boy growing up in poverty-stricken Magoffin County, Kentucky, a place so poor, say locals, that the biggest industry is jury duty, Flynt dreamed of becoming either a gynecologist or an evangelist. All of a sudden, it seemed, he had the opportunity to combine elements of both professions. In the wake of Flynt's religious experience, subscribers anxiously waited to see how his newfound Christianity would affect the contents of his magazine. He was quick to assure them they had nothing to worry about.

"I hope my finding God won't change the relationship I have with you, the reader," he wrote in his first post-conversion editorial. "I won't cram [religion] down your throat. . . . You will still see a tremendous amount of explicit sex in *Hustler*, no more explicit than what can be found in the Bible. And we will be sure to provide the references in our stories and picture features."

Four elaborately staged photographs illustrating nude scenes from the Scriptures were taken. Typical of Flynt, he predicted that the pictures would produce the greatest religious test case in history, but none of the pictures ever appeared in the magazine. After a 1978 assassination attempt during an obscenity trial in Georgia left him a paraplegic, Flynt prayed to God to heal him. When doctors determined he would never walk again, he said, "I stopped being spiritual."

That was the end of God's influence on Larry Flynt.

Flynt's new religion became the Constitution. As he explained five years after the shooting, "I've done more than anybody in modern history to protect the First Amendment—I've given up my manhood."

He elaborated in a *Hustler* editorial: "Nothing is more sacred to me [than freedom of speech] . . . not the poverty that gnaws at the land, the corruption of our political system, the insanity of the military who want to blow us all to hell, the phoniness of the venerable institutions or the churches. . . . *Hustler* exposed it all, irreverently satirizing everything. So *Hustler* was busted. And I was the one who was hauled into court. I am convinced my crime was that I appealed to the common man."

Despite his attempts to sound serious, Flynt is the nation's court jester. Courtrooms are his stage, and he appears every chance he gets. To protest a gag order, he once showed up before a Los Angeles judge wearing an American flag as a diaper. When he ran for president, he threatened to sue any station refusing to run his X-rated TV commercials. According to an attorney who used to represent him, "An awful lot of people would like to be able to do what Larry's doing—but they can't afford to pay the lawyer."

"I never believed in Flynt's conversion for one minute," said Jerry Falwell, who has personally officiated at thousands. From the day he began his first church, Falwell has been an advocate of "saturation evangelism," which he defines as "preaching the gospel to every available person at every available time by every available means." If religion is a business, Falwell is a one-man sales force.

"There are 227 million prospects in the U.S. to be reached with the message of Christ," he said. "I don't think we've even touched the hem of the garment."

When Falwell first started preaching, he got a big map of Lynchburg and drew six concentric circles around the proposed site of his church in the middle of the innermost circle, which he called "Judea." From there, he worked his way house-to-house until he personally delivered the same message to each resident in each circle: "I'm Jerry Falwell. I just came by to say hello and invite you to our services."

Thirty years later, he said the same thing to teary-eyed PTL members when he took over the bankrupt video ministry from Jim and Tammy Bakker. In response, they sent him millions of dollars. The man has economic charisma.

"The difference between me and other TV evangelists," he once joked, "is that they say to people, 'If you want to see God, put your hands on the television.' I tell 'em, 'If you really want to see God, put your hands in the television.'"

To raise funds to fight Flynt in court, Falwell mailed copies of the Campari ad to millions of potential contributors. "Will you help me defend my family and myself against the smears and slander of this major pornographic magazine—will you send a gift of $50, $25, or even $15 so that we may take up this important legal battle?" Falwell wrote. Along with the letter, he included a picture of him with his "dear sainted mother" who died "and went to heaven." Three separate pleas netted over $800,000.

He would never have sued *Hustler* if Flynt had only called him a drunkard, said Falwell, whose father, a hard-drinking bootlegger, died of cirrhosis of the liver. "But when he suggested my mother was a whore, a prostitute, I cannot imagine any red-blooded male in the world not being incensed by that."

Which was precisely the effect Larry Flynt intended.

The trial was held in December 1984, in Roanoke, Virginia, with Judge James Turk presiding. Turk was the judge who had tossed Falwell's suit against *Penthouse* out of court three years earlier. This time, Falwell was asking for $45 million. Winning would depend on proving the *Hustler* ad was purposefully malicious, and showing that would require an in-depth understanding of how Larry Flynt's mind worked.

Seven months before the trial, I took a videotaped deposition from Flynt, then serving time in a North Carolina federal prison for shouting obscenities in court. Wearing blue pajamas and a pair of government-issue glasses that looked like dirty windows, Flynt was rolled into an interview room strapped to a hospital bed. He said that the ad was not a parody at all, and that he had pictures and sworn affidavits to prove that Falwell really had committed incest with his mother.

"I have an affidavit signed by three different people from Lynchburg, Virginia . . . stating, okay, that purely and simply, that they had witnessed this act by Mr. Falwell," insisted Flynt.

He claimed that he got this information in 1978, but waited until 1983 to publish it because "I wanted to run for president."

That was followed by this exchange between Flynt and me:

Question: "Do you recognize that having published what you did in this ad, you were attempting to convey to people who read it that Reverend Falwell was just as you characterized him, a liar?"

Flynt: "Yeah. He's a liar."

Question: "How about a hypocrite?"

Flynt: "Yeah."

Question: "That's what you wanted to convey."

Flynt: "Yeah."

Question: "And did it occur to you that if that wasn't true, you were attacking a man in his profession?"

Flynt: "Yes."

Question: "Did you appreciate, at the time, that . . . for Reverend Falwell to function in his livelihood . . . he has to have an integrity that people believe in? Did you not appreciate that?"

Flynt: "Yeah."

Question: "And wasn't it one of your objectives to destroy that integrity, or harm it, if you could?"

Flynt: "To assassinate it."

This sounded to me like all the malice needed to prove libel. But Flynt was not finished. As he spoke, anger raging within him, he squeezed his face into a fist and his eyes narrowed to little slits behind his glasses.

Question: "Do you realize, Mr. Flynt, that you can injure people by inflicting mental suffering and disturbance on them that will cause pain that is as great or greater than physical suffering?"

Flynt: "You're goddam fucking right. And you're all gonna be on your knees before we finish."

The first thing Flynt did was hire Judge Turk's former clerk, Arthur Strickland, to be one of his lawyers. Working alone, Flynt's usual attorney, Alan Isaacman from Beverly Hills, would have been a distinct liability in Appalachian Virginia. Isaacman's wardrobe is 80 percent sharkskin; Strickland was "home-cookin'," as Southern lawyers say. Juries tend to respond more favorably to attorneys who look and sound the way they do.

Strickland got the case shifted from Lynchburg to Roanoke, fifty miles away, where Falwell had fewer supporters. Then Isaacman brought in his California academic experts on comedy and parody to testify that the Campari ad put Flynt in the same class with Chaucer, Shakespeare and Swift. The defense had assembled a neat package. But I had Flynt on videotape.

Isaacman started by declaring that all of Flynt's prison statements were the result of mental problems stemming from the 1978 assassination attempt. His client, he said, was deeply depressed and being treated with drugs. Faking insanity is one of Flynt's favorite tricks to play on a jury. However, this time it worked on the judge, who at first refused to let the jurors even see Flynt's deposition, although he later allowed an edited version to be shown.

Flynt's attorneys called the ad a satirical treatment of a public figure, and therefore protected by the First Amendment. Because Falwell had injected himself into the national debate on sex and morals, he was fair game for *Hustler*. I contended that Flynt had created an entirely new species of mudslinging so outrageous that nobody should have to put up with it.

Wheeling himself into court under his own power, Flynt testified that "[*Hustler*] readers know [the ad] was not intended to defame Reverend Falwell or any member of his family, because no one could take it seriously."

The pictures and affidavits Flynt had sworn he possessed apparently no longer existed. The point of the ad had been to instruct, not to harm. Now he was Larry Flynt the crusader, not Larry Flynt the exterminator. Upsetting Falwell was the farthest thing from his mind, Flynt said. The Hillbilly Houdini was at it again.

"At times," testified psychiatrist Dr. Seymour Halleck, "[Flynt] sees himself as a great human being fighting for noble causes and failing to achieve greatness only because of the malice of others. At other times he sees himself as a 'hustler' or a 'prankster' who is not really serious about anything. . . . The most basic psychological characteristic of Mr. Flynt is that he thrives on attention and being in the limelight. The world of plots and counterplots he has created with himself as the central figure is a world in which he cannot be ignored."

The fact the jury could not ignore was that Flynt had gone after Falwell with the intention of hurting him. Flynt was not held liable for defamation, but he was found to have deliberately inflicted emotional distress, and for that he was ordered to pay $200,000 damages.

No jury had ever reached such a verdict, a fact that almost guaranteed an appeal. In 1985, the Fourth Circuit Court of Appeals upheld the decision, and two years later the case went to the Supreme Court. In both instances it carried with it an unmistakable FYI: People who communicate information are responsible for its effect. How far that responsibility extends was the issue to be decided, and Larry Flynt, the most irresponsible communicator in America, would be the test.

In no time the media defense forces jumped into action. "Goodbye Saturday Night Live," wrote newspaper columnist Ellen Goodman. "Under the First Amendment you're allowed to inflict emotional damage," said Harvard law professor Alan Dershowitz. If Flynt lost, the opinion makers predicted, there would be no more editorial cartoons, no stand-up comedy. Larry Flynt had to be protected in order to preserve the wholesome chuckle everyone got from "Doonesbury." But the jury verdict recognized that Flynt was different from other sources of satire. This wasn't just a guy yelling "Fire!" in a crowded theater—he was more like the pyromaniac who started it.

• • •

One at a time, spectators passed through the metal detector, and as they came out the other end, Supreme Court guards ushered them to their seats. Flynt, shaped like an overstuffed bag of laundry, was wheeled to a niche in the press gallery by his attendants. Falwell, dressed in a made-for-TV blue suit and wearing a red-white-and-blue tie, arrived with his family and sat on the right side of the visitors' section.

Whenever I am due to appear in court, especially the Supreme Court, I like to be the first one there to check the feel of the room and look for anything that might give me an advantage when the action starts. Once I was arguing a case against Con Edison and found a book left on the opposing counsel's table from the day before. I flipped through it, came across evidence that the other side had been concealing, and as a result won the case for my client. Though discoveries like *that* are rare, I have learned that it pays to show up early.

After a walk around the courtroom, I headed for the lawyers' lounge. Inside, young attorneys were going over their notes, while a few old pros, sporting the optional uniform of cutaway coat and striped pants, worked the room like a law school reunion. If the Supreme Court is the ultimate club, the lawyers' lounge is the ultimate clubhouse. The country's greatest legal minds have limbered up there, which made the arrival of Alan Isaacman, Flynt's ferret-faced attorney, all the more noticeable.

A lawyer *should* represent his client, but Isaacman had sunk to the level of his. In order to show that Flynt was responsible for the Campari ad, I needed evidence that he approved it. Flynt's angry brother-in-law volunteered to get it. When he delivered the document—a memo signed by Flynt okaying the ad—and I confronted Flynt with it, Isaacman, as a defensive strategy, went to the U.S. attorney and tried to have me indicted for bribing Flynt's brother-in-law.

"*Hustler* has every right to say that somebody who's out there campaigning against us, saying don't read our magazine and we're poison on the minds of America and don't engage in sex outside wedlock, and don't drink alcohol—*Hustler* has every right to say that man is full of B.S."

That was Isaacman's opening salvo to the justices.

The First Amendment, he went on, gives *Hustler* the right to say,

"Let's deflate this stuffed shirt. Let's bring him down to our level, or at least to the level where he'll listen to what we have to say."

The courtroom broke into laughter, and all at once the judges rocked forward in their La-Z-Boys.

"I was told not to joke in the Supreme Court," Isaacman apologized. "I really didn't mean to do that."

None of the justices was smiling. In fact, they seemed a little concerned that the case was causing so much merriment. The Supreme Court is a temple of reason, and the justices pride themselves on not being swayed by public sentiment in any form. When the late justice William O. Douglas used to hike along the C&O Canal in Georgetown happily chatting with people he met, he was considered an eccentric nut. Nowadays, most justices are seldom seen outside of court. Tended by a battery of clerks and assistants, they have a schedule so tight that once when oral arguments ran five minutes past noon, making all nine of them late for lunch, Chief Justice William Rehnquist promised his colleagues it would never happen again. Connected to the rest of the country by the Word of Law, Supreme Court justices are America's answer to Tibetan monks; instead of praying, they make decisions, and by their collective wisdom lead the nation along the path of righteousness.

At least that's the concept. In reality, the Supreme Court functions more like nine competing courts, with each justice literally a law unto himself. They may not admit to being swayed by the public, but all nine got their jobs by being smart politicians, and it's politics that often leads to their most entertaining differences of opinion.

After the Court rendered a split decision in the 1989 *Webster* abortion case, conservative justice Antonin Scalia told Sandra Day O'Connor that her opinion was "irrational" and "cannot be taken seriously." Following a controversial case on flag burning that same year, Rehnquist dismissed an opinion by liberal justice William Brennan as "a regrettably patronizing civics lesson."

Fifty years ago, Justice Oliver Wendell Holmes called the Supreme Court "nine scorpions in a bottle." The description still applies, but the bottle is usually sitting on a shelf too high for most people to see inside. The Flynt–Falwell case opened the lid and gave everyone a good look.

When the laughter subsided, Justice Scalia, the most recent addition to the Court at the time, wanted to know if the same treatment *Hustler* had given Falwell might be used on other public figures. A few years before, the magazine had depicted the nine justices having an orgy, and the present case appeared to suggest that Flynt had similar projects in mind.

"The rule you give us says that if you stand for public office, or become a public figure in any way, you cannot protect yourself, or indeed your mother, against a parody of you committing incest with [her] in an outhouse," Scalia added. "Now is that a value that ought to be protected? . . . Would George Washington have stood for public office if that was the consequence?"

Then Isaacman reminded the Court that Washington himself was the subject of many cartoons, some even portraying him as an ass.

"I could handle that," Scalia said. "I think George could handle that. But that's a far cry from committing incest with your mother."

Reporters in their mahogany bullpen let out another chorus of chuckles. Despite the Court's official injunction against humor, this case had already produced a record number of laughs.

"Deliberate and malicious character assassination is not protected by the First Amendment," I told the justices when it was my turn to argue. "And deliberate and malicious character assassination was proven in this case."

As the chairs started rocking again, I could see a big cushion on Rehnquist's and was glad this was the first argument of the day. His mind would be on the case and not his back problem.

"But what if a cartoonist . . . says I'm going to show this person . . . as a windbag, a pompous turkey?" inquired the chief justice, a Western conservative whose sideburns hang down in front of his ears like loose stirrups. "He knows perfectly well that's going to create emotional distress."

What then?

Could someone like Gary Hart be able to make a similar claim of emotional distress when the press reported his sexual peccadillos? asked O'Connor.

"No," I said, "if what was reported by the newspapers was the truth."

A few of the justices nodded.

No one knows how much weight oral arguments carry when the Court gets down to making decisions. So just to drive my point home, I closed by calling Larry Flynt a blight on the Constitution. Nothing in his disgusting treatment of my client, I said, qualified as protected speech. And as Justice Byron White kissed his fingertips, the red light went on.

Leaving the Court and descending into a sea of waiting reporters, I had none of the doubts lawyers usually experience when a jury starts its deliberations. After all, these were the best jurists in America. They would not be distracted by thoughts of picking up the kids after school, or the four o'clock Dow Jones figures. I had just been to the mountaintop. The highest court in the land would study the facts in the case and make its decision. Flynt and Falwell, *Hustler* and the Moral Majority, not even Falwell's dear departed mother made any difference now. What mattered, I thought, were the principles at stake.

I firmly believe in free speech and the First Amendment and have defended these rights many times. But I also know there have to be limits on how far the press can go in defiling someone. By any fair and rational standard, Flynt had crossed the line, and I left the Court with the almost euphoric sense that justice would surely prevail for my client Reverend Falwell.

That feeling lasted exactly two days, the time it took to return to New York and business as usual—selecting a jury for a hit-and-run case in Queens.

The Queens courthouse is the lowest rung on the legal ladder. Inside, it reminds me of a busy delicatessen, the kind of place where customers crowd around the counter shouting their orders at the help. Comedian Lenny Bruce once said, "In the halls of justice, the only justice is in the halls." All you find in these halls are clients hunting for lawyers, lawyers hunting for clients and people screaming at one another in five different languages.

In the center of the lobby is a model of the Unisphere, the symbol of the 1964 World's Fair, with a plaque that reads, "Presented to Borough President Donald R. Manes to celebrate the tricentennial of Queens County by the Brooklyn Union Gas Co., April 15, 1983."

Manes committed suicide with a steak knife two years later, after being indicted in a kickback scandal.

Across the street there's a row of stores—a pastrami shop, a Chinese restaurant, a pizza carryout—and a bus stop advertising the legal services of Spellman and Speigal: "Had an accident?" The firm's specialties include: "No-fault cases, step-and-fall cases, faulty-product cases, building-construction cases." And—for your convenience—"Se habla español."

If the Supreme Court is the pinnacle of the legal system, the lower courts are the foundation. Regrettably, in Queens and elsewhere that foundation is cracking.

Nothing in the Queens court works—from toilets to telephones everything is broken. Ask a clerk for directions and he ignores you; ask a judge to explain a ruling and he tells you to shut up. The signs are not written in English; they are printed in symbols, the only form of communication the court's patrons all understand. Still, none of this seems to deter business.

People who come to the Queens courthouse are all looking for something—protection, stolen property, revenge, peace and quiet— things they think lawyers can help them find. But most lawyers who practice there are too busy looking for money to pay much attention to their clients' needs. Court sessions are like auctions, presided over by judges who handle dozens of cases a day, dismissing some, delaying others and sending the rest to decision clerks in the basement to be processed, filed or lost.

The Supreme Court elevates every case it hears; the Queens court sucks everything slowly down the drain.

As it turned out, my case was delayed, a tactic that defense attorneys use all the time to wear down the opposition and squeeze more money out of their clients. The practical effect is to clog the system with more and more backlogged cases.

Outside the courthouse is something that has always puzzled me, a cement statue erected in 1920 that depicts Civic Virtue as a gallant young warrior saving a naked woman from a dragon by chopping off its head. This work of art was commissioned by Mayor Hylan of New York at the turn of the century and originally intended to stand in the heart of Manhattan. However, the prudishness of the times prevailed and it was relegated to the hinterlands of Queens. The dragon is supposed to represent injustice, but the artist seems to have had mixed feelings about the results of the young warrior's deed. Dozens of snakes and a huge octopus are crawling out of the dead dragon's neck, and they appear to be heading straight for the courthouse.

Two months later I was taking a deposition from the head of the department of gastroenterology at Yale Medical School, an expert witness in a malpractice case, when the phone rang. It was someone from Frank Lorson's office at the Supreme Court. The deposition stopped, and with several lawyers and a stomach doctor looking on, I heard a voice on the other end say, "There's been a decision in the Falwell case."

Flynt had won.

Minutes before, my current adversary had been bragging about winning a "six-million-dollar bell ringer" in the Bronx.

"Well," I said, hanging up the phone. "I just lost one in the Supreme Court."

No one said a word.

I know some attorneys who are so floored by a loss that they are out of commission for months, sometimes years. Others train themselves to take defeat in stride and bounce back for more. Losing is part of the game, but it's never easy.

The vote was unanimous. The Court could find "no principled standard" to separate opinions on matters of public interest from any expressed in *Hustler*'s fake ad. In other words, Larry Flynt was simply exercising his right to free speech. After five years of trying to prove otherwise, it was hardly a decision I agreed with.

I thought back to the argument in which Justice Scalia asked me to provide the Court with a "painted red line" that would clearly define permissible speech. All judges love to make lawyers squirm by asking them questions like that. I replied by citing the law's tradition of dealing with glittering generalities, like "reasonable care," "due process" and other ideas that allow juries as times and circumstances change to render decisions consistent with the prevailing view of justice. But, ignoring that essential character of the law, the Court had chosen to enshrine an inflexible determination that all speech, even the repulsive ravings in *Hustler*, is protected by the First Amendment. Thus Larry Flynt left the fray the victor, and a more balanced legal principle, for the time being, was dead.

Only in the schizoid economics of the legal profession did the outcome of the case make sense. Flynt had spent a million dollars to win. Falwell collected $800,000 and lost. The $200,000 difference equaled the damages that the lower courts had awarded Falwell, but since the Supreme Court decision overturned those rulings, the only ones to profit were the lawyers.

THE BIG CASINO

To certain people, like Larry Flynt, lawyers are an everyday necessity. For others, needing a lawyer is the equivalent of needing major surgery—the ultimate horror. By the time they hire an attorney, clients usually feel they have been through enough, but since most lack the zeal of a Flynt or Falwell, a lawyer not only has to prepare their case, he also has to toughen them up for the long fight that lies ahead.

To find out what I have to work with, I give all my new clients a simple stress test. First I ask them to tell me everything they can about themselves and their case; then, using that information, I hit them with a barrage of insults and sarcasm. Some break down, go home and never come back; the serious contenders stick around.

A trial is a contest between two attorneys to see who has more nerve and whose client is more determined to win. People sue one another to inflict suffering. That's natural. To some extent trials are meant for revenge. Yet, for a growing number of litigants, lawsuits are not just a form of vengeance; they have become a way to strike it rich.

Just as there are corrupt lawyers like Burton Pugach, there are corrupt clients like Freddy Henderson, who made a career out of suing people. Referred to in New York legal circles as "Fall-down Freddy," he earned his living the hard way, as his nickname implies. Every year he had an accident in order to collect money from insurance companies. Then, conveniently, Freddy got a job as an investigator for a personal-injury lawyer and decided to arrange a fall that would set him up for good. He went into a movie theater, found a place on the balcony steps where the carpet was wrinkled and threw himself down a long flight of stairs. The result was broken vertebrae in his neck and back and a badly injured knee. Later, when his case came up, Freddy hobbled into court with a triumphant grin on his face. This was the jackpot he had been waiting for.

During the trial, however, Freddy's entire record of false injury claims was exposed, claims against everybody from his landlord to the U.S. Army. Eyewitnesses even testified that the fall had been staged. By the time the defense was finished with him, Freddy's career as a litigant was over. After the unfavorable verdict was announced, he left the courtroom in a walker. I happened to be in court that day, and as he got into a cab, I asked him if he had finally learned his lesson.

"Yeah," Freddy sighed. "I'm wiping the slate clean. It was my priors that got me. No more falling down stairs for me."

We said good-bye, and a half-hour later my office phone rang. It was Freddy.

"Hey, Mr. Grutman," he said, "I'm up in the Bronx. The cab I was in just got rear-ended. You want my case?"

Freddy believes in the legal system. Maybe a little too ardently. To him courts are a big casino and attorneys a means of improving the odds. He's not alone.

Centuries ago, justice was largely do-it-yourself. If someone harmed you, you harmed him back. There were no lawyers, no judges or juries, and the outcome was generally fast and final. The urge to get even still motivates people to fight it out in court, only today it takes longer to see the results.

One cause for the delay is the nature of the legal process itself; in America anybody can sue you for any valid reason. Another is the financial reward at stake. A principal function of the courts is to separate right from wrong through the redistribution of wealth. If a person injures someone and is found liable, he has to pay. If a company's product hurts someone and the company is at fault, it has to pay. Almost everybody who goes to court, from Fall-down Freddy to the nation's biggest corporate executives, expects to come out with money.

That's because a lawsuit is an investment in the legal economy. Taking someone to court is not simply an act of hostility, it's a complicated capital venture for attorneys as well as their clients. All it takes is a quick glance through the newspapers to see how profitable cases can be. Without them, lawyers would have nothing to do but write wills and close real estate deals. Suing and the threat of being sued are what scare people, and wherever there is fear, there are attorneys looking for bigger and better ways to make it pay off.

Looking the hardest are negligence lawyers, who literally comb the streets in search of clients.

In New York, if you happen to be driving along and your car hits a pothole, it is impossible to sue the city for damages unless the hole is officially registered. New York has so many potholes that it had to do something to curtail lawsuits. Requiring them to be registered as a precondition for recovering damages was the city's only solution. But enterprising negligence lawyers were not deterred. In their free time, teams of them examine the streets, recording unregistered potholes against the day an unsuspecting driver may hit one, get hurt and need their services.

The image of an ambulance-chasing lawyer waiting for customers outside a hospital emergency room is part of legal folklore. Obviously, no self-respecting ambulance chaser would be caught dead working that way today. Some pay police and paramedics to deliver their cards at the scene of an accident; others hire what are known in the trade as "steerers" to patrol hospitals looking for patients whose cases seem promising. Using newspaper stories about six- and seven-figure damage awards as enticements, steerers are paid a commission for signing up clients. This practice is against the law in most states; still it accounts for millions of dollars' worth of business every year.

Despite some of their methods, negligence and personal-injury lawyers offer their clients a way to change misfortune into money. Like medieval alchemists who claimed to make gold out of ordinary metals, they sell the promise of a fast fortune. And in that sense the service they provide defines the main economic ingredient in every lawyer-client relationship.

In addition, there is also a psychological bond that connects an attorney to the person he represents. Every day people are injured, hurt and abused. The rest of the world may be indifferent to their broken bones and broken hearts; lawyers not only listen to their woes, they make them the center of attention.

In the 1960s, a wealthy young New York socialite named Oakes Ames Plimpton was driving his date home after a night on the town when his car struck an elderly woman crossing a street on the Upper East Side. Oakes, the brother of author George Plimpton and the son of a former president of the prestigious Association of the Bar of the City of New York, was unquestionably at fault. Driving without his glasses, after downing several scotches, he had struck the woman as she was lawfully crossing the street while walking with her dog. His insurance carrier stood to lose a large sum of money if the case went to court. I represented the woman, a sweet little old lady named Mrs. Valentine. She was recuperating in the hospital when Plimpton, riddled with remorse, started to visit her. Before long, he was stopping by every day, watering her house plants, collecting her mail and showering her with attention. Mrs. Valentine, a widow, had no relatives or friends, and Plimpton, who genuinely felt sorry for her, soon became the most important person in her life.

As the trial date approached, Mrs. Valentine became more and more reluctant to go through with her suit. First she wanted to drop all the charges, then she wanted to delay. She had developed "litigation-itis," an addiction to long-drawn-out legal action. I have seen it hundreds of times. A legal dispute can change some clients' whole lives. Suddenly, lonely and neglected people are stars. The only thing that matters is their case, and when it's over, they are lost. That is what happened to Mrs. Valentine.

After her case was finally settled for $100,000, the excitement ended. A month later, all alone again, with no more lawyers or hearings to look forward to, Mrs. Valentine committed suicide. In her handwritten will she left the entire proceeds of the settlement to her only friend—the young man who had run over her, Oakes Ames Plimpton.

Most people hire lawyers for the same reason they hire doctors, to repair some damaged part of their lives. But in court, damage is in the eyes of the jury, and winning always depends on how well an attorney tells his client's story, no matter how unbelievable it seems.

Manny Katz, a New York personal-injury lawyer I know, likes to say he believes in "the reality of pain." The problem is conveying that belief to a jury. Pain, except to the person experiencing it, is an abstraction. In order to convince the court that his client deserves to be rewarded for his anguish, an attorney has to make it real, paint a picture of torment and sadness so vivid that no jury could deny his request for damages.

Katz, at eighty, with rings on every finger and dyed hair, looks like a Borscht-Belt pimp. He learned the routine when most lawyers conveyed the reality of pain with sound effects. In the old days, standing before a jury and discussing broken bones, his favorite trick was to hold up a Mongol No. 2 lead pencil and snap it in half. Today, assisted by his son Herb, an attorney with degrees from M.I.T. and Columbia Law School, he uses advanced technology to do the job. His clients are catalogued by computers, coded under headings like "PDK," for pedestrian knockdown, or "DCAP," for decapitation, each one cross-referenced by date, dollar value, and relevant body part. Now, father and son spend the better part of every day in front of their terminals, massaging cases. And when it comes to pain, Manny likes movies.

There are some lawyers who weep and wail to get their message across in court. Others bring in a cast of expert witnesses. Manny Katz does it with cinéma-vérité videos he calls "A Day in the Life of ———." One particularly lucrative production showed his client, a welfare mother, during a typical day, caring for a severely retarded infant while her normal children romped in the background. She was suing the hospital where the baby was born, claiming that doctors had botched the delivery. It was a complex case, asking for damages in the millions. Six physicians testified, but the only piece of evidence the jurors needed to see was the film, which had most of them crying their eyes out by the time it was over.

Juries are particularly susceptible to misery in movie form, and there is no doubt that the medium conveys the message with maximum impact. Yet there are still a few purists left in the legal profession who rely on the spoken word to do the job.

While it is hard for a fair-minded jury to turn its back on a person who sincerely needs help, there is a big difference between feeling sorry for someone and handing him a half-million dollars. For that the lawyer has to tell a sob story so powerful that the only sympathetic response is cash. One of the masters of the technique was Manhattan attorney "Mo" Levine, who never met a victim he didn't like.

Levine's voice choked with emotion when he described lost income. He could make a fender bender sound like the end of the world. In one particular case, he represented a man who had both hands amputated in an accident. The defense summed up its argument in the morning, and in the afternoon, Levine, a firm believer in high-impact imagery, got his turn.

"Ladies and gentlemen," he told the jurors, "I just had lunch with my client." Then, pausing between each word, he said, "He . . . eats . . . like . . . a . . . dog."

Period. That was his entire summation. The jury sat there in stunned silence, picturing the meal, and after deliberating for less than half an hour, gave Levine's client everything he asked for.

Levine was so good that he made money on the side by selling tape recordings of his final arguments. There are weepers for every occasion. Some lawyers bought the tapes and memorized every word he said. None, however, could copy Mo Levine's all-purpose sense of tragedy.

Orthodox Jews often hire people to cry at funerals. Chances are they have no relationship to the deceased; still, nobody puts on a better demonstration of grief. That's what Levine did in court. He was always crying about something. To him, life was a series of preordained catastrophes, and the only thing that provided temporary relief from floods of tears was a huge settlement or verdict.

The appeal of a lawyer's performance is based partly on reason and partly on what might be called emotional logic. On the surface, a trial may look like a presentation of hard, cold facts, but on the human level, where the lawyer talks directly to the jury, it has to be something entirely different.

In 1981, I tried the case of Daniel Cardone, a fourteen-year-old boy from Long Island whose family was suing the hospital where he had received heart surgery as a child. The operation had been a complete success; however, during surgery a heart-lung machine had accidentally stopped for a time, leaving Daniel severely mentally retarded, paralyzed and partially blind. It took twelve years and a dozen court hearings to get University Hospital in Manhattan, where the operation was performed, to release a copy of its records. Curiously, the data that had been missing showed up at the trial in three different versions. Once I finally had those charts, which graphically revealed the interruption, all I had to do was put Daniel on the witness stand for ten minutes to win the case.

After telling the jury the boy was trying to learn how to button his coat at a rehabilitation center, I asked Daniel what he wanted to be when he grew up.

In a halting voice he answered, "I want to be . . . a lawyer . . . like my daddy."

Everyone in the courtroom knew he was unable even to read and write and that his dream could never be realized.

Jurors, and even the opposing lawyers, were so overcome by emotion at the boy's hopeless aspiration that the judge recessed the trial for a half-hour. Several weeks later, as deliberations on the case were about to begin, the hospital settled.

Courts determine who pays whom, and the goal of every lawyer is to make sure that he and his client are the beneficiaries. In the most elementary kind of legal conflict, where party A hurts party B, that means proving liability. The results of an accident are usually obvious. The hard part is establishing responsibility. In a car crash, for instance, it's often one driver's word against another's, "a cussin' contest," as they call it down South. Having witnesses helps. But witnesses are notoriously unreliable, often saying one thing in a pre-trial interview and another in court under oath. To eliminate the chance of that happening, some lawyers pay them to make phony statements; others bribe policemen to alter their reports so the scene of a wreck can be moved to a better location. A few years ago I was contacted by a Maryland company that supplies lawyers all over the country with ready-made injury cases—real clients that it finds and sells for a percentage of the winnings. That particular company's services did not stop there. If clients needed financial advice after landing a big settlement, it offered a complete line of victim investment options. Here was a business providing one-stop shopping that included everything except funeral arrangements.

Airplane crashes, fires and construction cave-ins are made for attorneys who know how to build up a case. Paying doctors to exaggerate injuries is a common method for inflating damage claims. Some attorneys even defy medical science to make money. After a resort hotel in Puerto Rico burned down in 1986, disaster master Melvin Belli was fined $5,000 for filing a lawsuit on behalf of a dead man. The suit claimed that the plaintiff's wife, who was injured in the fire, was unable "to perform her duties as a spouse" and cited the loss of family income from the woman's missed earnings. An astute judge determined that the man could not have authorized Belli to file the suit, since he had been dead for twelve years at the time the litigation was started.

Lamentably, these kinds of shenanigans occur everywhere law is practiced. They especially thrive when an attorney's fee is based on how much he earns for his client. That is not to say the contingency-fee system lacks necessary and important benefits. Without it, how could poor people ever have their day in court? In England contingent fees are prohibited and the client bears all the costs and risks of legal action. There only the rich can afford a lawsuit. Although Britain is considering a contingency-fee plan similar to the one available in U.S. courts, under the present arrangement the client pays for everything, including the other side's legal expenses, if he loses. It would be hard to call that justice. But it certainly is one way to curtail lawsuits.

Wealthy clients, regardless of how unpopular they are, can always find good lawyers. Oil spills, chemical pollution and plane crashes may mean bad press for big business, but they are easy money for elite law firms, most of which have no moral qualms about representing anyone who can pay their fees.

"Hail me, I'm a cab," said Simon Rifkind, a partner with the respected New York firm of Paul, Weiss and one of the top American litigators. Still, no cabbie gives away free rides, and good attorneys rarely work for nothing. The choice of clients, even in charity cases, can be a business decision. Lawyers like to pay lip service to the idea that no individual, corporation or foreign country should be denied legal representation; however, from Bhopal to Bedford-Stuyvesant, the cases they fight the hardest for are the ones they can take to the bank.

A negligence lawyer, working on contingency, is like a boxer who only gets paid when he wins. "You don't need an Ivy League education in our profession," said a New Jersey attorney in the field, understandably proud of his ring record. "A Phi Beta Kappa key never won over a jury," he added. "For that, you have to be street smart."

It also helps to be tenacious. Take, for example, the saga of my own Phi Beta Kappa key, which I finally got after seven years of waiting. Although I had the necessary good grades when I graduated from Yale, the head of the chapter blackballed me for being, as he put it, "too flamboyant" for their staid society. He may have been right about that, but he underestimated my persistence.

After the man expired, and long after my graduation, one of the greatest moments of my life came when I reapplied for membership. I was invited back to New Haven, and in Nathan Hale's room I signed the Phi Beta Kappa book on the page with the rest of my class. The experience taught me as an attorney how to persist on appeal.

All lawyers are essentially confidence men, some in the best sense, many in the worst. What they market is the belief that for a price they can solve their client's problems and put cash in his pockets. In most cases the problems are not solved comfortably, and the money usually travels in the opposite direction. But knowing that does not stop some people from calling a lawyer every time something goes wrong.

We live in an imperfect world, and attorneys are part of it. However, an imperfect world is full of economic opportunities, and given the right legal advice a person can pick up a nice piece of change.

Joe Flom of the New York firm of Skadden, Arps may be the highest-paid attorney in America. The Harvard-educated mergers-and-acquisitions expert would never be confused with an a leg-off man. Yet every year Flom earns between $3 million and $5 million cleaning up after corporate collisions.

A generation ago, the American business world was a far more peaceful environment than it is today. Bankers, CEOs and their lawyers closed as many deals at the country club as they did at company headquarters. Competition followed a sportsmanlike set of rules, and hostile takeovers—buying businesses not wanting to be sold—were strictly out of bounds.

Skadden, Arps changed all that. Under Flom's guidance, the takeover has become a commonplace corporate strategy—and his firm's device for charging whatever it wants.

Using the grandfatherly Flom and a bloody proxy fight as an implied threat, Skadden, Arps has converted fear of unfriendly buyouts into a private cash machine. If a lawyer works for you, he's not available to help someone else take away your business. That would be a conflict of interest. So just to be safe, corporations reportedly pay Skadden, Arps over $20 million a year in retainer fees to avoid facing Flom and company in court. Keep in mind, this is money Skadden, Arps collects for being on call. In the event that actual legal work is required the cost goes up.

Normally, law firms charge 1 percent of the total dollar value of a deal to handle a takeover. Skadden, Arps is generally more expensive, yet that has not hurt business. It's easy to see why. The fact that clients include such notorious corporate raiders as Sir James Goldsmith and Carl Icahn (whose Flom-assisted takeover of Trans World Airlines inspired the movie *Wall Street*) is encouragement enough for most companies to sign on.

Corporations live in terror of Flom, and even those that hire him do not like to talk about it. In today's corporate world, Flom is the modern equivalent of a Wild West gunfighter. When he rides into town, every businessman wants to be his friend, since to be anything else is suicidal.

"Takeover insurance" is just one of Skadden, Arps's protective services. If a corporate war goes to trial, the firm calls in its corps of cutthroat litigators. A kinder, gentler world would not have lawyers from Skadden, Arps in it. Their instinct for the bottom line is legendary, and so are their bills, structured to reflect both the time they spent working on a case and how well they performed. The more lucrative the outcome is for clients, the more Skadden, Arps takes off the top.

Like negligence lawyers, mergers-and-acquisitions specialists can be a mean and reckless breed. "Watching these deals get done," said an investment banker who helps do them, "is like watching a herd of drunk drivers take to the highway on New Year's Eve." One of their favorite maneuvers is the scorched-earth discovery process. Takeover lawyers are experts at depleting the other side's resources with endless motions for documents and data. There are attorneys in takeover firms who are assigned to do nothing but create correspondence and bury the opposition with paperwork. The issues in a case become secondary to bombarding the targeted company with demands for more and more information until it finally gives up.

Defensive strategies, known as "shark repellent," require even more ingenuity. One is the so-called Nancy Reagan defense, where companies "just say no" to buyout offers. Another more elaborate maneuver known as the "onion shield" was devised for Unocal, the Southern California oil company, when it became a target of takeover king T. Boone Pickens. Designed by the New York firm of Sullivan & Cromwell, the onion defense called for the creation of a series of holding companies between Unocal and its parent Union Oil of California. Under the plan, if Pickens succeeded in buying Unocal, he would acquire a business in name only. Every time he took aim at one of the holding companies, another would be created. Like peeling the skin off an onion, Pickens would have to spend years looking for the real Unocal.

When the company settled with Pickens by going deeply into debt to buy back its stock, Unocal chairman Fred Hartley triumphantly described the long struggle and its outcome this way: "Mad dog bites man, man bites back; man, with superior intellect, defeats mad dog." But the mad dog in this instance claimed to have taken millions of dollars with him.

Other takeover-avoidance techniques are more ruthless than clever. In one case, Joe Flom acted on behalf of a corporation that eliminated 27,000 jobs to avoid an unfriendly buyout. The decision, he explained later, was in the "best interest of the company."

A philanthropist in his spare time, Flom justifies what he does as a way to increase earnings for his firm and the raiders he works for. "This is capitalism," he declared after a recent victory. "I thought profit was what it was all about."

But lawyers do not add value to the economy, they add cost, and in the mergers-and-acquisitions business the amounts of money involved can be staggering. When a law firm can earn $15 million for a month's work, not an unusual payoff for handling a big takeover, realities like cost and labor tend to lose all their normal meaning.

"I remember spending months on a billion-dollar buyout," said one acquisitions specialist. "We were talking about seven figures for this and that as if it was chump change. One night my wife was complaining about how expensive everything was, and when she said tuna fish just went up a nickel a can, I told her to let me know when it hits a million. How jaded can you get?"

According to Carl Icahn, one of Joe Flom's big clients, "The takeover boom is a treatment for the disease . . . destroying American productivity: gross and . . . incompetent mismanagement." Viewed another way, takeover mania, like the glut of negligence suits, is the symptom of a different sickness. Under the guise of improving corporate efficiency, buyouts are a way of rearranging assets for the benefit of the investment bankers and lawyers who make the deals. In 1988, the

$24 billion takeover of RJR Nabisco produced "professional fees" totaling over $1 billion. Roughly two-thirds went to bankers and the rest to lawyers. Whatever happened to productivity?

This is the Age of the Middleman, and never before have so many earned more for doing less. Arbitrageurs and acquisition attorneys have become entrepreneurs in reverse, buying companies in order to break them up and sell the pieces. If productivity is suffering from mismanagement, as Icahn claims, it's because making deals and money has become more important than making products.

Lawyers thrive in a hostile environment where doing business means doing unto others before they do unto you. As a rule, the more unfriendly the opposing parties, the longer they fight, and since, for attorneys, time is money, drawn-out conflicts can be a valuable source of revenue. Quick-strike takeovers and mega-payoffs may get headlines in *The Wall Street Journal*, but sustained legal warfare is what lawyers love.

The predatory psychology that attracts clients like Icahn to firms like Skadden, Arps is the same thing most attorneys rely on to generate business. Just as the only protection against Joe Flom is to hire him, the only way to be safe from someone else's lawyer is to hire one of your own.

Whether the case involves personal injury or a multimillion-dollar merger, a lawyer is always the weapon, an instrument for threatening harm and inflicting damage. The strongest incentive to retain an attorney is the thought of what might happen to you without one, and it's that fear that lawyers use to intimidate their opponents and profit from their clients.

The first step in the litigation process, and frequently the last, is putting the other side on notice that legal action is about to begin. This is usually done by a letter, whose main purpose is to scare the recipient into immediate surrender.

Recently I took the case of a love-torn lady in Seattle who was suing her gynecologist. The doctor had just ended their affair and, in addition, left her with a nasty case of herpes. Under ordinary circumstances the woman's claim for damages might have been difficult to prove in court, but before their breakup she had tape-recorded a conversation with the doctor in which he not only confessed to infecting her but also admitted having affairs with other female patients as well.

THE BIG CASINO   63

The gynecologist was cornered. He had to be convinced that it would be in his best interest to resolve the matter quickly and quietly, and here (with appropriate name changes) was the letter I sent him:

[First the bad news]
Dear Dr. Jones:
We write to you in our capacity as counsel to Jane Smith, on whose behalf we have been instructed to promptly initiate an action at law against you, if necessary, to recover for the severe damages she has suffered at your hands.
[Then a dilemma]
To place before you in the clearest way possible the nature of Ms. Smith's grievances, the bearer of this letter is delivering the accompanying copy of a proposed draft of a complaint which will be served upon you within two weeks in the event that you do not give this matter the immediate attention it requires.
[Then the solution]
We invite you and your counsel to meet with us next week at the earliest mutually convenient time to discuss the possibilities of an out-of-court resolution of this matter.
[Then another dilemma]
We have fully investigated the allegations contained in the complaint. We are also perfectly aware that they involve highly sensitive material that could result in severe damages to you with attendant unwelcome publicity.
[Then a warning]
This matter should not be sloughed off. We have in our possession incontrovertible evidence, proving beyond a doubt that the allegations contained in the complaint are the facts and are true.
The evidence to which I refer consists in part of your own confession and admission. We also have evidence that what my client suffered on account of you is no isolated episode.
[And finally, the handshake and the ultimatum]
On behalf of Ms. Smith, we are prepared in the spirit of cooperation to explore the possibility of settling this matter with you. If you are amenable to meeting and conferring for that purpose, we will be reasonable, but if you are otherwise disposed, then you will have only

yourself to blame for the consequences, distasteful as they may be, which appear to us to be inescapable.

Trusting that you yourself or your counsel will respond to us within the next week, we remain,

Very truly yours

To protect himself and his reputation, the doctor had no choice but to settle with my client. Sometimes, though, the tables are turned and it is the attorney who needs protection. The agreement between a lawyer and his client is like a military alliance. The objective is to defeat the enemy or at least push him back into his own territory. For some clients winning is never enough. They want to demolish the opposition and frequently end up venting their anger by turning on their lawyers and refusing to pay.

Once I represented a Florida real estate executive who was so determined to get revenge on his ex-partner that he hired five different law firms to go after him. His plan was to drive the man crazy. With so many lawyers second-guessing each other, that idea soon backfired. Several years—and several law firms—later the irate executive is still obsessed with destroying his former partner, but the only people going crazy are the attorneys who have yet to be paid.

People who need lawyers are either angry or afraid. The ones who are afraid can overcome their fear by getting angry; those who show up angry only get worse.

Clients who see attorneys as a necessary evil when they have a legal problem often see no reason to pay them when the problem is solved. Indeed, they can be very ungrateful. The assumption is that lawyers get paid for winning arguments and vanquishing their foes. Actually, they get paid when, and if, their clients feel like it, and in certain cases that can mean never.

A few years ago, an international financier came to me for help in a complicated and potentially lucrative case. An offshore bank had moved several million dollars from one of his accounts to another without his permission, leaving him with obligations to his stockbroker he could not readily meet. He wanted to sue. I told him that if he did, the IRS would probably investigate, since the money had never been taxed. He was adamant about litigating. I agreed to take the case as long as he signed a letter saying that I had warned him of the possible consequences. No problem, he said, so I prepared the complaint and sent him the letter. After weeks of work went by without a reply, I assumed the letter was lost in the mail. I was wrong. The client had not planned on signing—or paying—anything. From his point of view he had me over a barrel. If I dropped his case, he would refuse to pay me a penny for all my work. And if I worked without his signature on the letter, he believed he could sue me for malpractice in the event he ever got in trouble with the IRS. This was not the basis for a good working relationship.

"As long as I don't acknowledge that letter, I've got you by the balls," he said. And despite his indelicate way of putting it, he was right. Although the case itself was going well, I could see where it was leading and bowed out while I still had the chance.

Every attorney has been stiffed dozens of times by clients, and many clients probably think they have been cheated by their attorneys. This does not mean that all lawyers are thieves and every client is a deadbeat. It only means that money is on the minds of most people who go to court.

There are two things at stake in every legal case: profit and principle. The system works best when all parties get what they deserve, but that does not happen by accident. Before attorneys sit down to cut deals, they always separate "the issues" from the bottom line. Lawyers and clients should do the same by agreeing on who gets what before either side gets anything. That way there is less chance of a misunderstanding when principles are compromised for money—and the money (as it usually does) turns out to be less than everyone expected.

Liking each other is not a requirement for a successful lawyer-client relationship, but trusting each other is. I have had clients who lied to me about everything: women who claimed they were being sexually harassed by men they were sleeping with; businessmen who were stealing from people they accused of stealing from them; and, in one case I'll never forget, an acquitted murderer who wanted me to bring a libel suit against the district attorney who tried him for homicide and the unfriendly newspaper that had written about the case. It made no difference to the man that he had committed the crime, as he freely confessed. The trial had inconvenienced him, and he was determined to make everyone who had anything to do with it pay, although I declined the offer to help.

No attorney can ever do enough for his client. If he loses a case, it's always his fault; if he wins, he should have gotten more money from the other side. The only predictable thing about people in legal distress is that they always take out their worst dissatisfactions and frustrations on their lawyers.

Clients come to attorneys with complaints, some justified, some exaggerated and some totally imagined. There are those who truly need help and those who chronically require it. People in this latter group are not just shopping for legal advice, they need psychotherapy.

Several years ago, a client of mine thought he was being followed by spies from Mars. His predicament was laughable, although to him it was very real. Substitute a hated boss, an ex-spouse or a corporate raider for the Martian spies and you have just the sort of paranoia that attorneys depend on for their livelihood. Spies from Mars are exactly what lawyers are to most people—mysterious creatures from another planet who invade their lives. The only way to beat them is to join them. The man had come to the right place for help.

With him sitting there in my office, I picked up the phone and pretended to call the FBI.

"J. Edgar? Roy Grutman . . . Fine, and you? . . . Great. Listen, J. Edgar, I've got someone here who's being followed by spies from Mars. That's right. From Mars, and I was wondering . . . You can? . . . A dozen agents? . . . I'm sure they will. Thanks a million. I'll tell him. . . . You too, J. Edgar, and keep up the good work."

The long-deceased FBI chief, I assured the man, had promised to take care of everything right away.

A few weeks later he stopped by to thank me, obviously happy with the results of his first visit. "The spies from Mars are still following me," he said. "But I'm happy to see the FBI agents are right behind them."

The service was free, and I have never had a case with a happier ending.

CHAPTER 4

FEEDING THE
SHARKS

America is a nation of laws. Which means it is also a nation of legal fees, and with many lawyers now charging over $400 an hour for their services, a law office is hardly the land of the free. Attorneys routinely bill clients for meetings, interviews and telephone calls (whether the phone is answered or not). However, few have the nerve of a famous lawyer I know in Chicago who tried to collect money in his sleep.

The attorney's firm represented some of the most important businesses in the city, so large bills were common. One particular client felt he was grossly overcharged for twelve hours of work. After getting no satisfaction from the lawyer, he took his complaint to the local bar association, which examined the attorney's records and found that his billings for the day in question covered the entire twenty-four hours! Asked how he could practice law while he slept, the lawyer imaginatively replied, "I dream about my cases."

Not all attorneys have that kind of earning power, but a lot come close.

Unlike most economic activities, the legal profession has never been seriously affected by the law of supply and demand. The more lawyers there are, the more ways they seem to find for expanding business horizons. Now there are lawyers who specialize in sports law, animal law and surrogate-mother law. If it pays, or just gets publicity, it exists as part of the practice. Stock market crashes and political power shifts—

revenue-threatening disasters for some people—are opportunities for attorneys to create new profit centers.

Since 1960, the number of lawyers in this country has doubled to more than 650,000. Today there is one attorney for every 400 Americans. That's nearly three times the lawyer-per-capita ratio of England and twenty times that of Japan, but it is very close to the same proportion that existed in New York City when the first American law firm began there in 1818. At that time, New York's population of 123,706 contained 236 attorneys, or one for every 524 inhabitants.

Then as now there was plenty of work for lawyers, particularly ones specializing in bad-debt cases. Failure to repay a loan could have tragic consequences in early America, and often the only thing standing between a financially embarrassed debtor and years behind bars was a skillful attorney. The first Wall Street lawyers frequently handled nothing but debt cases, arranging high-interest loans to free imprisoned borrowers, then serving as collection agents to make sure lenders got their money back.

The field was so busy that two enterprising attorneys, John Wells and George Strong, got an idea. The only way to beat the competition, they decided, was to pool their talents and their earnings. The result was the country's first law partnership and a whole new concept in marketing legal protection.

Strong and Wells were a perfect team. Strong supplied the management know-how and Wells, the only survivor of an Indian raid that had wiped out his family, tried cases in court. Before the two joined forces, lawyers had been independent operators whose income was limited by the number of cases one man could handle. Strong and Wells revolutionized the profession. Dividing the labor not only enabled them to work more efficiently and make more money, it raised the practice of law to a new level of commercial respectability.

Gradually, as debt collection became a sideline for the two partners, their clientele grew to include banks, factories and insurance companies. By the 1840s, when Strong's son George Jr. and grandson Charles took over the office, law firms had become an indispensable part of the business establishment. In transportation, industry and technology, new companies, generating huge fortunes, needed teams of lawyers to look out for their wealth. The Strongs were ready. To attract top customers, they realized, their firm needed a certified dealmaker, and for that they called on the services of a friend, John Lambert Cadwalader, assistant secretary of state in the influence-for-hire administration of President Ulysses S. Grant.

Before he left for Washington, Cadwalader, a successful New York attorney, asked the Strongs to mind his clients, a lucrative arrangement that George Jr., as a professional courtesy, felt deserved some token of gratitude.

"Do you suppose that I will consent to pocket the good fat things which are to a certain extent the culmination of your professional labor?" he wrote to Cadwalader. "I should not feel comfortable, my dear Boy, to have you serving your country for $3,500 a year while I enjoyed the emoluments of the business you built up."

The Strongs, however, had more up their sleeve than a few friendly kickbacks. Cadwalader's upper-crust contacts could give their firm just what it needed to tap some of America's biggest legal clients. The plan to join forces was a stroke of genius, and in 1877, when Cadwalader left the government, a new partnership was formed.

Almost immediately Strong & Cadwalader was doing business with railroads, overseas fruit companies and some of the richest families in the country. Thanks to Cadwalader's pulling power, the firm's client list soon read like a page from the Social Register. The Morgans, the Fearings and the Huttons joined the fold. That attracted the Manhattan Trust Bank, which shortly became a source of other business, including Macy's department store and the Rapid Transit Construction Company, original builders of New York's subway system. By the end of the century, the first American law firm had become a legal conglomerate.

Cadwalader, who rose to managing partner after the last Strong departed, believed in the value of good connections, which he kept current by sitting on dozens of civic boards and committees. As the firm hired new attorneys, it changed its name to Cadwalader, Wickersham & Taft, with offices in New York, Washington and Palm Beach (where most of its rich clients spent the winter), but it never changed its basic credo.

"Law firms have grown in number, but not always in quality," observed Cadwalader, who had a theory that "every large firm should have among its partners at least one gentleman," as a reminder that the law is a noble profession.

Cadwalader never thought there was anything wrong with law firms earning money, only that certain rules of behavior should be followed in the process. If the world is full of thugs and crooks, attorneys, he believed, should make it a better place by helping others while they help themselves.

Cashing in on good deeds is a time-honored tradition in the legal profession. Lawyers like to call this charitable notion *pro bono publico*, a Latin term meaning "for the public good." The concept goes back to the Middle Ages, when champions often beat each other up at bargain rates to advertise their services.

Today, thanks to firms like Cadwalader, Wickersham & Taft, the medieval motif plays an important part in the legal system, giving courts their gothic pomp and lawyers their Sir Lancelot complex. Most law firms operate just like King Arthur's castle. At the top of the firm are the senior partners, the lords who make all the major decisions and reap the greatest gains; then come the associates, the knights who roam the countryside looking for trouble; under them are the new recruits, the vassals who learn the business by polishing the in-house torture equipment. Every year, as a reward for faithful service, knights and vassals move up the pay scale, receiving a larger share of the profits until they eventually become lords of the castle themselves.

Law firms have worked this way for centuries. Lately, with many firms as affluent as some of the corporate clients they represent, the climb to the top has been shortened.

Even before they are taught the first tricks of the trade, today's apprentice attorneys are exposed to all the "good things" the profession has to offer. Competition for top law students from Harvard, Yale, Stanford and Columbia is so fierce that major firms spend enormous sums wooing them as summer associates. In Washington, one firm pays its summer interns $1,000 a week, plus extras, including free lunches, yachting parties and theater tickets. Lavishing high pay and perks on ambitious beginners is common as a way of advertising clout. In a profession that measures quality by cost, firms that spend millions of dollars on untried talent are seen as the best in the business. They pay more because they charge their clients more, so they can afford to splurge on hot prospects.

"The effort is to treat recruits to a considerable degree the way you treat regular associates," said a senior partner from a large East Coast firm. The practical effect, though, is to let them know that a law degree is a license to get rich.

Annual salaries for first-year associates at prestige firms in New York, Washington and Los Angeles now exceed $70,000. At Skadden, Arps in Manhattan, newcomers make over $80,000 a year. With bonuses for racking up billable hours (the time devoted to performing actual work for a client), a young hotshot at a major firm after two years on the job can be earning more than the attorney general of the United States.

The money that makes all this possible is supplied by clients. And what starts the cash flowing is the threat of court action, when opposing lawyers declare war on one another—and on the people they represent, who always pay no matter which side wins. Few attorneys have understood the economics of this arrangement better than Steven Kumble, founder of Finley, Kumble, the second-largest law firm in the country before it went bankrupt in 1988.

"Praise your adversary" was Kumble's advice to his troops. "He's the catalyst for billing your client. Damn your client. He's your real enemy."

If Cadwalader believed lawyers should be gentlemen, Kumble thought they should be salesmen. For him, a law firm was first, last and always, a business, and every client's problems the raw material of profit.

When it began with a half-dozen lawyers in 1968, Finley, Kumble was an ordinary Manhattan law office, indistinguishable from hundreds of others, except for Kumble's determination to play by his own set of rules and always get cash up front.

It takes years for a big-name firm to earn a reputation, years that Steven Kumble did not have to waste and, in his genius for shortcuts, saw a way around. Respected firms like Sullivan & Cromwell or Cravath, Swaine & Moore did not just suddenly erupt on Wall Street. They grew slowly over decades, servicing accounts, building resources and competing with one another for business the way wealthy friends play golf. Stealing another firm's lawyers or another firm's clients was out of the question. There were some things a gentleman did not do. For the old-line partnerships the practice of law was like the practice of religion. But Kumble, a graduate of Yale and Harvard Law School and a former Marine, had a different idea.

"You put together a law firm the way you put together a baseball team," he once said. "You need a third baseman, you go out and get one."

Instead of being like other firms, Finley, Kumble was like the New York Yankees. When Yankees owner George Steinbrenner needs players, he buys free agents from other teams, enticing them with fat contracts full of incentive clauses and bonuses. Kumble used a similar technique to sign frustrated attorneys from other firms. What he offered them was a bigger piece of the take, and what he got in return were the clients that new lawyers brought with them.

I fell for the idea in 1970. Kumble needed a trial lawyer to handle his commercial cases, or so he said, and I was looking for new surroundings. I had tried so many personal-injury suits that I relished the opportunity to work on contracts, mortgages and bank notes. Of course, what Kumble really wanted was my practice. I headed the Finley, Kumble litigation department for the next six years, while Kumble proceeded to turn his firm into a bicoastal bait-and-switch operation. When I realized what was happening and that it did not bode well in the long run for Kumble's partners, I looked for even newer surroundings. Kumble's talent was pretending his firm could do anything. From what I saw, clients to him were meant to be fleeced, and nobody knew better what makes them give lawyers their money than he did.

Steven Kumble was a slightly more polished version of Burton Pugach, the infamous Bronx ambulance chaser. Both were experts in the uses of greed, but instead of hiring tow-truck drivers and traffic cops to solicit business the way Pugach did, Kumble hired lawyers with big names and legal mystiques. And anyone who failed to bring in new business was out. Kumble made being greedy respectable.

A client is a creature of habit. Knowing that, some law firms milk the same ones for generations, inheriting corporate and individual accounts usually without even trying. But Kumble knew that clients have favorite lawyers, not favorite law firms. Lure the attorney away, and his customers will follow.

The waiting game that's part of every law firm's graduated salary plan was the key to Kumble's initial success. Rather than paying lawyers on the basis of years served, Kumble devised a plan to pay them for business delivered. The more money you produced, the more money you made, and the more money its attorneys brought in, the more Finley, Kumble would grow.

All law firms make a distinction between major partners and associates, but at Finley, Kumble the difference was dramatic. In 1975, Finley, Kumble moved to Park Avenue, home of some of the most prestigious firms in the world. The firm's old offices had been above a Midtown dime store, but the new headquarters, Kumble declared, would be the embodiment of his philosophy of sell more, climb higher.

For economic purposes, Finley, Kumble partners were divided into two categories: those who attracted clients, the "rainmakers," and those who were assigned the drudgery of working on cases, or as Kumble called them, the "shitniks." If 425 Park Avenue, the firm's new address, was to become the nerve center of a nationwide legal network, it had to reflect the division of labor that made Finley, Kumble Finley, Kumble.

Law offices are usually decorated by committees that spend years arguing over where the portraits of the firm's founders should hang, but the Finley, Kumble offices were Steven Kumble's unique creation. He wanted the walls washed in dignity. The artwork, a major part of the overall design, was eighteenth century, with pictures of anonymous barons and earls (Kumble's instant ancestors). After his marriage to New York socialite Peggy Vandervoort, a thoroughbred horse dealer, equestrian paintings were added. In the cafeteria, English muffins replaced bagels, and following Kumble's motto, "Think Yiddish, Dress British," the partners began showing up for work in custom-made worsted suits and carrying umbrellas.

The centerpiece of his grand design was an ornate spiral staircase that joined the eighth-floor lobby and ninth-floor executive suites. It was an exact copy of the one in the Madison Avenue salon of makeup maven Georgette Klinger. To Kumble, it symbolized the firm, and only the rainmakers, the A partners, could use it. The rest were restricted to the service stairs in the rear of the building, with the warning that any of them caught going up or down the limited-access "stairway to the stars" would be fired on the spot.

The look of a law office is intended to put clients at the mercy of attorneys. It is an unwritten rule among lawyers that a potential client entering the lobby of a law firm should be as afraid to be there as he is to leave. Defying tradition, Kumble did not try to scare customers; he courted them with show business.

His first headliner was former New York mayor Robert Wagner, whom Kumble immediately made a senior partner. Wagner was the firm's original floor-model celebrity, the kind of ex-politician law firms use to fool clients who think name recognition equals quality legal work. In the same way the Strongs had exploited John Cadwalader's government connections a century earlier, Kumble used Wagner as a come-on. His office was a veritable shrine of grin-and-grab photos, and a drop-by was the high point of every important client's first visit.

Having Wagner around worked so well that Kumble gradually expanded his stable of out-of-work public servants to include former New York governor Hugh Carey, who had pardoned Pugach, former senator Russell Long of Louisiana, and former senator Paul Laxalt of Nevada, famous for being one of Ronald Reagan's best friends. Long and Laxalt drew salaries of $800,000 a year—over ten times what they had made in the United States Senate.

Like Kumble, the top partners at his firm seldom practiced law. As salesmen, Kumble decreed, their job was to court new clientele. The problem was that few of them wanted to work that hard. One exception was Marshall Manley (salary: $1.5 million), who had come from Mannett, Phelps in Los Angeles after being fired in 1978 for bragging to *Esquire* magazine about "stealing . . . lawyers and clients from other firms."

By then, having caught a whiff of Finley, Kumble's future, I had left the firm to practice on my own. But knowing Kumble, I suspect that when he read about Manley a light flashed in his mind that said, "Hire this guy!" It was as if fate had produced an exact clone of Kumble on the West Coast.

A successful lawyer seduces clients, charms them out of their worries and into a fat retainer agreement. Not many were better at it than Manley. Within four years, largely because of his nonstop sales pitch, *The American Lawyer*, a trade paper that drools over attorneys' salaries, praised Finley, Kumble as "the ultimate meritocracy."

With sixteen offices around the country and one in London (where Kumble was rumored to buy his suits), Finley, Kumble had merged and expanded into a gigantic business. No longer would hometown juries have the upper hand. Kumble's firm was in every major hometown. It represented a hundred companies on the New York Stock Exchange, forty-seven in the Fortune 500, banks, foreign countries and even Ronald Reagan. What it sold was the look of success, the right connections to solve any problem. Clients hire winners, and that is what Finley, Kumble seemed to be.

"We could open an office in Ames, Iowa, and make it work," boasted Kumble.

The business operated more like an automatic teller machine than a legal practice. Despite claims of yearly revenues above $100 million, the top partners' salaries were draining the firm dry. Kumble's superstars were not attracting enough new clients to pay the bills, and the over-worked shitniks, responsible for most of the day-to-day labor, were quitting constantly.

Kumble, however, had a plan worthy of Ivan Boesky. To supplement the growing shortfall, he devised a scheme to hide the firm's losses by selling accounts receivable to a shell corporation. That corporation then borrowed from banks, pledging the law firm's receivables as collateral. To create the appearance of affluence, Kumble paid salaries with the bank loans. The banks were perhaps unaware of the problem, because they were accustomed to using law firms as customer referral services, and could not imagine that one as big and flashy as Finley, Kumble would ever default. By the end of 1987, though, the firm was in bankruptcy, a victim of its own massive overhead and the greed of its management committee headed by Kumble and Manley.

Long before the final collapse, most of Kumble's high-priced partners had fled to other firms, or, like Laxalt, started new ones. Laxalt even managed to get a $15 million line of credit from Manufacturers Hanover, one of the banks that unhappily had lent money to Finley, Kumble. Officials seemed perfectly willing to lend money to another promising law firm, no matter how suspect its history.

The investment, said one banker, is "an innovative way to remove the specter of association with Finley, Kumble." Just the same, lawsuits to determine who will pay back over $150 million in Finley, Kumble debts should keep its name on lawyers' lips for a long time.

Not all law firms are like the high-gloss scam Steven Kumble created. Yet Kumble's influence on the legal profession is hard to miss. "If you are dealing with an important question," he used to tell me, "and the answer doesn't involve money, you have the wrong answer." Kumble showed his brethren at the bar how they could profit by selling law the same way insurance companies sell insurance, by acting like entrepreneurs instead of undertakers. Finley, Kumble may have self-destructed, but its legacy lives on.

It's easy to see why. Kumble never talked about the intellectual income that law is supposed to provide. He only talked about money, and in the process cleared the air so other attorneys could talk about it too. He also exposed the myth of collegiality as nothing more than a code word for the uneven distribution of income. Today, lawyers change firms the way star athletes change teams, going wherever they can make the most money. To hear some attorneys, you would think that law firms used to be like Robin Hood and his band of merry men. "Partners really aren't partners anymore," one lawyer I know sadly observed. But that's because the practice of law has more openly become what it really has been from the start: a form of highway robbery where the merriest men are the ones who take home the most money.

Law firms market protection. The marketing used to be done with some degree of finesse. A less affluent economic environment and a sharp increase in the number of lawyers have forced even the most conservative firms to change. Once anxious to avoid publicity and required by law to seek cases only through professional contacts, attorneys of every persuasion are now merchandising themselves any way they can.

Some advertise on taxicabs; other use a more sophisticated approach. Finley, Kumble was one of the first partnerships in the country to hire a public relations agent to keep its name in the news. In 1981, the Washington firm of Heron, Burchette went a step further by combining law and PR to create "America's first full-service law firm."

"People come to us with problems," said co-founder James Lake. "If it happens to be a company with a legal problem, there's usually a PR problem to go along with it. We're equipped to deal with both." Packaging is the key, explained Lake, predicting that any firm that does not aggressively sell itself "will be cycled right out of the marketplace."

Putting that theory to the supreme test, Heron, Burchette, in the endless quest for new clientele, recently became the first American law firm to open a satellite office in Moscow.

Even WASPy old-line firms like Milbank, Tweed are starting to worry about such things as image and positioning. Two years ago Milbank hired camera-ready lawyer Thomas Puccio, best known for his successful defense of Claus Von Bülow, to give it more visibility. Puccio created a special unit designed to conduct friendly investigations of corporations. In this he is assisted by former U.S. attorney general

Elliot Richardson, a standard-issue Milbank, Tweed partner. One of Puccio's goals is to find indictable offenses before the government does. Another is to produce up-to-date PR. The announcement of the new service actually made ye olde Milbank, Tweed sound cutting edge.

Since collecting fees can be the most challenging part of practicing law, lawyers spend a great deal of time pondering what services clients will and will not pay for. Frequently the magic formula has less to do with real customer care than creating the right illusion. A client is more willing to accept a large bill from an attorney who is in demand, or at least pretends to be. By the same token, successful law firms get that way by generating an aura of indispensability, the feeling that nothing important can happen without their assistance.

Still, attorneys in the top firms are always disposable. A lawyer is a tool for problem solving, and if one has trouble finding the right solution, there are a thousand others who think they can.

While companies and individuals may use the same lawyers for years, nothing is more impermanent than the makeup of law firms, most of which change names on a regular basis as new partners join and others depart. In its twenty-year history, Finley, Kumble's front door was like a movie marquee, recording more than a dozen name changes. Big firms are forever merging with mid-size firms or having members leave to form smaller ones. The law is a nomadic profession, and whether they are rotating in and out of partnerships or auctioning themselves off to the highest corporate bidder, attorneys tend to be in constant motion.

The cause of all this movement is the hunt for clients. Sharks have to keep swimming forward or they die; lawyers have to bring in new business or they go belly up. At the high end of the income pyramid that means attaching themselves and their firms to big companies, banks and industries: first by doing legal work, then by moving into board-level and executive positions. At the low end, it often means taking anything that comes through the door.

When a major corporation has a legal problem, its counsel springs into action and business goes on as if nothing has happened. When the average person needs a lawyer, everything in his life comes to a stop. And since he usually needs help in a hurry, there is little time for comparison shopping.

The typical civil case begins with a trip to an attorney's office. If party X is being sued by party Y, his lawyer will ask him for details, then get in touch with the attorney for party Y to see how much money he wants. As the plot thickens, both sides flex their muscles. The lawyer for party X answers the complaint, motions are filed, letters and phone calls are traded and a settlement may be offered, accompanied by more muscle flexing. If Y accepts, the case if over. If Y isn't interested, a trial date is set, briefs are filed, a jury is selected and the two sides get ready to face one another in court. On the big day, lawyers for X and Y meet, have a private discussion and the case, more often than not, is settled.

Seventy-five percent of all civil cases follow this pattern. The rest are resolved in court or, are continued once or twice for dramatic effect and then settled. In the meantime, lawyers log hundreds of hours of billable time, while their clients usually have no idea what is actually going on.

If you know a good attorney or know someone who does, you are ahead of the game. But taking your problems to a lawyer you trust does not necessarily mean he's the one who will handle your case. Chances are good that he will refer you and your troubles to someone else. There is easy money in legal referrals, and some attorneys, working on a split-fee basis, broker clients the way Hollywood agents sell movie ideas. The practice is considered unethical, but so are a lot of things lawyers do. Just for making the call that sent you next door an attorney can pick up a sizable percentage of any money you gain by going to court. At best, if your case is referred, you will be funneled to a lawyer who knows what he's doing and does it at no added cost. At worst, several attorneys from several different firms could get involved, with each taking a cut and each adding his own extras to the final bill.

Since legal problems are often emergencies, law firms, in the great tradition of price gouging, charge whatever the traffic will bear. But like everything connected with the profession, attorneys surround their fees in mystery. Until the first bill arrives, smart lawyers try to keep the emphasis on what the client stands to gain from his case, not how much it will cost.

Some firms, like Wachtell, Lipton in New York, are so expensive that price is no object for most of its clientele. Last year the firm made $20 million for two weeks' work representing Kraft Foods in its takeover by Philip Morris. "Our feeling is that if our services aren't going to satisfy you, we're not going to have a good working relationship," said managing partner Martin Lipton. If, for some reason, a client does not like the bill—retainers reportedly begin at $250,000—Wachtell, Lipton lawyers simply ask him to pay what he thinks is fair and never come back.

For years, local bar associations suggested minimum price guidelines, and most run-of-the-mill attorneys followed them. Several antitrust suits put an end to the practice, and legal fees are now largely a reflection of what a firm thinks it is worth—or thinks it can get away with charging.

As a rule, small firms are less expensive than big ones, mainly because they operate on less overhead. (It helps to remember when selecting a law firm that the Oriental carpets and rare antiques in the lobby are paid for by clients.) Small firms are frequently started by ambitious lawyers from big firms who leave to prove themselves. What they lack in interior design they often make up for in special skills and hard work. Still that's no guarantee you will find the right talent to handle your case.

Big firms have resources that small firms lack. The largest, Baker & McKenzie, the McDonald's of law, has offices around the world. But size can be deceiving. Among larger firms it is common for name partners (the "finders") to sign up cases, then hand the actual work over to junior associates (the "grinders"). As a result, clients frequently pay for top-quality attention they never get.

A classic example is overbilling for routine court appearances. Large firms file dozens of motions on various cases every day. This is often done in one mass dumping by a legal underling, but at first-class hourly rates for each motion. Few people ever know that all they buy when they hire a big-name lawyer is his name.

Billing tricks are common, and large and small firms have many ways to disguise doing nothing as work. Assigning more lawyers than needed to a case, then passing the added cost on to the client is standard practice. "Review, analysis and study," a phrase that often appears on legal bills, can mean virtually anything from opening mail to reading the newspaper. "Conference time" is another favorite billing term. It sounds important, but it usually means the client is paying for a lunch.

Most firms charge by the hour. Billing clients for every six minutes of work is the wave of the future. Advocates say the new system makes accounting more precise, even if it misses some of the hidden costs. When I pressed him for his firm's hourly rates, a New England tax specialist told me the average was $350, then quickly added, "That doesn't include photocopying."

He was not kidding. Copying can be a very expensive extra. In big merger cases a million dollars is cheap. Photocopying documents for a divorce or a contested will can increase a lawyer's fee by hundreds of dollars. Although knowing the cost per page up front may not minimize the bite, it will lessen the surprise when the time comes to pay.

The most common complaint from clients, aside from being overcharged, is that their lawyers never pay any attention to them, never call, never write, never keep them informed. This goes for corporations as well as individuals. The worst cases of neglect can be remedied by a malpractice suit, which will require you to hire a second lawyer to sue the one you hired in the first place. But smart shopping to start with can help separate the knights in shining armor from the shysters.

Trust your instinct. Whether your legal problem involves the breakup of a business partnership or the end of a marriage, a good lawyer should be able to put you at ease without putting you in a coma.

Beware of attorneys who agree with everything you say. You want a lawyer who will tell you the truth from day one, even argue with you, not one who nods understandingly while the meter is running overtime.

Even though you may need consolation, watch out for the attorney who encourages you to pour out your soul every time you meet. His mission is usually mercenary.

Trust your wallet. When people need a lawyer it is usually because they feel economically threatened. Do not compound the problem by hiring a thief. Lawyers are in business to make money. Make them earn it.

Any attorney who is not willing to draw up a budget for your case may be setting you up for the kill at billing time. The same is true of attorneys who advertise low-cost wills and divorces and try to sell you other legal services the minute you walk in the door.

Trust the record. The law is based on precedents, past cases and opinions that tell the courts what to do. Before you hire a lawyer, apply the same principle. The best way to know what kind of attorney you're dealing with is to know what he's been doing lately.

Ask him for information about past cases, about clients and about lawyers he has argued against in court. If he fails to comply, consider him history.

Law is a capital-intensive industry. It may be inspiring to read about attorneys righting wrongs out of the goodness of their hearts. But goodness is a luxury few lawyers and law firms can afford. Most are too busy hunting for paying customers—lately a pursuit with an entirely new set of demands. Not only are large corporations minding their legal budgets more carefully than ever before; so is the average client. Like other businesses, law firms that last will have to prove themselves, and those that sell expensive imagery instead of cost-effective service are headed for a Finley, Kumble tumble.

Lawyers do not like to look back. In the legal profession, however, the past is never far away. Two blocks from my office on Park Avenue is the old headquarters of Finley, Kumble, where six months after the firm's demise a court-appointed trustee held an everything-must-go sale to help pay off its staggering debt.

Watching lawyers from other firms walk away with furnishings and artwork that Steven Kumble thought would give his firm the look of a Milbank, Tweed had an added touch of irony, since the bankruptcy trustee, a lawyer from Milbank, served as the de facto auctioneer. For its part in overseeing Finley, Kumble's final reckoning, Milbank, Tweed picked up a fee of nearly $15 million, paid from the received portion of the infamous accounts receivable.

The Kumble collection of prized British hunting scenes was the first to go, followed by portraits of Robert Wagner, Hugh Carey and other firm heavyweights whose pictures decorated the lobby leading to the spiral staircase.

As the dust settled, one item that remained—a box of one hundred monogrammed ties—suggested how far-reaching Kumble's Ozymandian vision had been. Made by an exclusive Madison Avenue tailor, the ties were adorned with the initials of the final lineup of partners (FKWHUMMC, for Finley, Kumble, Wagner, Heine, Underberg, Manley, Meyerson & Casey) and the scales of justice.

"Anyone in Milbank, Tweed caught wearing one," said the trustee, "will be fired."

Steven Kumble could not seduce enough eight-figure clients to support the vast and costly empire he created. Nor was he, or any of his big-name partners, willing to do the heavy labor good lawyering requires. Like most people who become attorneys only to make money, Kumble and some of his cronies were for a while fantastically successful. The difference between Finley, Kumble and too many other firms is not that its managing partners were greedier but that they were found out.

HIDE-AND-SEEK

"**A** murder is the ultimate puzzle," said Jack Kassewitz, a private detective in South Florida. "But just because all the pieces fit, doesn't mean you know who did it."

Two years ago, Miami lawyer Ellis Rubin, who represented a Delaware man accused of killing his girlfriend, asked Kassewitz to listen to a taped interview with his client. Over and over again, the man repeated that he had nothing to do with the crime. The problem was that no one could explain how else the woman ended up nude and strangled to death in *his* bathroom.

"I've talked to hundreds of murderers, ones who beat the rap and ones on death row," Kassewitz said. "After a while you know what a killer sounds like, and something in this guy's voice told me he was innocent."

Just the same, his story was a prosecutor's dream. According to what he told police, he was watching television with his girlfriend one night when he fell asleep on the sofa. He woke up an hour later thinking she had gone to bed. When he went into the bathroom, she was dead on the floor with a cord around her neck.

The man was charged with first-degree murder and had already spent a year in jail awaiting trial when Kassewitz joined the investigation.

"I studied the layout of the rooms, pictures of the body, whatever

I could get my hands on," he said. "Then I thought, What if the woman killed herself? Nothing else made any sense."

There were no signs of struggle, yet it was hard to overlook the possibility that sex may have played a part. Kassewitz went to the Miami medical examiner, told him everything he knew about the case, and the doctor gave him a book on autopsies that he thought might help. In a section on accidental suicides, Kassewitz found the answer he was looking for.

"Her boyfriend didn't kill her," he explained. "The woman was masturbating and choking herself at the same time. The kick is getting high by putting a noose around your neck and reducing the supply of oxygen to the brain. All the evidence was there. The cause of death was autoerotic asphyxiation. After getting off, the woman fainted, and instead of slipping loose, the rope stayed tight around her neck and she died."

When the case went to trial in Delaware, the jury agreed and found the woman's boyfriend not guilty. Maybe his attorney would have won anyway, but it helped having a detective who knows the obvious answers aren't always the right ones.

Lawyers—even those who never play by the rules—do not like to get their hands dirty. The law is a profession practiced in offices and courtrooms. Attorneys are negotiators, and usually out of their element at the scene of a real crime. Their talent is manipulating the facts; digging them up—or sometimes covering them up—is work for the police and private detectives.

A private eye is like a pair of gloves that a lawyer puts on whenever he has to touch something unpleasant. Every smart attorney knows a dozen good investigators, each with his own special skills for making and unmaking cases.

"I'm hired to hunt for loose ends," said Joseph Thompson, a former philosophy professor who now runs a detective agency in San Francisco. "The real world is essentially ambiguous; my job is to coax that ambiguity to the surface." Teaching philosophy, he soon discovered, was the perfect background for investigating crime. Whom do you trust? Where do you find the truth? A private eye asks the very same questions a philosopher does.

Armed with a gun and a Ph.D. from Yale, Thompson, like other detectives, gets most of his work from attorneys. His typical case is a criminal defense, and his typical assignment is to locate evidence and witnesses the authorities have overlooked.

"The first thing you learn in this profession," he said, "is that nobody is as willful as the prosecution claims or as will*less* as the defense lawyer says. The truth is always somewhere in the middle. The second thing you learn is that the middle can cover a lot of territory."

Private investigators are rarely as glamorous in person as they are in novels and movies. Most tend to be ex-cops, frustrated claims adjusters and chronic night owls. Their offices are their cars, and their business, as Thompson puts it, is being there "when what *really* happened reveals itself in all its weirdness."

That was the case when New York private detective Bob Janoff, whom I first met in the Bronx, was investigating accidents for a cab company. Taxi wrecks are so common in Manhattan that Janoff wore a beeper, and one day it summoned him to the worst chain-reaction pileup he had ever seen. The usual routine is to pay off accident victims on the spot, thus avoiding more costly settlements later when personal-injury lawyers get involved. This time Janoff hardly knew where to begin.

"Our cab was heading south on Seventh Avenue a little after noon," he recalled. "The driver went through a red light, hit the rear end of a car going west on 57th Street, spun it around and knocked it into the front of another car heading in the opposite direction. The cab crashed into a newsstand, and the two wrecked cars on 57th caused a dozen more crashes in the intersection. When I got there five minutes later, wrecked cars were everywhere, and the cab, with the driver and passenger both out cold, was totaled."

It did not look good for the taxi company. Still, like any seasoned investigator, Janoff knew looks can be deceiving.

After talking to a couple of witnesses, who were too stunned to say much, he came across a man who was standing on the corner and saw the whole thing.

"Sure, the cab went through a red light," the man said. "But there was a guy in the back seat with a knife to the cabbie's throat."

That was all Janoff needed to hear. The police pulled the passenger out of the wreckage, arrested him for attempted robbery, and the cab company never had to pay a cent.

Little details like that can win or lose a case. It's not enough just to know that a spark from a cigarette butt thrown from a passing car started a fire that burned down an abandoned warehouse. That's in the morning papers. Detectives, no matter who they happen to be working for, need more information. What brand was the cigarette? Did the car have out-of-state license plates? Was the building insured? When was the insurance policy written? Where was the owner at the time of the incident? Was the car registered to anyone in his immediate family? Does the owner smoke? Does the owner's favorite brand match the cigarette butt? Etc. . . . Etc. . . . Etc.

Investigators are gluttons for details, particularly in a criminal case where the verdict often depends on a single witness pointing at the accused and saying, "That's the one who did it."

What makes him so sure? Details.

A part-time sleuth in a city down South tells the story of being hired by an attorney to find a go-go girl who owed his client a small fortune in unpaid liquor bills.

"The only description he gave me," said the detective, "was that she had very large knockers, with a three-inch scar from a bullet wound on the left one. Not a lot to go on, but I started hitting go-go bars all over town studying left tits. After nine or ten places, I found her. Naturally she denied who she was. But what gave her away was the scar on her boob."

That's detective work. It's part of the discovery process, and can include anything from researching documents and interviewing witnesses to taking pictures of people having sex in a motel. (Bedroom work may have fallen off since no-fault divorce; still, with the increase in sexually transmitted diseases, investigating the mating habits of prospective spouses is a growth industry.)

Fifty years ago, before the adoption of discovery rules by the courts, trials were full of surprises, since both sides kept what they knew to themselves until the moment they faced each other in front of a judge. That's when law was a true sport. Today, with opposing attorneys in civil cases required to share their pre-trial findings (in criminal cases only the prosecution has to), the biggest surprises generally occur outside the courtroom while a case is being investigated.

Private detectives work from the ground up. Literally. Often they are the first ones at the scene of an accident, gathering statements for attorneys while the victims are still flat on their backs. The real hustlers make the rounds of local police stations every morning to collect the names of people arrested for drunk driving the night before and sell them to DWI specialists by the dozen.

In a world where secrets are a prized commodity, private detectives are the street vendors of hot tips. If an attorney wants someone's credit rating checked or needs to track down the address of a runaway husband, he hires a detective for the job. Private investigators are far more than data retrievers. They are also social intermediaries. Detectives can talk to informants who would run from a lawyer. The police can use threats to get what they want; private eyes have to be more creative.

"The whole game is to make the person your friend," said a detective I know in Boston. "Some of it's phony," he confessed. "But it's a natural phoniness. You have to be able to deal with people to get information. Whatever the witness is, I am. If he's into music, I'm a musician. If he's into art, I'm a painter. I'm a good guy, a bad guy, an intelligent guy, a stupid guy. You see what's going on, and you do what the situation demands. It's no different from having good manners in high society. Act the way people want you to, and they always tell you things."

Detectives call this a "setup," and it comes in many forms. Janoff, a veteran of 2,000 cases, does magic tricks while he asks people questions. He can pull a quarter out of somebody's ear, make his pinky ring disappear and extract his complete work history all at the same time.

A West Coast divorce attorney, whose work deserves credit, likes to use women detectives because of their "conversational" skills. In one case where those skills paid off, he represented the ex-wife of a well-known politician. The politician was living the high life, thanks to several wealthy businessmen who were funding his career under the table. On the other hand, a botched support agreement was forcing his former wife to work two jobs. She wanted more money, and she hired the lawyer and his "female dicks" to help her get it.

Some preliminary snooping revealed that the politician's girlfriend liked to visit an exclusive Palm Springs health ranch, so on her next trip a lady detective went along on a fact-finding mission. After a week of aerobics and massages the two women became best friends, and the detective had enough information to start a major scandal. Understandably, when his ex-wife's lawyer laid it all out, the politician signed a generous new support agreement.

A person is only as good as his worst instincts, and an investigator who can expose them is a valuable asset, like a private eye I know who happened to be questioning an unfriendly witness in a traffic case several years ago. The police had the man's statement, so did the victim's lawyer, and he wasn't going to change it for anybody.

"I know what I saw," he told the detective, who was working for the driver's insurance company. "The guy hit the lady in the crosswalk and knocked her twenty feet. It was his fault."

In a case like this, where the witness refuses to budge, detectives look for anything they can use to discredit his testimony. Maybe he's blind in one eye. Maybe he has a drinking problem. Or maybe he can be bought off.

"The only thing I can do is tell the truth," boasted the man.

"That's not the *only* thing," pointed out the detective. "The other thing you can do is lie. Hey, I have a girlfriend who used to say she'd never go to bed with me. Now she wants to get married."

When this failed to impress the man, the detective took a more direct approach.

"If I gave you a million bucks, I bet you'd lie?"

"If you gave me a million bucks, *I'd* go to bed with you," the man laughed.

Here was the opening he was looking for, and the detective started talking to the man about all the things money could buy. "Wouldn't it be great to be rich? You could travel, buy anything you wanted and never have to worry about bills."

Then came the hook. Was there something the man really wanted? A car? A barbecue pit? A big-screen TV?

He did have his eye on a nice television set, he said. But with his salary, forget it.

"Suppose that TV showed up at your house next Wednesday?" the detective proposed.

Next Wednesday, the man reminded him, was the day he had to appear in court.

"Right," said the detective. "But what if the TV came to your house? Think you could manage to be out of town?"

The man thought about it for a minute, then said it was a deal— so long as the set came with remote control!

The entire conversation was captured on tape, and after hearing it, the attorney for the other side realized that his star witness was a major liability and settled the case out of court.

And the television? It never arrived. That was just part of a setup to trap the witness.

"I can't change a person's character," said the detective who pulled off this piece of artistry. "I can only take advantage of his flaws. When you put out the right bait, it's amazing what you can catch."

Making sure people appear in court is just as tricky as making sure they don't. A reluctant witness can always be subpoenaed, but that often produces hostile testimony. On the other hand, there are lawyers who would never call someone to testify without paying him first. The practice is not as unethical as it sounds. Expert witnesses are paid all the time, and in some states, like Minnesota, the law requires attorneys to reimburse businessmen for their time at depositions. Often, however, buying testimony amounts to pure bribery.

"My job is to keep the lawyer holy," said a private investigator familiar with the routine. "When I want to give a witness money, I tell him that I get a bonus from the attorney if he shows up at court. Then as a favor I offer him half. But there's one condition. He can't mention it to the lawyer I'm working for or I'll get fired. Bingo, we're business partners. It works every time. The witness gets a few dollars; the lawyer gets a happy witness; and nobody ever hears a word about it."

There are two kinds of detectives: con men and moles; one finds things out by disguising his real intentions, and one by exposing other people's disguises.

"Looks are the last thing you believe," said Josiah Thompson, who once served as a consultant to *Life* magazine on the Kennedy assassination and later wrote a book that used the laws of physics to refute the Warren Commission's single-bullet theory.

"Kennedy was murdered in broad daylight, in front of a thousand eyewitnesses," said Thompson. "Nevertheless, what appeared to be happening and what really happened were two different things."

That's why the only pair of eyes a true detective trusts are his own. Most of what a private investigator does falls under the heading of "surveillance." The assumption is that, given the time and opportunity, anyone with something to hide will eventually betray himself, if one of his friends doesn't beat him to it.

It's a good bet that 50 percent of the people you know don't like you, and finding them is never a problem. Ex-wives and husbands are a good place to start. Then come former employees, lovers and business associates. Next-door neighbors see you come and go; so do janitors and maintenance workers. A private eye in New York told me he used to pay a building superintendent $50 a week just to find out what five or six prominent residents of an Upper East Side apartment building did in their spare time. You never know when an important executive's jogging schedule might come in handy.

Like scientists who monitor the progress of rats going through a maze, detectives are born observers.

Businesses hire them to watch employees suspected of stealing. That's what the owner of a clothing warehouse in New Jersey did when he thought one of his custodians was robbing him. While he was unable to prove anything, the signs were obvious. The man was only making $200 a week, yet he was driving a new car, wearing expensive clothes, living much better than anyone could on his wages.

The detective dressed like one of the janitors and started trailing the man, only to learn he was a perfect employee, the best worker in the warehouse. Until the day before payday, that is, when he approached the detective and asked him if he wanted to buy a ticket in a raffle. The prize was his $200 paycheck, and he was taking in over $800 a week from co-workers trying to win it. Instead of being fired for stealing, he was arrested for running an illegal lottery.

Investigating money crimes is like inspecting a cheap suit. Pull a loose thread—whether it's a bank document or a telephone message—and pretty soon the whole thing falls apart.

Unlike private detectives who try to con the truth out of people, moles such as California "investigative" lawyer Mike Aguirre can spend years searching through paperwork to find the single mistake that tips someone's hand.

I hired Aguirre during the La Costa Country Club trial to learn how the organized-crime bosses who infested La Costa were laundering millions of dollars through a San Diego bank. He discovered that C. Arnholt Smith, one of the most influential men in town, had been allowing mobsters to keep their gambling receipts in his U.S. National Bank since the early 1960s. In addition to crime funds coming into the bank, Aguirre found evidence showing that illegal loans were also going out, most of them to Smith himself, who regularly borrowed money secured by nonexistent assets, then defaulted on payments.

If that sounds farfetched, it shouldn't. The same basic activity caused the savings-and-loan crisis when thrift officials used deposits to fund risky, and in some cases fraudulent, loans that were never paid back.

"The first thing you have to understand," said Aguirre, "is that in a big segment of the money industry deception is the norm rather than the exception. . . . What goes on in the economic world is a mystery to most people. Anyone can call himself a financial planner or an investment counselor and start raking it in just like a casino. Everybody's after easy money. In most cases the victims are just like the perpetrators, only dumber."

Greed makes people take shortcuts, and shortcuts cause mistakes. There are very few perfect crimes for the simple reason that few people are careful enough not to slip up at least once, and one mistake is all a smart investigator needs.

With proxy fights and leveraged buyouts now standard practice in the corporate world, detective services are considered a cost of doing business. Companies use private eyes in two ways: to assist in takeovers by locating soft spots in a targeted firm's defenses, and to fend off hostile deals with damaging information about a corporate aggressor. That was what happened in 1988, when investigators working for the Avon cosmetics company learned about several embarrassing lawsuits pending against an Amway Corporation executive suspected of financial mismanagement. The revelations produced a wave of bad publicity on Wall Street that soon halted Amway's unfriendly bid for its door-to-door rival.

Corporate sleuths have cracked insider trading scams and company spy networks, often simply by eavesdropping on secretaries. Once, a trail of insider tips led detectives to two lowly proofreaders and a computer operator who were stealing important documents from a major law firm and selling them to stock market speculators.

Aside from their ability to penetrate the opposition, much of what detectives bring back from their forays into the corporate underground is regarded as "work product," gray-area data generally protected from pre-trial discovery. Whereas lawyers in civil cases are required to show their opponents any evidence they plan to use in court, material that private detectives unearth is usually off limits to the other side. This makes investigators especially valuable in paving the way for mergers and acquisitions or any other transaction involving hidden assets or hidden problems.

Private citizens are even more vulnerable to snooping than corporations. You never know when you're being videotaped or tape-recorded, when your financial records are being looked into, or who's doing the looking. IRS agents, bank examiners and run-of-the-mill accountants can hunt through files and credit data without leaving the slightest hint they were ever there. And the only information needed to get started is your name, date of birth and Social Security number.

But fiscal excavations are not the only kind of digging detectives do. Mass disasters, like plane wrecks, chemical spills and building fires, require a completely different kind of mole work. The opponent in most cases is an insurance company defense team trained to keep damage awards at a minimum, and in order to beat them to the bank, speed is critically important.

After the victims' lawyers and their investigators have gotten to the scene of the accident with a court order to stop cleanup operations from destroying any evidence, the next step is looking for as many causes as possible. The more defendants brought into a case, the better the chances of winning a big settlement.

Stanley Chesley, the Cincinnati attorney who tried the landmark Beverly Hills supper club case in 1977, is known for converting disaster areas into archeological sites. The location is like a document in a contract dispute. You have to read it over and over, and Chesley, whose career has taken him from one catastrophe to another, believes in examining every punctuation mark at the scene of the accident.

For someone who specializes in what to do when things fall apart, Chesley is a firm believer in strong foundations—finding the facts that prove what happened, then building the case story by story until the other side surrenders. Construction experts working as investigators for Chesley spent months combing through the Beverly Hills debris until they found out why a fire that barely damaged the club had killed dozens of people. The cause of the blaze, they determined, was faulty aluminum wiring; the deaths were the result of toxic fumes from plastics used in the walls of the building. But learning why so many died was just the beginning.

In the past, "crowd cases" like this had been tried one by one. "That's great if you're the first of 200," according to Chesley. "Not so great if you're the last." Chesley's theory was to have "one forum, one judge, one resolution," and, hopefully, one huge payday for him and his clients.

There are usually many smoking guns in large-scale disasters, and as the discovery of other contributing causes in the Beverly Hills case added new defendants, Chesley applied his vacuum-cleaner approach to the litigation process, joining all the plaintiffs and their lawyers together in a single lawsuit. The judge approved, the insurance companies settled for $50 million and the tactic has been an accepted practice in the field ever since.

Whenever a disaster occurs anywhere in the world, lawyers descend the next day. In most cases, investigating what caused a catastrophe is less important than signing up clients as fast as possible. After the initial competition for business ends, clusters of individual attorneys then pool their cases and form a committee to do battle with the insurance companies.

In Bhopal, India, where a Union Carbide chemical leak killed and injured thousands of people, some lawyers, with the help of bribes to local authorities, represented entire neighborhoods. While involvement of an American company simplified the litigation, the fact that the accident occurred in India added a level of corruption to the proceedings that amazed even regulars on the circuit.

In 1986, Chesley, a veteran of the Agent Orange case, helped work out a $350 million settlement that would have given money directly to some 1,200 Bhopal victims and their families. But Indian officials, who wanted a cut, disapproved. The case was finally settled three years later for roughly the same amount, only this time funds went to the Indian government for distribution. The kickback is S.O.P. all over the world

Charges that he and his colleagues are no more than global ambulance chasers, Chesley says, simply aren't true. "Who else was there for the victims?" he once protested. "Somebody's got to be right up front to protect [their] interests."

He has a point. Nevertheless, lawyers who show up at catastrophes like Bhopal are not there to help others as much as to help themselves. Victims are every attorney's best friend. Without them there would never be a single case, and without a case how many lawyers would be in Bhopal?

You rarely hear detectives or their follow-up act, the process servers, talk about helping anybody. Their business is finding the clues to bring a case to court or else delivering the official papers that insure all invited parties are there to participate. As soon as someone gets a summons, a legal clock starts ticking. The recipient has to answer the complaint against him, and that sets in motion a costly chain of events involving court clerks, lawyers and judges.

"People do whatever they can to avoid me," said Bruce Pascal, one of the most successful process servers on the East Coast. Pascal once delivered a summons to officials in the Reagan administration when movie producer George Lucas sued to prevent the use of the term "Star Wars" to describe the strategic defense initiative. In a driving rainstorm, he served corporate raider Herbert Haft by putting a subpoena under the moving windshield wiper of his Mercedes after Haft locked himself inside and refused to come out.

For obvious reasons, no one is happy to see a process server. Pascal has been beaten on the head with a hammer, shoved down steps and run over twice, all in the line of duty.

"I love it when they try to escape," he laughed. "But I always catch up with them."

In some states that can be easier than others. Under California law, papers are considered served if they are given to a co-worker or relative of the intended addressee. The strictest laws are in states like Maryland, where a summons must be handed directly to the person being subpoenaed. Some states have statutes that prohibit process servers from pursuing their prey on Sundays, and others exempt foreign ambassadors from being served on embassy property.

None of those exemptions, however, applied to Peter Dixon, England's "most wanted man," when Pascal found him living on a country estate in Virginia. A former underwriter with Lloyd's of London, Dixon and an accomplice had allegedly embezzled more than $50 million from the famous insurance company before leading investigators on a trail that took them from the French Riviera to TV star Chad Everett's mansion in the Shenandoah Valley, which Dixon bought with his share of the stolen money.

A British law firm, working through an American attorney, hired Pascal to serve the subpoena. Time was a factor, since several London tabloids had also learned where Dixon was hiding. If the news got to him before Pascal did, he might escape.

Pascal dressed up like a delivery boy and on the way to Dixon's house bought a $50 bouquet of flowers and stuck the subpoena inside.

"All process servers have a sixth sense that tells them the guy that just walked by is the one they're supposed to serve," said Pascal. "As I was standing in the doorway, somebody walked past me without saying a word, and I knew it had to be Dixon."

He handed him the bouquet and told him to read the message.

"What's this?" Dixon said.

"You're served," replied Pascal.

"He asked me how I found him," Pascal recalled. "And when I said, 'We have our ways,' he started to cry. I kinda felt sorry for him."

That sympathy lasted five minutes, then he was off on his next delivery.

Business executives are the hardest people to serve. Finding them is only half the problem. Shielded by secretaries and assistants, they have a built-in defense against intruders, particularly those bearing bad news. The more important the person, the more limited the access. One of the most elusive CEOs of all time was Ernest R. Breech, former chairman of Ford, and famous for dodging subpoenas. Car-company officials are often the targets of product liability suits, but few possessed Breech's evasive skills. In one case, the server caught up with him on a plane. As the flight passed over a state that allowed court papers to be delivered in midair, the passenger next to Breech introduced himself with the familiar words "You're served," and the job was done.

Sometimes even more inventive delivery methods are required, as I learned in the famous Nigerian cement case. In 1975, Nigeria was ruled by General Yakubu Gowon. Following a civil war that left his country in ruins, General Gowon devised a plan to turn Nigeria from a backward nation of thatched huts and dirt roads into the envy of the civilized world. His idea was to corner the market on cement. Free-ways, shopping centers, everything modern societies depend on is made with cement. If he could control the supply, the general reasoned, Nigeria's economy would skyrocket and he would become a cement-mix version of Goldfinger.

When his plan became known, suppliers from around the world signed contracts to bring cement to Nigeria. Soon ships of every size and description were steaming for the African nation loaded with tons of the suddenly precious cargo.

General Gowon's grandiose scheme, however, had a built-in flaw. In a few months an armada of ships, all carrying cement, started arriving in the Nigerian port of Lagos. But the cement they brought with them was too much for the primitive facilities to handle. If dockworkers had unloaded nothing else besides cement, it would have taken them seventy-five years to finish the job. Yet that did not mean that shippers were losing money. For every day a vessel remained unloaded in the harbor, Nigeria was required by maritime law to pay a demurrage fee of $3,500. Multiplied by hundreds of ships, the cost soon climbed into the millions.

General Gowon's dream of a new economy based on cement mix had turned into a fiscal nightmare. At the rate it was accumulating debt, Nigeria would have saved money if it had let all the ships in the harbor sink. Some did sink on their own when the cement they were carrying hardened.

To remedy his country's growing problem, the general called a halt to all new cement contracts and set up the Cement Renegotiation Commission, which was designed to settle accounts with foreign shippers. In reality it was a means of limiting liability and funneling bribes to Nigerian officials.

I represented one of the companies involved. Traveling to Nigeria to deliver a summons would be useless without some means to make General Gowon respond. The courts provide a partial remedy in such cases. It's called "long-arm" service, a departure from the normal procedure that allows a faraway defendant to be served a subpoena by mail. Clearly, a simple piece of paper was not going to make the general pay up. For that I needed to bite into Nigerian assets in America. First, though, they had to be found.

I suspected that no self-respecting dictator would ever store all his money in his own country, and while I never discovered General Gowon's main safe deposit box, what I did find was just as good. The Morgan Guaranty bank had bookkeeping entries showing that the government of the United States owed the government of Nigeria $15 million in gold, more than enough to pay my clients. I hired a process server to deliver a writ of attachment, and the general was trapped.

After jurisdiction was established in New York, my clients, a disreputable group of Spanish businessmen, one of whom even suggested settling their bill by bribing Nigerian authorities, were the first among some forty cases to be heard. I had done the groundwork for the rest of the plaintiffs by finding Nigeria's hidden assets. But the judge ruled against the band of overly aggressive international entrepreneurs I represented, finding that they had entered into a substitute contract with the commission and had probably already been paid more than their due. He seemed to suspect that they were as corrupt as the Nigerians, and he decided to wash his hands of the entire affair.

In every case, court papers have to be delivered in precise compliance with the law. If they're not, it can be grounds for dismissal. Evictions are the most common of all legal actions, and many summons bearers handle hundreds of them a week. Due process requires that each potential evictee be officially notified and given a chance to respond. With court proceedings often costing more than back rent, a landlord's goal usually is not collection, it's removal. Most, in fact, would gladly settle for a default judgment, the legal version of a forfeit win in sports. And the best way of guaranteeing that is never to notify the party in question he's wanted in court.

The ploy is called "sewer service," which literally means throwing the summons into a sewer. It happens all the time where there's a big demand for housing. Bogus records show that service was attempted and a notice was posted on the defendant's door, but he never showed up in court. A default judgment is entered and eviction occurs. Of course, if the tenant can prove he was never served, he can have the ruling overturned and live rent-free while the landlord tries again.

It's all part of the elaborate game of hide-and-seek that the legal system not only allows but encourages. Having the evidence on your side is first a matter of finding it. The same applies to witnesses, but getting them to tell the truth almost always means disguising your true intentions.

The basic assumption that process servers and private eyes always make is that no one can keep secrets. Become a smart talker and chances are you'll hear as many as you want. In another context, that's called acting, and in the next chapter I will show you some of the things that happen when lawyers take the stage.

CHAPTER 6

STAGE MANAGING

The baseball shot off the bat at an angle that sent it high into the dark sky above the stadium, where it stopped, made a U-turn and headed downward. The Baltimore third baseman was ready to make the catch, then held both hands out in a gesture of bewilderment. He had lost the ball in the lights. Two innings later, the 1988 Orioles lost the game—their twenty-first in a row—a new record for the worst losing streak in American League history.

Edward Bennett Williams could barely stand it. The defender of Mafia bosses, counselor to crooked politicians and owner of the winless Birds did not like to lose—at anything.

When he worked as a criminal lawyer, Williams earned the nickname "Get-'em-off Ed" for his skill at winning cases no one else would take. "All of the problems of humanity can be broadly divided into three categories—physical, spiritual and social," he once wrote. "The physician, the clergyman and the lawyer devote their lives to the solution of these problems. No doctor worthy of the name turns away a patient because he suffers from a loathsome disease. . . . No clergyman worthy of the name turns away a suppliant sinner because his sins are too heinous. . . . Only a lawyer is expected to turn away a client because society regards him as socially, morally or politically obnoxious. Only the lawyer is expected to withhold his help from those who need it most."

Williams had no interest in charity cases, but a client's legal dilemma never deterred him. He won acquittals for Teamsters boss Jimmy Hoffa, New York mobster Frank Costello and former Texas governor John Connally, who was charged with accepting bribes from a Washington milk lobbyist in 1974.

In planning a defense, Williams left nothing to chance. Connally's trial was a case in point. Using opinion polls to test local reaction to the issues involved, he selected witnesses with the care of a casting director. Williams knew that the jury, made up of middle-class, churchgoing Washingtonians, would examine his client's character as closely as it would the prosecution's evidence, so early in the proceedings he put evangelist Billy Graham on the stand to testify in Connally's behalf. Graham was asked to state his occupation, and when he answered, "I preach the gospel of Jesus Christ around the world," one juror responded with a loud "Amen."

Williams took that as a good sign. In fact, he stage-managed every aspect of the trial to such perfection that by the time it was over he had convinced the entire jury that Connally was close to being a saint and innocent on all charges.

One client he could not save was Bobby Baker, a top assistant to then-senator Lyndon Johnson, indicted for fraud and corruption. After the guilty verdict, the two left court together, and Baker described in his memoirs how Williams began to cry uncontrollably: "He did not cry a silent gentlemanly stream of tears. His body shook and jerked almost convulsively as he sobbed. Mucus ran down his nose. I wiped it off . . . and tried to comfort him."

If it was all an act, Baker had never seen a more convincing performance.

In fact, few actors know their business as well as Williams did. To him a courtroom was a theater, and win or lose, he never stopped practicing his dramatic technique. In 1986, he was in Miami defending financier Victor Posner against charges of income-tax evasion. On the day he was to make his final summation, Williams, exhausted from cancer treatment, spent half the morning rehearsing in front of an empty jury box. When court convened, he spoke for more than two hours, standing the whole time and never consulting his notes.

"Most people go to work, come home, and kiss their wife hello," Williams once told an interviewer. "If things went well, they say,

'Things went well today.' They didn't win and they didn't lose. It's not . . . a victory or defeat. Some 98 percent of the people live that kind of life."

But not Williams, who practiced what he called "contest living," where "every effort is marked down at the end as a win or a loss." If things went well for him, it was because he came out on top.

The contest is what defines the attorney's role in the legal system, just as the ordeal defines the client's. The difference is that for clients the ordeal is an unavoidable fact; for lawyers the contest is an act, the purpose of which is making the other side lose—and pay.

As in a baseball game, the outcome of a trial is direct and unambiguous. The trick in both cases, Williams learned, is to maximize the chances of winning by doing everything possible to make sure you do not lose. The key is preparation, but the goal is always outperforming your opponent.

"You have to get ready for the contest. You burn your body, burn your spirit [and] your psyche," Williams said shortly before his death. "I prepare for everything. In court, I never ask a question to which I don't know the answer."

In the parlance of Washington, where he worked, Williams was a "player," defending criminals one day, advising movers and shakers the next. His firm represented John Hinckley after he tried to assassinate Ronald Reagan. Later when Reagan asked Williams to head the CIA, he turned the offer down. The stakes were high enough, but unlike trials and athletic contests, espionage never has a final score.

Washington Post editor Ben Bradlee called Edward Bennett Williams "a primitive man." The same description could easily apply to any successful attorney. What Bradlee meant was that Williams operated on instincts so finely attuned to the basics of human nature they were almost infallible. An expert in managing facts and emotions, Williams knew that a court case is an acting contest. Instead of fighting with clubs the way ancient champions did, each attorney uses a different version of the truth—or maybe no truth at all—carefully arranged to show his side's cause in the best possible light and his opponent's in the worst. In every trial the client is the hero, the witnesses are the supporting cast and the script is what each lawyer tells the judge and jury.

Some cases are tragedies, some are comedies, some combine elements of both. An attorney unaware of the difference will not win many decisions or put on a very good show.

To be sure, a courtroom reveals more than acting ability. Besides being a form of theater, it is a place where secrets are told. The hidden workings of major corporations, the misdeeds of government officials, the private lives of celebrities and ordinary people are all exposed in legal proceedings. Fear is a lawyer's best weapon, and often the fear of having embarrassing information made public is enough to end a case long before it ever gets to court.

Prior to a trial, opposing attorneys have the opportunity to conduct question-and-answer sessions with one another's clients. While these interviews, known as depositions, are part of the discovery process, they can also be psychological strip searches aimed at forcing the other side to settle out of court or else drop its case altogether.

In 1987, former secretary of state Henry Kissinger sued *Penthouse* for $10 million for publishing an interview with him. The interview had been voluntarily given to two freelance writers who sold the story to the highest bidder. Since Kissinger had not imposed any restrictions on the journalists when he agreed to meet with them, he had no case for an injunction or for damages. As Jerry Falwell had a few years earlier, Kissinger claimed that the interview, which he thought was going to be used as part of a book on foreign policy, had harmed his professional reputation. I was *Penthouse*'s lawyer, and it was my job to prove differently.

Kissinger has an immense ego forged by a decade of trying to run the world. His years in government also had made him a master of the non-responsive reply. Unless he is locked into very tight-fitting questions, leaving him no room to wiggle or squirm, he always gets away. Interrogating someone with Kissinger's evasive skills can be a rhetorical wrestling match. However, there was one hold I thought might work. Since Kissinger had made his reputation the central issue in the case, I decided to use the deposition to show his lawyers how their client's public image would suffer even worse damage if his suit went to trial.

The session took place in my office, and Kissinger sat stone-faced at the conference table, daring me to penetrate his defenses.

I began by asking him how he knew his reputation had been harmed, and he replied that two people who worked for his consulting company had said so. When I inquired about who else had expressed the same opinion, he could not offer any names.

The following exchange then took place:

QUESTION: Has any government entity declined to do business with you or Kissinger Associates because of the interview that appeared in *Penthouse?*

KISSINGER: Not to my knowledge.

QUESTION: Would you say that the publication of the interview has in any way interfered with your ability to act as a statesman or a person?

KISSINGER: Not to the best of my knowledge.

QUESTION: As a diplomat?

KISSINGER: Not to the best of my knowledge.

QUESTION: Would your answer be the same with respect to your ability as a writer?

KISSINGER: Yes.

QUESTION: A consultant?

KISSINGER: Yes.

QUESTION: A lecturer?

KISSINGER: Yes.

QUESTION: And a businessman?

KISSINGER: Yes.

QUESTION: Have you lost any sleep over the publication of the interview in *Penthouse?*

KISSINGER: No.

QUESTION: Have you seen a physician for any care or treatment for health in connection with any problem arising from the publication?

KISSINGER: No.

QUESTION: That I take it would include not having to see any health care provider of a psychiatric or psychological nature as well, correct?

KISSINGER: . . . That's correct.

There are inescapable body signs that a person displays when he is unsure of himself; it may be a blink, maybe a gulp or a nervous twitch. Kissinger the diplomat was right at home in a pressure cooker. Citizen

Kissinger, the private person, was not. As the tension increased, his manner became almost Wagnerian, his accent more like Dr. Strangelove's. He seemed to realize that his answers were putting his claim of a damaged reputation on shaky ground. I sensed it was time to make him really sweat.

> QUESTION: Were you aware at the time that you first saw an issue of *Penthouse* that in addition to publishing the pictures of attractively unclad figures, it was also a publication which, among other things, published investigative journalism and political comment?
>
> KISSINGER: I was aware that, occasionally—that it occasionally published, yes, investigative articles. I think that is when I saw it the first time.

That was the signal I had hoped would appear. Kissinger's legendary precision of language was breaking down. His back-up lights were on. Super K was in retreat.

> QUESTION: Well, were you aware that, among other things, *Penthouse* is one of the foremost photographic men's entertainment magazines, which frequently published pictures of beautiful nude ladies?
>
> KISSINGER: Of course, I am aware of that.
>
> QUESTION: Have you ever sought to cultivate a public image of yourself as a lothario?
>
> KISSINGER: No.
>
> QUESTION: Are you aware of the fact that you have had a reputation of being something of a ladies' man?
>
> KISSINGER: Certainly, when I was unmarried.
>
> QUESTION: And did you ever do anything to refute that image?
>
> KISSINGER: I did nothing to promote it or to refute it.
>
> QUESTION: As a matter of fact, you were married to the present Mrs. Kissinger in what year?
>
> KISSINGER: 1974.
>
> QUESTION: I draw your attention to a newspaper article that appeared on January 19, 1987, in the *New York Post*, in which

you are quoted as saying, "Spread it around that I am sexy, says Henry," speaking of you, originator of the immortal line "Power is the ultimate aphrodisiac." Did you say that?

KISSINGER: If it was quoted, I must have said it.

QUESTION: So, by your public statements and public activities you have not portrayed yourself as being shy in some respects in sexual things.

KISSINGER: Sexual subjects is different. If you are saying— This was, anyway, a joking conversation with the author at the dinner table.

QUESTION: Was that at Cafe Mortimer?

KISSINGER: Yes, but . . .

At that moment Kissinger must have envisioned the tabloid headlines that would make him and his eight-figure lawsuit a coast-to-coast laughingstock. Johnny Carson would ridicule him in his monologue; gossip columnists would have a field day. The deposition had served its purpose. In less than an hour the Great Negotiator had talked himself out of a $10 million litigation. A few days later, after weighing the pros and cons of continuing the case, Kissinger's attorneys, led by Oliver North's chief prosecutor, the spaghetti-haired Arthur Liman, called to say their client was dropping his suit.

The law is supposed to be a search for answers. Actually, making it hard to find information is one of the things lawyers do best. The more money there is at stake, the longer a case takes to resolve, as lawyers for the side that stands to lose the most delay the proceedings any way they can.

Recently, I handled the case of comedian Richard Belzer, who sued wrestler Hulk Hogan and actor Mr. T. for conspiring to break his neck. The two appeared on Belzer's TV talk show, promoting an event called Wrestlemania, when the anemic-looking host suggested that wrestling was fake. Hogan and Mr. T. took exception, and to prove Belzer wrong Hogan put him in a headlock that sent him to the hospital.

The result was a sort of athletic Scopes trial. The issue was not just the injury inflicted by Hogan but the legitimacy of professional wrestling. Lawyers for Titan Sports, wrestling's biggest promoter and profiteer, were in a "prevent defense" when Hogan came to my office to give his deposition.

During a deposition, many of the same rules that apply in court are in effect, including the right to note objections to questions, which a battery of attorneys for the wrestling industry used like a half nelson to protect their employer's interests.

Hogan, a bleached-blond creation of the media, sat at a conference table, glaring into my video camera, while his lawyers had their camera trained on me as I tried to question him.

> QUESTION: "Were you aware, Mr. Hogan, of there being a public controversy at the time when Wrestlemania was about to be presented concerning whether or not wrestling was real or whether it was fake?"

Then the litany began.

THEODORE DINSMORE (Hogan's lawyer): Objection.

BARRY ROTHMAN (Titan Sports's lawyer): Objection.

MARK VAN NORMAN (Mr. T.'s lawyer): Objection.

QUESTION: Was it your understanding that it was the intention of the promoters of [Wrestlemania] to give the impression to the public that what they witnessed at wrestling events was a real competition as distinguished from something that was purely staged or fake?

DINSMORE: Objection . . .

VAN NORMAN: Objection . . .

HOGAN: Not real competitions, but real issues.

QUESTION: Issues? What is the issue that was involved as you understood it between two wrestlers in a wrestling ring?

HOGAN: Good guy versus bad guy.

DINSMORE: Objection.

QUESTION: Was there any effort that you were aware of to dispel the notion that these wrestling events were rigged with the outcome being predetermined before the event took place?

ROTHMAN: Objection.

VAN NORMAN: Objection.

DINSMORE (to Hogan): Do you understand the question?

HOGAN: No. I don't.

QUESTION: In fact, in wrestling events, such as Wrestlemania, the wrestlers knew in advance who would win and who would lose?

DINSMORE: Objection.

QUESTION: Is that a trade secret?

DINSMORE: Yes.

ROTHMAN: Objection.

QUESTION: When you appeared on the Richard Belzer Show did you have an understanding of what professional wrestling was?

ROTHMAN: Objection.

DINSMORE: Objection.

QUESTION: Did you understand that professional wrestling was an activity in which the participants struggled in hand-to-hand combat primarily for the purpose of providing entertainment to spectators, rather than conducting a bona fide athletic contest?

DINSMORE: Objection.

ROTHMAN: Objection. Instruct the witness not to answer.

This case was headed for a media blitz. By court order the trial was to be televised. It was even listed in *TV Guide*. Unfortunately for viewers, the matter was settled just before airtime, and the truth about wrestling was never told.

Once you begin legal action, particularly in a libel case where your character and reputation are the central issue, your life becomes an open book. If you do not want all the phrases in that book to be read out loud in public, stay out of court.

American diplomat Alger Hiss might have been president of the United States if he had refrained from suing Whittaker Chambers for libel. Instead, information came out during the trial that sent Hiss to jail and ended his career in disgrace. The same thing happened to British playwright Oscar Wilde when he sued the Marquis of Queensberry for calling him a "sodomite." There is a long list of famous plaintiffs who should have left well enough alone, but instead they never considered the consequences of a lawsuit, or else severely overestimated their tolerance for bad publicity.

Almost everyone has something to hide. Several years ago I was hired to defend a small computer company against a wily corporate raider from New York named Ascher Adelman. Fond of high-budget maneuvers, Adelman had spent $5 million on a proxy campaign to take over the company. To his dismay, after the stockholders' votes were counted, he had won only a four-seat minority on the new board. When he informed company officials that he wanted to be reimbursed for his proxy expenses, they refused. So Adelman sued them for libel, claiming that false statements had been circulated about him during the campaign.

In the course of my investigation of the case, an interesting pattern began to emerge. In a number of previous takeover attempts, Adelman had employed similar tactics: muscling in on targeted companies, then, if his financial demands were not met, he would file similar suits. I put Adelman through a deposition that lasted over four hours, and by the time it was over, he knew someone was on his case. He also had to realize that a trial would expose his past history, making it difficult, if not impossible, to use the same business methods in future takeover attempts. Not long after the deposition, Adelman decided that suing the computer company was not such a good idea after all and withdrew his action.

Dan Burt, Adelman's lawyer, had another client, General William Westmoreland, who came to the same conclusion in his libel suit against CBS. A network news program had accused the Army of doctoring Vietnam casualty figures, and the general wanted to clarify his role in announcing those figures. After a few weeks in court, Westmoreland realized that retrying the entire history of an unpopular war would only make matters worse, and he too dropped his case.

Court cases are won by people who know how much they can afford to lose. There is a simple risk analysis that anyone contemplating a lawsuit, especially a plunge into the libel lottery, should consider before calling a lawyer: Think of the worst thing that could be said about you. Now imagine hearing it announced in a courtroom by an attorney with a very loud voice whose job it is to tear you to shreds. Then ask yourself if winning—or losing—is worth it. And if your answer is anything less than a stout-hearted YES—do not sue.

Everything trial lawyers do is designed to reduce the opposition's willingness to fight. Even before a case reaches the deposition stage, attorneys love to test each other's macho. Some try a barrage of court motions to wear their adversaries down; others use the media to leverage a surrender. Press and television coverage can easily scare off opponents or, if that fails, give them so much negative publicity that an effective defense is impossible. I know of several major lawsuits that were settled the minute one of the attorneys threatened to call "60 Minutes." It is the rare client who wants to go *mano a mano* with Mike Wallace.

Televangelists Jim and Tammy Bakker hired San Francisco lawyer Melvin Belli to defend them against charges of stealing church funds, but Belli's ego got more attention than his clients' case, and the public relations project failed.

"I like a minister who's been tempted and sinned," he declared at a press conference. "That way he can counsel his flock better. . . . Give me a sinning minister any time."

I represented the Falwell faction in the TV holy war, and at times Belli's misdirected media efforts were my secret weapon.

"Really, Melvin Belli has been found not to be a shining human being," I told the press as part of my own media campaign. "I am not trying to become personal. I am not talking about Melvin Belli and his multiple stewardess wives, or about the arrogance of naming his one son Caesar. Every step that Belli makes is one step lower down."

By the time the two of us met on the TV program "A Current Affair," even Belli must have realized that the more exposure the case got the less his clients benefited, and just as the show began he stalked off the set in a huff. After reporters were through with them, the beleaguered Bakkers barely had a legal leg to stand on. With their defender Belli nowhere in sight, Jim and Tammy appeared on "Nightline," and Ted Koppel finished them off as they replied to his questions with quotes from the Bible.

The media giveth and the media taketh away. Nobody knows that better than lawyers. If it were not for newspapers and television, many attorneys would be only half as threatening as they seem. Gerry Spence, the legendary Wyoming trial lawyer—best known for his ten-gallon hat and $10 million wrongful-death recovery in the Karen Silkwood case—pretends he's the Lone Ranger, a message he likes to deliver to his foes by sending them silver bullets. It's his way of saying, "You're next, pardna."

Spence mailed one of his fabled cartridges to me shortly before we met on his home turf, Cheyenne, Wyoming, in the $26 million Miss

Wyoming libel case. Only days before, he had filed a suit claiming that his client was the intended subject of a fictional short story in *Penthouse* about a beauty queen who dreams of saving mankind. Her "talent" was fellating world leaders and raising them off the ground. Spence was shooting from the hip on this one, so after receiving his bullet I fired back this reply: "If you persist in seeing yourself as Wyatt Earp . . . I would suggest you seek psychiatric help. . . . But yes, I will be happy to meet you at the O.K. Corral, as you so banally put it."

The issue in the case boiled down to the legal difference between fact and fiction, and during the deposition I zeroed in on Spence's client, Kimerli Jayne Pring, Miss Wyoming 1978.

"Now you understand," I asked her, "that having received his blowjob and ejaculating, the man in the story is levitating. Isn't that what the story is saying?"

"Yes, sir," she demurely answered.

"Now, Miss Pring," I continued, "in the real world, do you know or have you ever heard of anyone who could ever levitate?"

"No, sir," she said.

"Whether connected with a blowjob or otherwise?"

"Correct."

Miss Pring, whose official beauty-pageant talent was baton twirling, was an attractive young lady with an active social life. After some digging we turned up an old boyfriend who claimed to have been on the receiving end of her oral skills. However, once he found out what his story was worth, he wanted $300,000 to tell it in court.

Without the boyfriend's testimony, Spence easily won the trial by turning the case into an attack on Wyoming womanhood. But the verdict was reversed on appeal. The lone dissenting vote came from a judge who said, "I consider levitation . . . as fiction. Fellatio is not."

The victory became a landmark. Almost as satisfying was a paragraph it got me in one of Spence's books: "Norman Roy Grutman," he wrote, "was cunning, crafty and tough. He would do whatever was necessary to win. His style was to attack straight on—everybody and everything—relentlessly. He gave no quarter until his opponent was subdued, prostrate, and begging for mercy, and—having none—he gave none."

In a line of work where threatening behavior is a virtue, I could hardly have asked for a better endorsement.

Of course, going to trial is the ultimate threat. That's because the outcome is the ultimate uncertainty. But a trial is not the only way to win a case.

"There is no glory in a settlement" was the favorite saying of John "Eyebrows" Reilly, one of the vanished greats of the legal profession. A settlement, though, can often be more rewarding than winning a court verdict, since it eliminates most of the risks that come with a trial. Because lawyers often use settlements to increase their profit and decrease their work, the problem for the client is knowing when to settle, and for how much.

Crowded court dockets can keep a case on hold for years. Instead of speeding up the process, attorneys have turned slowing it down into an art form. The longer a criminal case is delayed, the better the chances are that evidence and witnesses will disappear. In civil cases, defense lawyers know that money delayed is money saved, and will try every maneuver they can to keep the plaintiff's side waiting.

Discovery motions, appeals and continuances are typical ploys to frustrate indigent plaintiffs and get them to settle cases for less than they are worth. In negligence and personal-injury suits, delays have another advantage to the defense. Given enough time, a plaintiff facing a long hospital stay could always die, a turn of events that can save the defendant a fortune in extra charges.

"Delays or a continuance are almost as good as an acquittal," said Edward Bennett Williams. "The only trouble is they don't last as long."

Then there are those cases where clients refuse to give up, no matter what. Once I had a client who was severely injured in a construction accident. As his suit against the company he worked for dragged on, the man's condition deteriorated, and with his doctors predicting he had only days to live, the insurance company finally offered him $50,000. The judge was adamant we settle, but my stubborn Italian client would not budge.

"Itsa not enough," he groaned from inside his oxygen tent. "Getta more. That money's a gonna send my kids to medical school." I told him that getting any more looked impossible. "No way," he said with what sounded like his last ounce of strength. "Go back. Getta more."

The judge could not believe it, and neither could the defense lawyers. The plaintiff was playing hardball from his deathbed. But his determination paid off. To everyone's surprise, he pulled through. The insurance company raised the settlement to $150,000, and the man's two children became doctors.

Nothing convinces an opponent you mean business like sticking to your guns. Still, every case has moments of maximum and minimum settlement value, times when a plaintiff stands to gain the most and a defendant to lose the least. It is up to the lawyer to know when those moments have arrived and take advantage of them. Sometimes that can be more of a gamble than a science.

A few years ago, I represented a man in a suit against the manufacturer of a defective pacemaker. Midway through the trial the other side offered to settle for $20,000, which seemed like peanuts at the time. I had Dr. Denton Cooley, the famous heart surgeon, as an expert witness, and figured the jury would award much more than that. I finished my summation with a self-confident flourish, and the case went to the jury. But before long, questions started coming back that made me very nervous, questions about the pacemaker, not what it did to my client.

I became so concerned that I asked the opposing lawyer if the $20,000 offer was still good. He said yes, and my client took it.

Afterward I met the jury foreman in the hallway. What did I get for a settlement? he wanted to know. I told him. "Oh, that's too bad," he said. "We were going to give you $100,000."

"What about those pacemaker questions?" I asked.

"They all came from the same guy," he replied. "He was only showing off."

Reaching settlement is part of the game lawyers play with one another and their clients. Most attorneys make it their practice to inform a client of a settlement offer twice: first at a figure less than what was offered; then, after pretending to get tough with the other side, the real figure is disclosed as a triumph of negotiation. In a system where profit depends on dispensing information in carefully controlled amounts, most lawyers like to keep their clients guessing, which puts them at a distinct disadvantage if their case ends up before a judge.

Anyone who comes to court as a plaintiff or a defendant is there to be tested, to have his prejudices probed, his memory questioned, his reaction to stress observed. Nowhere is an individual more vulnerable than he is in a courtroom. The pressure of having to take the witness stand causes some people to lose their voices; others get so nervous they self-destruct. I once saw a Mafia boss come completely unhinged when a lawyer simply mentioned the name of his mistress.

In days of old, the basic element of every trial was the ordeal. Now it's called cross-examination, and it has two basic aims: to reveal testimony that can help a case and to undermine any that can hurt it. This is the point at which the plaintiff's and defendant's stories collide. Rather than being a vehicle for determining which side is telling the truth, a cross-examination is more like a demolition derby to see which one survives. Sometimes it takes several laps around the track to produce a wreck; sometimes a crackup is almost immediate.

Sneak attacks on a witness's character are a favorite weapon. So are questions devised to elicit responses like "I don't know" or "I don't remember," either of which, said often enough, can make any testimony sound suspect. No matter how honest a person's statements may seem, a crafty attorney can always find ways to weaken or even reverse the effect. Accusing glares, shrugs, smirks and the most powerful courtroom gesture of all—a pointed finger—are a few of the dramatic touches lawyers use to type-cast and discredit a witness.

Some attorneys are document wavers, others are railing slappers. I like to use props, and any object that gets attention will do.

The perfect opportunity presented itself in a case I tried in Miami in 1989. My client, the owner of 116 Florida gas stations, was seeking $60 million in damages from a major oil company, which had abruptly ended a long-term supply agreement, citing his failure to meet his quarterly quota of gasoline sales. The fact that he had been one of the company's best dealers and was even awarded an expensive clock to mark his fiftieth anniversary in the business made no difference. Big oil companies are ruthless, and when negotiations failed to produce a settlement, my ruined client was forced to go to trial.

Hundreds of file boxes filled the courtroom. Both sides called expert witnesses; the oil company used six of them at a disclosed cost of over $2 million. However, the evidence made it clear that my client was not at fault and that the oil company itself had contributed to the drop in sales by not pricing its gasoline competitively.

On the jury were several retirees and senior citizens, and when it was my turn to deliver a final argument, I reviewed the high points of the case. Then in a great show of contempt, I held up the anniversary clock and glared at the defendants. "For fifty years," I said, "the hands of this clock have turned 400,000 times. That's how long my client has worked for you. Here, take back your clock and give him back his business."

Every person on the jury who had ever felt cheated by the company he worked for got the message, and so did the company, which lost the verdict.

With most lawyers the theatrics are only an act. Occasionally you encounter one who absorbs his client's anger and uses it to badger witnesses and opposing attorneys. Richard Golub, an obnoxious attorney I faced once in a breach-of-contract suit, would call me "a fat lesbian" whenever we met in the hallway outside of court. Since the insult made no sense (although I was slightly overweight), I assumed he subscribed to the fallacious theory that getting on the other side's nerves with insults automatically increases the chances of winning. In this case, I stayed cool, while Golub became so obsessed with making me mad that he forgot about the need to prove his case at the trial, which he lost.

I agree with Edward Bennett Williams. The best defense is not necessarily the truth, it's a thorough rehearsal. Even when they appear to be losing, savvy attorneys give off a feeling of being in charge. Witnesses are a different story. Some you can wind up and say, "Sic 'em," and they know exactly what to do. Others have to be almost anesthetized. A client on the witness stand is like someone with a toothache throbbing in his head. The normal response is to scream. But to survive a hostile cross-examination and at the same time score points with the jury, it's important to keep normal responses under control. And the only way to do that is to be ready for anything.

Every answer a witness gives sends a message to the jurors. Some messages speak louder than others, and it's up to the lawyer to be sure that each one supports the central theme of his case. Nobody has ever expressed this idea better than New York defense attorney John Gardner, whose theory is that the plaintiff should never answer a single question on the witness stand without plugging his theme. If the opposing attorney asks his name, the reply, says Gardner, crudely but correctly, should be: "They screwed me." Where do you work? "They screwed me." What kind of car do you drive? "They screwed me."

Gardner may be overstating the importance of consistency. Yet not by much. Repeat something often enough and it starts to sound true. A trial is a contest between two actors, and the side with the most consistently believable lines almost always wins.

Sometimes getting a person ready to appear in court can require no more than making sure he shows up on time. Then there are those who go blank or, what's worse, completely change their stories. I have had clients unable to testify without taking tranquilizers. I represented a man in California who became so afraid when he saw the courthouse that he had to be pried out of the taxicab and dragged inside.

Then there was Wilfredo Beltron. He was recommended to me by another lawyer, and when I met him, he was wearing a back brace and a neck brace, and one of his legs was in a cast. He said his car had been pulverized by a bakery truck. Despite his pitiable condition, the insurance company refused to settle. After the case got to court, I found out why. The company's lawyer showed movies of Wilfredo changing a flat tire, fixing his front door and doing all sorts of things inconsistent with his injuries. At which point, he tugged on my sleeve with tears in his eyes, and sobbed, "I want to go home."

The stress of a court appearance, even when they're telling the truth, can make clients very unpredictable creatures, and saving them from themselves is always a lawyer's hardest job. Testifying at a trial is a dialogue, not a chat. What a good attorney tries to do when he's cross-examining a witness is draw him into a conversation, get him to drop his defenses and make an unguarded comment that, either by itself or combined with other information, will help his client's case.

How questions are answered in a deposition or a trial dictates the result. Which is why teaching clients what to say—and what *not* to say—is so crucial. The key to stage managing is directing your players, and I give everyone I represent in court three basic acting instructions:

Answer defensively. The opposing lawyer is your enemy. He's trying to catch you in an admission of wrongdoing or, the next best thing, a series of inconsistent responses that will ruin your testimony. If you do not understand a question, ask for it to be repeated. That provides time to formulate the answer you want to give—not the one your opponent's lawyer is looking for. It also makes the attorney respond to you instead of the other way around. A jury respects someone who fights back in a hostile cross-examination.

Say less. What you have been hearing on TV police shows for the past twenty-five years is true. Anything you say *can* be used against you. With that in mind, dispense as little information as possible to unfriendly lawyers. If the opposing attorney asks if you know what day it is, don't give him the date and a full weather report. The answer should always be a simple yes. Why make his job easier or your situation any worse? Keep the burden of proof where it belongs—on the other side.

Do not guess. If you understand the question the opposing lawyer asks but do not know the answer or have forgotten it—never guess. Once a witness starts saying "I think" or "I suppose," the advantage shifts to the questioner, and when that happens, the ball, so to speak, is in your court.

In a trial, one side wins and the other side loses, but before that can happen, it's up to the lawyers to blame somebody, and make it stick. Whether the case involves a murder, a breach of contract or a hostile takeover, the jury has to be persuaded first that the law has been broken and then that one side is responsible. Within the either-or framework of the legal system that may sound like the difference between right and wrong, but it's actually the result of a selective disclosure of information. Law is not a science. In court, truth is a matter of opinion based on impressions that have filtered through a confusing maze of procedures, and how those impressions are created can dictate the outcome of a case.

In every legal matter, procedures define reality. The way facts in a case are revealed—or whether they are revealed at all—depends on hard-and-fast procedural rules. A case can be knocked out of court because the statute of limitations has expired; there could be a conflict of interest, an abuse of discovery or an improper police search. Those are all procedures, and the lawyer who uses them to his advantage has the best chance of winning.

In a trial where it is one man's word against another man's alibi, what matters as much as an attorney's procedural know-how is his ability to conduct the performance, to make his case look good by making his adversary's look bad.

In 1988, Bess Myerson, the former Miss America and New York culture queen, was charged with bribing a judge, Hortense Gabel, to get her boyfriend's alimony reduced. The circumstantial evidence was probably enough to convict Myerson, but when the prosecution brought in the judge's daughter, Sukhreet Gabel, as a witness against her mother, the psychodrama of the whole trial changed.

What had been a bribery case turned into a violation of the scriptural commandment to honor thy father and mother. Bess Myerson was no longer on trial. Sukhreet Gabel was. Defense attorneys went on the attack, questioning the key witness for the prosecution until the jury couldn't stand her. And when they summed up their case, who did they invite to sit in the front row but Sukhreet, by then a full-fledged camera hog. Myerson, her boyfriend, sewer king Carl Capasso, and Judge Gabel were only supporing players. Myerson was found not guilty.

A court case is like a Broadway play. There are auditions, rehearsals and opening night. Whether the play is a hit or a flop hinges on which version of the plot the jury wants to believe, and which players win the Tony awards.

Good lawyers know how to reduce a complicated case to human proportions, give dry statistics drama, turn witnesses into heroes and villains and give a big part to someone like Sukhreet Gabel.

The point of going to court is walking out a winner, and the attorneys who do that most often can put on a convincing show with any available talent—even if it belongs to the other side.

CHAPTER 7

THE MYTH OF THE IMPARTIAL JURY

Trial by jury is a basic right of every American. The theory is that twelve people with no special skill or learning can hear the facts in a case and by using what lawyers like to call "their God-given common sense" decide who should win and who should lose.

As theories go, few are more sacred in the abstract or less reliable in real life. In big antitrust cases, for example, judges often spend weeks trying to find jurors smart enough to understand the issues involved. Imagine being on the jury that heard the famous case several years ago in which Memorex sued IBM for unfair competition. The billion-dollar lawsuit was a test of physical stamina as well as the jurors' grasp of economics, engineering and corporate psychology. The trial lasted three months, as jury members listened to eighty-seven witnesses, examined three thousand exhibits and then spent nineteen days in deliberation before informing the judge they were too confused to reach a verdict.

Not every case calls for jurors with brains. Recently in Washington, the judge in the Oliver North trial was determined to find a jury that knew absolutely nothing about North and the much-publicized Iran-contra scandal. In less than two days he had fifty qualified candidates. The legal system thrives on an uninformed populace.

"I don't like the news," declared one potential juror. Whenever anyone in his family talked about politics, he said, "I go into my room and lock the door."

Another prospective juror said she never read a word about North, Iran or the contras. "Just hearing about that stuff made me mad," she told the judge. "It was on television all day . . . and there were reruns at night. I couldn't stand it."

Was this a jury of North's peers or a cross section of global-village idiots? The jurors who were finally selected not only knew nothing about the case, they knew almost nothing at all. Here were a dozen noble savages, residents of an information society with no information but, in theory, plenty of untapped common sense.

In the eyes of the law, the perfect juror is Rip Van Winkle, someone who has been snoozing in the hills for the past twenty years; every name he hears in court he is hearing for the first time, every event is a revelation, every piece of evidence he is shown is like a chunk of moon rock. If finding people who fit that description is not easy, consider how much harder it is keeping them awake once the trial begins.

A lawyer who cannot keep juries entertained usually puts them to sleep. Most jurors are reluctant to be in court in the first place, and if the show isn't that interesting, they simply fade out.

In the same District Court in Washington where North was tried, former White House aide Lyn Nofziger had been on trial six months earlier for violating federal lobbying laws. During final arguments in the case, one juror was dismissed for dozing off and falling out of his seat. After noticing that other jury members were closing their eyes, the judge ordered all of them to stand and do wake-up exercises.

It happens all the time. Cross-examine a murderer, and the jury follows every word; call a banking expert to testify, and you might as well pass out pillows.

I always tell jurors that I am looking for people with open minds, not empty minds. The truth is that I often have to settle for anyone who appears able to stay conscious for three straight hours.

As a rule nobody sleeps at a sex-crime trial. But there was a legendary case in Brooklyn where even that failed to keep one man in the jury from taking a nap. During questioning, a woman testified that the male defendant had forced her to engage in oral sex.

"Could you tell us exactly what he said?" asked the defense attorney.

"I can't say it," she sobbed. "It's too embarrassing."

"Well, then write it," the lawyer told her.

The woman wrote down the defendant's request, and the attorney gave the piece of paper to the jury foreman, telling him to read it and pass it along. When an attractive female juror nudged the sleeping man next to her and handed him the paper, he read it and, thinking it was a secret message from his neighbor, slyly put it in his pocket.

"Sir, would you please give me that note," the attorney demanded. "What note?" the man replied, totally unaware it had anything to do with the case.

Sleeping jurors are symptoms of a much greater problem that exists in every court. It's not that most trials are boring, it's that most trial juries these days simply are not willing or able to absorb what's going on. In courtrooms across the country, juries with tenth-grade educations are responsible for deciding complicated civil and criminal cases, not because they are sufficiently uninformed to be fair, but because they are the only ones available.

In fact, the best people for the job are usually the most eager to avoid it. And who can blame them?

In most places, being on a jury differs little from being on trial. Jurors are prisoners of the justice system. Barred from any contact with lawyers, they are herded by the hundreds into bus-stationlike holding rooms and ordered to stay there until further notice. Sometimes the wait can last weeks. Yet being chosen to sit on a trial hardly qualifies as a reprieve.

The bigger the case, the greater the hardship—and the risk. Some high-profile trials can drag on for months, even years, while jurors spend their days in the courtroom and their nights under virtual house arrest in tamper-proof hotels. In cases involving organized-crime figures, courts in New York now try to protect jury members from reprisals by having them watch the proceedings on closed-circuit television. At the 1989 trial of a notorious drug dealer in Washington, the judge recognized the safety factor, but instead of installing closed-circuit TV, he surrounded the jury box with panels of bulletproof plastic.

The longest and costliest criminal prosecution in U.S. history, the McMartin Preschool child-molesting case in Los Angeles, began in 1986 and ended two and a half years later after 124 witnesses filled 60,000 pages of trial transcript. When it finally concluded, the case was on the verge of a mistrial because there were no more alternate jurors left. Various members were dismissed one by one for gallbladder surgery, chronic back pain and the threat of a lost promotion.

"There are limits to what jurors can endure," said the judge in glorious understatement just before the last alternate suffered a stroke. "A trial should not take so long." By the time this one ended with verdicts of acquittal, the cost to taxpayers in California was $15 million.

In the "pizza-connection" drug case, a New York jury was cooped up for seventeen months. During the trial, which lasted from October 1985 to February 1987, jurors heard 236 witnesses and examined literally tons of documents, so much evidence that it took nearly a year to introduce all of it in court. Aside from the work load—there were eighty-seven defendants involved, all members of a Mafia group accused of running an international heroin operation—jurors had to cope with long-term separation from their families and jobs and, for the final months, complete isolation from the outside world.

Six months into the trial, the confinement got to one member of the jury, who went berserk and began attacking marshals in the hallway. At the one-year mark, a defendant was murdered in a gangland execution. Shortly afterward, a juror received a death threat, and the judge decided to sequester the entire panel. When both sides ended their arguments, each member of the jury carried with him into the deliberation room a 59-page verdict sheet, a 100-page copy of the judge's instructions and, just in case they had forgotten the opening argument in the intervening months, a 410-page summary of the government's case.

Not all trials require that kind of sacrifice, but word about the general unpleasantness of jury duty gets around. Which is why so many people would rather skip the experience. Any excuse usually works. I know of one case where a man was dismissed after claiming he was in "a poor frame of mind" and another where someone was excused because there was nobody to walk his dog.

In many jurisdictions court administrators pick the names of would-be jurors from the voter registration rolls. Knowing this probably keeps millions of people from voting and assures that most juries are made up of the elderly, the unemployed and anyone else with nothing better to do.

A jury is a psychological road map of the community it comes from, all the fear and loathing of the local population concentrated in twelve average citizens. Juries are not selected at random. They are made to order for each case, and how they're put together, the ingredients purposely added and left out, has more to do with who wins or loses than anything else that happens in court.

Grand juries are made up of twenty-four people and function like a neighborhood review board, passing preliminary judgment on anyone accused of a crime. These jurors are different from trial (or petit) jurors. Instead of being drawn from the masses, they are generally a town's leading citizens—businessmen, bankers, builders—chosen for the job by their friends in politics. In New York City, where their terms can run for years, grand jurors even have an elite social club known as the Chowder and Marching Society whose members regularly meet for dinner parties and high-level back slapping.

Operating more like establishment inquisitions than trials, grand juries are controlled by district attorneys, whose choice of which cases to prosecute and which ones to drop is never purely legal. Unprotected by a lawyer or the rules of cross-examination, anyone who appears before a grand jury is naked prey for vicious, ambitious assistant DAs. Guilt and innocence are determined later. The grand jury's job is to send the best cases to court, and that's a decision influenced as much by the political climate as it is by the evidence.

Subway vigilante Bernhard Goetz, who is white, shot four black teenagers because he thought they were going to rob him. New Yorkers are "experts" in life-threatening situations, and a Manhattan grand jury, no doubt feeling Goetz was only defending himself, indicted him on one count of possessing an unregistered firearm. As national re-action to the shooting mounted, prosecutors went to another grand jury and persuaded it to indict Goetz on more serious charges, in-cluding attempted murder.

During the seven-week trial, Goetz's lawyer, Barry Slotnick, who specializes in defending high-profile, low-esteem public figures, made the "double" indictment a major issue in the case, claiming that the district attorney, responding to political pressure, had coerced the sec-ond grand jury into doing what the first one refused to do. The trial jurors must have agreed, since Goetz was found guilty of only the original charge, carrying an illegal gun.

Critics complained that the outcome of the case was a triumph of primitive emotions over reason. They were right. Primitive emotions are a lawyer's best friend. The secret is finding ways to make them work for your client.

Trial juries are chosen during an elaborate question-and-answer session known as the voir dire, French for "to see and tell." In most state courts, with the judge looking on, lawyers for both sides audition candidates, asking them about their jobs, their income, their sex life and whatever else might affect their opinion of the plaintiff or defendant or the situation.

Of course, there is no guarantee anyone is telling the truth. Most people would probably believe an arresting police officer's testimony before they would believe the person he arrested, but when it comes to saying so in front of a judge, few will admit it. Everyone always insists that he can be fair. Even the most diehard bigots try to hide their true feelings in court. Yet true feelings are what the trial lawyer must try to divine, any way he can. It is a myth that trial attorneys are looking for an impartial jury. Experienced litigators know no one is ever unbiased. What they are looking for are jurors who will be *partial* to their client's case and prejudiced against their opponent's.

The jurors in the Bernhard Goetz trial clearly accepted Slotnick's invitation to see themselves and the defendant as victims. In effect, their verdict said if they were in Goetz's position they would have done exactly what he did. It is that kind of sympathetic connection that lawyers try to build into every jury.

In another part of the country, even another part of the city or state, jurors might have seen things in a completely different light. Wealthy communities like Fairfield County, Connecticut, or La Jolla, California, are not places to look for fat damage awards in civil suits or a forgiving love tap in criminal cases. On the other hand, jurors in poor communities not only tend to be more lenient, they love to play "Wheel of Fortune" with other people's money.

Plaintiffs in cities with large minority populations have a big advantage in negligence cases. Defense attorneys like to pick the best-educated jurors they can, believing they will be less emotional about the issues. But educated white-collar jury candidates often find ways to get out of serving, which leaves most urban juries made up of poor blacks and others, who feel, with good cause, they have been cheated by "the system." They have a natural tendency to reward the underdog, no matter what the facts in a case show, and appealing to that urge is standard practice among plaintiff's lawyers.

When it comes to juries, geography is destiny. I once tried a medical malpractice case in New York in which the victim of a traffic accident was first treated in a Bronx emergency room, then taken to a Manhattan hospital where the real damage was done. The plaintiff could have sued in either jurisdiction, but I moved to have the case heard in the Bronx, where juries are a well-known source of big payoffs. The motion was granted, and the verdict awarded was $1.6 million, considerably larger than it would have been, even in overly generous New York County.

In a similar case twenty-five miles away in White Plains, New York, the headquarters of IBM, a client of mine with far worse injuries was awarded half that amount when the jury, dominated by a stingy IBM engineer, felt sorry for a local quack, who is probably still dispensing faulty medical aid to his unsuspecting patients. After the trial the juror who had held the line on spending sent the quadriplegic victim a bouquet of flowers to show how sorry he was.

In federal courts, where juries are chosen by the judge, lawyers have to take what they get. In state courts, where attorneys make the picks, the selection process is a Q-and-A version of musical chairs, with opposing sides trying to fill seats with as many friendly jurors as they can.

Nobody grows up wanting to be a juror, but some people are better at it than others. In every case, each lawyer has a certain number of challenges he can use to dismiss jury prospects he does not want. When there are only a few minutes to determine a person's qualifications, the first thing I do is weed out undesirables. Lawyers and anyone else with legal training are the first to go. Why put someone on the jury who already knows your tricks, or will be second-guessing every move you make? I also have a general rule against using bachelors. They tend to be too selfish. I like to avoid retirees for the same reason. Intellectuals confuse the facts; and military people, airline pilots and government bureaucrats always believe the authorities, good enough reason to steer clear of them too.

Lawyers do not like to waste their challenges, especially when they can get the judge to excuse a juror for conflict of interest. Whenever a Dallas attorney I know sees a juror he wants to get rid of without using up a challenge doing it, he asks him where he works. If the person has a job with the phone company, the lawyer tells the judge it's one of his clients. A local department store? Sorry. That's a client, too. No attorney ever thinks a jury will be objective. Most, in fact, work under the assumption that just the opposite is true, that all jurors are predisposed to certain choices that have nothing to do with the evidence in a case, that short people are vengeful, fat ones are generous with damage awards and women jurors always hate pretty female witnesses.

Barry Slotnick, this time representing former New York congressman Mario Biaggi on bribery charges, relearned the pretty-woman rule the hard way. Slotnick had Biaggi's girlfriend on the stand, but quickly realized the women on the jury loathed her.

"I saw it in their eyes," he said. "Those answers she gave about going to a spa 'to maintain herself' . . . the way she preened . . . I wanted her off fast."

Apparently his "fast" was not fast enough. The jury found Biaggi guilty of accepting illegal gratuities in the form of several Florida vacations with his girlfriend.

Choosing juries is an experiment in group psychology, where factors like social status, income level and race can tip the balance of opinion in either direction. In a weak case it's often wise to pick jurors preprogrammed to disagree with one another. Angry minorities, gun nuts or militant gays are always good choices. If all goes well, they will turn the deliberations into a shouting match and the trial will end with a hung jury and, with any luck, an out-of-court settlement.

Other times, attorneys battle it out for the ethnic advantage. When your client is Irish, you try to seat as many Irish jurors as you can. If he's Jewish, you look for Jews. One place that was never a problem was the old Second District Municipal Court on Manhattan's Lower East Side. The surrounding neighborhood was made up entirely of immigrants, and the only language you heard was Yiddish.

Lawyers like to give friendly signals to jurors. Often it's something they say during selection, or it could be a comment they make in their opening statement. The aim is to recruit the jury to their client's cause.

The boldest practitioner of the art I ever saw was an attorney named George Grabow. The Second District was his home court. Grabow spoke Yiddish, and whenever he argued against a lawyer who did not, he would slip little ethnic asides into his speeches. He would extol the flag and the Constitution. He would compare George Washington to Moses. He would talk about the Declaration of Independence, life, liberty and the pursuit of happiness, all the great concepts our forefathers believed in, including the cherished doctrine of *yentzim goyim*, which basically means "Screw the gentiles" in Yiddish.

Grabow got away with this for years, since judges in the Second District usually could not speak the local language. Then one day he faced Jimmy Dougherty, a Yiddish-speaking Irish lawyer who understood every word Grabow said.

"Waddaya mean, *yentzim goyim?*" Dougherty shouted as he sprang to his feet. "I want a bench conference."

He translated for the judge, and Grabow, for the time being at least, had to revert to English.

Every jury has its own personality, its own leaders and followers. No attorney can ever be sure he has found the right combination. That feeling of uncertainty, plus a dramatic increase in the stakes, has given rise in recent years to the jury-research specialist, a kind of group-behavior guru who helps lawyers analyze, select and influence jurors.

In cases where billions of dollars may hang on the verdict, attorneys try not to leave anything to chance. When MCI Communications won a major antitrust suit against AT&T a few years ago, it did so with the aid of a crack team of corporate lawyers and a jury-research company. Months before the real trial took place in U.S. District Court in Chicago, specially chosen mock jurors were studied by experts from Leo J. Shapiro and Associates, a market-research firm. Their findings not only helped attorneys pick jurors likely to line up on MCI's side, they also showed them how to beef up the bottom line.

During practice sessions it was discovered that the practice jurors were more generous with damage awards when no mention was made of specific lost-profit figures. So after casting MCI as the little guy and AT&T as a rich giant, attorneys encouraged the real jurors to let their imaginations run wild when it came time to decide what the losing side should pay. The strategy paid off with a $1.8 million award.

Research firms have taken the basic techniques that trial lawyers employ every day for selecting and rejecting jurors and turned them into a social science, complete with terms like "decision clusters" and "predictor variables." I took on a law firm once that hired someone to chart the body language of prospective jurors while they waited to be questioned. Companies that offer these services make no guarantees; just the same, few big-money cases are conducted without adding their charges to the bill.

Some lawyers have gone a step further and hired psychics to help them pick juries. In 1985, Florida defense lawyer Ellis Rubin used

Micki Dahne, a clairvoyant, to select jurors in a grisly Miami murder trial. On four separate occasions—twice in court—the female defendant admitted shooting her husband, cutting his body into little pieces, then scattering them all along Rickenbacker Causeway.

"I tried to find jurors who looked like they'd be kind to their mothers," said Dahne, who had helped Atlanta police locate dead bodies in the Wayne Williams murder case there.

Dahne not only assisted Rubin in choosing a jury, she also sat in court for the entire trial.

"The effect of having her there was incredible," said a detective who worked on the case. "Here you've got a woman who confessed to doing everything the prosecution said she did, and the jury still let her off. They probably figured if a famous psychic thought she was innocent, who were they to disagree."

Juries are not always that easy to persuade. To win a case a lawyer has to convince them that his argument is right, or at least that his opponent's is wrong. Some attorneys single out the one juror they think will be the leader during deliberations and focus their efforts on him. Others resort to flattery, constantly complimenting juries on their intelligence and patience. If jury members believe the things a lawyer says about them, they are likely to believe the things he says about his client.

New York defense attorney Pete Johnson takes a slightly different approach. If he can get the jury to believe in him, his theory goes, he can get them to believe anything he says. Trust the teller and you trust the tale.

Nightclub entertainers and stand-up comics talk about being on a roll, a phenomenon that occurs when they have an audience not simply under control but under their spell. Any lawyer who has ever had a jury in the palm of his hand knows the feeling: twelve sets of eyes following your every gesture, twelve heads nodding in agreement with everything you say. The first step in the process is establishing an emotional bond between the lawyer and the jurors, and Johnson has the act down pat.

The show starts with his opening statement. Johnson came up the hard way, and every jury he meets hears a version of his life story, how he struggled to make ends meet, how he held three jobs to support his family and pay the bills. Not many lawyers could pull it off, but by the time he has finished his opening statement, Johnson has jurors thinking he is as honest and hardworking as they are. Here is somebody who knows the value of a dollar.

"Nobody gets something for nothing," Johnson tells the jurors, and it's not long before he has them convinced that plaintiffs looking for big awards in accident cases are lazy freeloaders.

I faced him in court in the late 1960s. My client was seeking damages for a back injury, the result of a serious car wreck, and Johnson made him sound like the worst whiner in the world.

"What's the matter with this guy?" he asked the jury, pointing an accusing finger at my client, who was wincing in pain.

"He wants $150,000! For what?" demanded Johnson. "Because his back hurts? There are American boys over in Vietnam getting their arms and legs blown off every day, and I don't hear them moaning for a hundred and fifty thousand bucks."

My client and I ran for cover and settled out of court for a lot less.

Juries only hear what the judge lets them hear. If procedural questions are discussed, the jury is generally removed from the courtroom, or else left waiting there as talks go on in the judge's chamber. In typical fashion most jurors never know the rules of the game being played until it's almost over, when the judge tells them how to apply the law.

While they're in court, jury members are supposed to take in all the facts of a case, but considering how events are often presented out of context and participants' roles in them redefined by special arrangements, they rarely see the whole picture. In cases with multiple defendants, juries are expected to follow several story lines, each managed by a different attorney, some of whom are trying to complicate the issues even further as a defensive tactic.

If things get confusing, that's the idea. Keeping the jury guessing is standard practice, particularly in criminal trials where "reasonable doubt" is cause enough for a not-guilty verdict.

In robbery cases, lawyers frequently get their clients off by using what's called "the missing-dude defense." This is the way it works: It was eleven o'clock at night, and the defendant, who has been accused of stealing $1,000 from a convenience store, was standing on a street corner, minding his own business. All of a sudden, according to his lawyer, a stranger runs by, throws $1,000 at him and keeps going. As his client picks up the money, the police arrive and arrest him.

The cops have the stolen money and the store clerk's positive identification. But his client is innocent, the defense lawyer protests. The "missing dude" did it. And by definition, he's nowhere to be found.

It happens to be one of the oldest tricks in the book. But to many jurors hearing it for the first time the story sounds plausible. The contest in every criminal trial is between reason and reasonable doubt. So while the prosecution tries to appeal to common sense, the defense attorney is busy blowing smoke.

Did the police make a mistake? Was the man arrested and charged only an innocent bystander? This is classic courtroom confusion, and more times than not it works well enough to make the jury wonder if the prosecution hasn't made a serious mistake.

"We can't send this young man to jail for a crime he didn't commit," pleads his lawyer, hoping the jury will think the missing dude is the real culprit, and many times they do.

In civil cases, expert witnesses can serve the same purpose. They supply information that can salvage a lost cause or turn a winning case into a loser by purposely misleading the jurors. A lawyer who presents false evidence can be held in contempt of court. Yet there is nothing wrong with using professional opinion that puts the jury in a trance or leads them off on a tangent.

Some doctors are so adept at swaying jurors they earn more money from testifying in court than they do treating patients. There are engineers and psychologists who have made careers out of being expert witnesses. I once had to pay a Washington cancer specialist $42,000 to appear in court for a day and a half in a malpractice case. That, he informed me, was his "bargain price."

Expert witnesses sell their services like anyone else in the legal profession, and the best in the field can sound convincing defending either side of an argument. Their function is to snow the jury. The job of the opposing attorney is to melt the snow, and the process starts by letting jurors know how much expert witnesses are paid to testify. It comes as a shock to most of them, who make under thirty-five dollars a day for their time in court, that someone else could make thousands.

The best experts introduce just enough arcane information into a case to make the jury doubt the other side. Demystifying their mumbo jumbo is essential.

In 1971, I represented a couple whose newborn child was left permanently retarded after being dropped on its head by a hospital nurse.

The damage was obvious. The child could not have been responsible. Still the hospital refused to take the blame. At the trial the hospital's lawyers produced an expert witness who testified that the infant was not injured by a blow but suffered from a rare condition he called "transient neo-natal hypoglycemia" or, properly translated, "a temporary, intermittent lack of sugar at birth."

In a nation where newspapers and television shows introduce new diseases every week, jurors can hardly be blamed for falling for such nonsense. In this case the doctor who appeared in court brought along charts and slides to show how the dread affliction claimed its victims, how powerless medical science was to stop it or predict where it would strike next, and therefore how no hospital could be held responsible for the consequences of the condition. I eventually won the case, but only after convincing the jury the doctor had no idea what he was talking about and that his hypothesis was an insult to the jury's common sense.

The best way to undermine the testimony of any expert witness is to ask him questions he can't answer. So when it was my turn to cross-examine the doctor, I put him to the test. After inquiring about his medical training, which I tried to portray as inadequate to the demands of the case—despite his knowledge of this strange disease that had somehow escaped detection by other doctors—I asked him to name for the court the twelve cranial nerves. It was a risky move if he knew them, but a potential knockout punch if he did not, and I figured him for a bluffer.

I gave the jury a friendly nod that said, "Let's see how smart this guy really is," then turned to the doctor, who was beginning to falter after naming one or two nerves.

"Well, sir," I said, careful not to suggest any special competence by calling him doctor, "has your knowledge failed you?"

Whatever he replied after that hardly mattered. The jury could plainly see there were things the other side's expert witness did not know.

A variation on that technique in medical malpractice cases is calling hospitals "corporations" or health-care providers "syndicates." This makes them seem more sinister and, more importantly, gives jurors the impression of big businesses with enough money to pay a million-dollar damage award and never miss it.

The testimony of any expert witness can be turned against him. Sometimes, if events require a change in strategy, it's even necessary to sandbag a friendly witness. Take the *Caligula* case. In the late 1970s, the film was the subject of several obscenity suits. One went to trial in Atlanta, where a fervent local prosecutor claimed the movie violated the moral standards of that fine Southern community. Having seen the film three times, I found it hard to disagree, but since I represented *Penthouse* publisher Bob Guccione, who produced this $14 million Roman orgy, it was my job to prove otherwise.

With Guccione's help, I imported an Italian priest to testify that *Caligula* was a great work of art. The jurors seemed impressed, until the prosecution introduced a pompous New York monsignor with the opposite opinion. It soon became clear that a jury of Baptists was not about to let Catholic priests tell them the difference between right and wrong. So I quickly altered course to make that the theme of my defense.

"I don't know what your religious preference may be," I told the jurors in my closing remarks. "However, I can think of no other institution on earth that has been responsible for more suffering than the Catholic Church. It caused the Thirty Years' War, the Hundred Years' War, the Spanish Inquisition. And now the prosecution has brought one of its representatives here to tell people in Georgia what to think and believe. You should be outraged."

As I spoke, I could see looks of anger and indignation on several jurors' faces. True, I was appealing to their worst suspicions. But sometimes that's what lawyers are paid to do. The next day, *Caligula* was playing to standing-room-only crowds in Atlanta.

Just to prove that no two cases are alike, I achieved the same result in Boston in a different way by convincing a judge that the movie, based on a screenplay by Gore Vidal, was a serious literary commentary on politics. This time, I appealed to the local sense of intellectual superiority. And it didn't hurt to have a Harvard professor of philosophy testify on the film's artistic merit. "By showing revolting incidents," he declared, "*Caligula* assaults the audience's passivity . . . as does Ingmar Bergman in *Cries and Whispers*."

Case closed.

People respect titles. Remove the title, and often the respect goes with it. Rather than call expert witnesses who have borderline credibility, some lawyers, used to trying certain kinds of cases, play the role themselves. A jury is usually more impressed by the real thing, but that never stops an attorney who thinks he can be just as good. I remember a case where a lawyer for the plaintiff's side described in gruesome detail all the injuries his client had sustained in a horrible industrial accident, how his limbs were crippled, his face was mangled and his internal organs so damaged that he had to relieve himself through a tube. The man's life was ruined, and his attorney thought he had the jury in his hands, until one juror in the front row leaned over the railing and vomited. The result was a mistrial.

Although most lawyers swear by the jury system, few trust it to be predictable. Attorneys read hidden meaning into everything a jury does and does not do. Once the jurors leave the courtroom to begin their deliberations, every request for more information, every long period of silence is a sign that one side or the other may be losing.

One of the nastiest cases I know involved a bitter struggle between two groups of relatives for control of their family's business. The warring factions hated one another. There were screaming matches on the witness stand, shoving contests in the corridors and fights in the parking lot. By the time the case went to the jury, the opposing lawyers and their assistants were yelling at one another as if they were part of the family too.

The jurors were out for two days before sending word they just could not reach a verdict. The judge told them to keep trying. Two more days passed and still there was no decision. This time the judge called them back to court to find out what the problem was. With family members staring daggers at each other, he asked the foreman for an explanation.

"Well, frankly, Your Honor," said the kindly-looking old man, "we feel this is the sort of case where we shouldn't mix in."

But mixing in is what courts and juries are designed to do. The legal system demands decisions. In most states it takes a unanimous vote by the jury to get a criminal conviction and a five-sixths majority to win a civil case. In bench trials, where the judge constitutes a jury of one, a single opinion is all that matters.

Nevertheless, the side that wins the verdict does not always win the case. A lower-court decision can be reversed on appeal, or a mistrial can be declared and the process started all over again, a prospect that encourages settlements and often leads to having the case dropped.

That's why losing attorneys go to any length to find evidence that the jury may have acted improperly. Something as innocent as a casual exchange of words between a juror and a lawyer can be enough for a mistrial. Often when the jury makes a monetary award, lawyers for the side that has to pay will examine the deliberation room for proof that jurors arrived at the amount by taking the average of several figures, also grounds for a new trial. So are prejudicial remarks by a juror, and unauthorized visits paid to the scene of a crime. I once represented the victim in a shooting case where a mistrial was declared when a juror brought in some pistol bullets from home for his colleagues to study during their deliberations.

Lawyers and judges like to think that juries, despite their shortcomings, invariably make the right decisions. Actually, so much can go wrong in the process that any verdict a jury reaches is suspect.

Our belief in the jury system reflects our blind faith in basic human understanding, the idea that people will know the truth when they see it (assuming nobody has paid them to look the other way). In fact, every day innocent people lose cases in court because jurors were intentionally misled or simply not paying attention. That's one reason judges at all levels of the legal system have the power to reverse any jury verdict with which they have a valid disagreement.

Courts exist to resolve the ambiguity of events, to decide what happened in the past and who should pay in the present and future. In a courtroom, though, truth can be an elusive commodity. When motives and actions are defined by legal concepts like "proximate cause," "concurrent cause" or "continuing cause," asking jurors to decide who or what really caused anything frequently means inviting them to guess. That does not mean that juries are failing to do the best they can. It simply means that anybody would be wise to think twice before trusting his fate to "twelve tried men and true." Yet given the choice, there are many times I would sooner trust a jury than a judge.

DISORDER IN THE COURT

William Marcy Tweed, the infamous political boss who ran New York City in the late nineteenth century, had a favorite saying that still applies. "It's good to know the law," he would tell his Tammany Hall henchmen. "But it's better to know the judge."

Tweed obviously understood how the legal system works.

In a courtroom the judge *is* the law. He decides what evidence can be used at a trial, what questions lawyers can ask and what answers witnesses can give. He tells the jury how to weigh the facts in a case, and if he disapproves of the resulting verdict, he can throw it out.

Part of every judge's power is real, but part is also symbolic. "When a judge walks into a courtroom, and everybody stands up, they're not standing up for that person, they're standing up for the role he's about to play," said the late historian Joseph Campbell. "When someone becomes a judge, he's no longer just a man . . . he's a mythological character who has to sacrifice his personal desires . . . to the role he now signifies."

That may be true in principle; however, not all judges put principle above other considerations. The list of judges thrown off the bench for misconduct gets longer and more impressive every year. Recent departures from federal courts include: Nevada judge Harry Claiborne, convicted of income-tax evasion; Judge Walter Nixon of Mississippi, found guilty of perjury; and Florida judge Alcee Hastings, impeached by Congress for suspicion of taking bribes.

"I took an oath to uphold the law," Hastings said in his defense. "I did not take an oath to love the law. And I don't."

The record goes on. Unfortunately, judicial corruption is nothing new. The godfather of bad judges was William F. Manton, who served on the Second Circuit Court of Appeals in the 1920s. Before being convicted of larceny, Manton for years collected "non-refundable loans" from lawyers whose cases he heard.

Justice is too frequently for sale, often at cut-rate prices. But the worst judges are more likely to be incompetent than corrupt. When Richard Nixon chose Florida circuit judge G. Harrold Carswell to fill a Supreme Court vacancy, critics protested that Carswell's mediocre record made him a poor selection. As the debate in Congress turned into a referendum on the nominee's IQ, Senator Roman Hruska, a Carswell supporter from Nebraska, declared that "mediocrity deserved to be represented" on the Court. Carswell was ultimately rejected and not long afterward was arrested for soliciting sex in a Florida shopping mall men's room.

The priestlike trappings of their job make it easy to forget that most judges are politicians elected to the bench in their cities and counties by campaigning for votes just like any other candidates. In theory, judges who run for office have to follow certain rules set forth in the Judicial Code of Ethics. Rule Seven of the code actually states that they should stay out of politics altogether, except, naturally, when they are up for election. It also states that campaigns should be dignified and tasteful, and that judicial candidates cannot take positions on controversial issues.

It goes without saying that few if any judges who campaign for their jobs ever pay attention to these guidelines. I have heard radio commercials for law-and-order judges with the sound of gunfire in the background. Judges use ads to tell voters they intend to be tough on crime, lock up drug dealers and punish foreign terrorists. As ludicrous as many judicial campaigns are, however, it is just as absurd to imagine that voters can make an intelligent choice between two judicial candidates without the slightest idea of where they stand on abortion, the death penalty or any other important legal subject.

What all of this illustrates is the schizophrenia of a system that expects judges to be saints, then generally looks the other way when they sin.

At the federal level, politics also plays an important part in the appointment of judges. The American Bar Association, which screens judicial nominees, stated in a 1988 pamphlet on the subject that "ideological philosophy is not considered [in the selection process], except to the extent it may bear upon . . . other factors." "Other factors"? What could *they* be?

One recent critic called the politics involved in choosing federal judges "a bottomless pit of subjectivity surrounded by an insurmountable wall of secrecy." The process may be a mystery, but the results speak for themselves. A half-dozen recent Supreme Court nominations show how important ideology is in selecting the nation's most important jurists. So it should come as no surprise that the least important are often little better than party hacks.

If justice is local, it makes sense that every judge, to some extent at least, represents the attitudes of the people he serves. In conservative communities there are usually conservative judges; in liberal communities, liberal judges. Yet legal decisions are rarely free of other influences that are not so apparent.

In politics and law, appearance is never reality. Politicians do not like to be wrong, and in pretending to have all the right answers they often hide crucial information from voters. Judges who do the same thing in their courts, who help to conceal rather than reveal the truth, are even more of a menace to society.

Not all trials take place in the open. In a convenient arrangement for anyone with something to hide, every court has a secret justice system where aspects of cases are resolved behind closed doors. For example, attorneys for either side can petition to have certain sensitive material in a lawsuit kept confidential, or they can ask a judge to seal the files for an entire case, removing any trace of legal activity. Many judges readily comply, since it usually means that a time-saving out-of-court settlement will follow. Defense attorneys like secrecy agreements because they put a lid on bad publicity; plaintiffs' lawyers like them because they help get more money from the other side. But secrecy can also mean stealth.

In a series of cases, lawyers for General Motors used several cooperative judges to keep important safety data sealed and out of sight for nearly twenty years. Company records indicated that GM officials learned as early as 1970 that gas tanks on their cars were vulnerable to fires during crash tests. Nevertheless, a decision was made not to move the tanks to a safer location, since the design change was deemed to be too expensive for the company.

In subsequent wrongful-death suits against GM, opposing attorneys were allowed to see the crash-test material provided they promised to keep it confidential. Over the years, General Motors settled dozens of cases out of court without ever admitting fault—and twice even asked judges to punish lawyers who violated secrecy orders by revealing lifesaving information.

In case after case, facts about unsafe consumer products, harmful drugs and bad doctors are routinely kept from the public. Peter Wolf, a Washington, D.C., Superior Court judge who sealed the files of a lawsuit accusing a psychiatrist of having sex with a patient, confessed to a reporter that some days he's so busy "that I may approve four or five . . . [of these] things before I say, 'Wait a minute.' "

Some judges, like Conrad Cyr of the Federal District Court in Maine and Richard Wallach of the Appellate Division of the New York Supreme Court, treat each case before them as if the fate of the world depended on it. Other judges run their courts the way dictators run their countries, seizing property, imposing gag orders and coercing guilty pleas and settlements as their whims direct. Still, the tendency is to give judges more power, not less. Under special provisions of the Racketeer Influenced and Corrupt Organization Act, known in the trade as RICO, a judge has the power to do almost whatever he wants in the name of the law, including confiscating the assets of any person or company accused of a crime. That explains why the Drexel Burn-ham Lambert investment firm entered into a settlement with the government and gladly paid a $650 million fine for insider trading. If they had not paid up, the RICO statutes could have enabled a judge to put them out of business without ever going to trial. Of course that's all a moot point now.

Even the ordinary power of judges is enormous, and nothing is more futile than arguing a case before one who is determined to control the outcome. A judge is a legal referee whose job is enforcing the rules of the court. When he fails to apply those rules evenly, or, what is worse, actively favors one side over the other, a trial can turn into a tragedy. Or a farce. Which is what happened in the case that pitted the La Costa resort against *Penthouse* magazine and its publisher, Bob

Guccione. In more than thirty-five years of practicing law, I have seen trials that were fixed and trials where the judge was so arrogant that going to court became a psychological stress test. I have never seen anything before or since to match this case or the judge who presided at it.

There are two kinds of lawyers—those who become like their clients and those whose clients become like them. The first is a mouthpiece who does what he is told; the second is a performance artist who puts his client's case on stage. Of course, some people are too distressed to play along, but that was never a problem for Guccione, whom I represented for eighteen years.

I first met Bob Guccione at the London Penthouse Club in 1970. Dressed in a white suit and an unbuttoned Hawaiian shirt and sporting an array of gold chains, he looked like a psychedelic Beau Brummel. Five years earlier, Guccione had launched his famous magazine by inadvertently using the wrong mailing list and sending brochures advertising the first issue to a collection of church vicars, schoolboys and members of Parliament. The mistake turned out to be a brilliant publicity coup. When copies began arriving, there was such a public uproar that the entire issue sold out immediately. *Penthouse* became an overnight sensation and Guccione an instant success.

What interested him about me the night we met was a case I had recently tried involving a white Southern urologist whose wife had reportedly run off with a black man. The insulted jealous doctor got his revenge on the next black male who visited him by amputating his penis. In fact, on his desk the doctor had a cookie jar of amputated penises floating in formaldehyde. When I asked about the collection, he responded, "I'm interested in organ acquisition." I represented the victim, but it was the doctor's "hangup" that fascinated Guccione, who saw penile envy as his motive. Sex and the law were two of his favorite subjects, and by the end of the evening we were talking business.

At one time, Guccione spent nearly $4 million a year on lawyers. The money bought more than just legal advice. For Guccione, like many business executives, lawsuits are a form of corporate sport, a challenge to his adversaries to stay in the game as long as he can. When an Eastman Kodak film lab refused to print slides of the 1979 Penthouse Pet of the Year, Guccione went after the company in court until he got his slides back. He spent nearly a million dollars in legal fees with another firm before I made a simple telephone call to Kodak and the matter was settled on the spot. A few months later when the same Pet sued him for exploitation, he retaliated with equal determination.

Guccione loves to litigate. As with most people who are fond of going to court, he is addicted to argument. Legal terminology is part of his daily vocabulary, although he often uses the wrong words to describe what he means. Whenever someone failed to do what he wanted, he would call and direct me to "injunct" them. Guccione kept me busy, and I had a lot of fun "injuncting" and countering injuncting on behalf of *Penthouse* and its innovative publisher.

Lawsuits are Guccione's way of expressing himself. His elaborate deposition answers almost always hurt his case, but it hardly matters. After the bedroom, a courtroom is his favorite venue. In that connection, Guccione has probably been sued by more women than any man in America. Some of his most hard-fought legal battles, in fact, have been against former Penthouse Pets. Guccione regards all Pets as his creations. He discovered them. He even made up most of their names. And when one takes him to court, he considers it an act of treason. Yolanda von Szmuda, a former Miss Poland, directed by her disturbed husband, a former attorney, tried to sue him for "rape" and other irregularities.

Isobel Lanza, a onetime Pet of the Month, on the advice of a PR agent took Guccione to court for elevating her to Pet of the Year, then denounced him in a fervent pro-feminist speech during her coronation at Lincoln Center. Despite her rejection of the title, Miss Lanza, represented by Richard Golub, insisted on receiving the cars, furs and jewels that go to all Pets of the Year. When she lost her case, Golub in his irrepressible rage wildly accused the judge of smoking marijuana. He also accused the court stenographer of falsely recording the testimony.

Another ex-Pet, Anneka di Lorenzo, charged Guccione with everything from breach of promise to forcing her to have sex with one of his 200-pound Rhodesian Ridgeback dogs.

"Did you do it doggie style?" I asked her.

"No," she replied, as if I were suggesting something uncivilized. "I was on the end of the bed and the dog on top."

Guccione, she also claimed, had ruined her film career by making her perform unnatural acts in his movie *Caligula*. She and another Pet were the stars of a lengthy lesbian interlude in a portion of the film that Guccione directed himself.

One of Guccione's most renowned female opponents was non-Pet Vanessa Williams, the dethroned Miss America, who tried unsuccessfully to sue him for publishing nude photos of her. That case, noted Guccione, proved his longstanding theory about bad publicity. "The Vanessa Williams experience tends to underscore something particularly American," he said, "that out of scandal, especially scandal of these proportions, ultimately everyone profits."

Guccione, who once worked as a cafe artist in Morocco, told me he "pays no attention to sex." And in a way he meant it. What he is interested in is making money, and whoever tries to stop him meets with an all-out counterattack.

After making a fortune in England, Guccione decided to bring *Penthouse* to America, where *Playboy* had owned the upscale men's magazine market since the late 1950s. He thought he was smarter than *Playboy* publisher Hugh Hefner, and to prove it he jumped out ahead of him in 1970 by breaking the pubic-hair barrier. The result was a sales bonanza.

Guccione was not just selling a magazine. Like Hefner, he was marketing a way of life. *Playboy* offered its combined version of the sexual revolution and the American dream, while *Penthouse* pushed Guccione's idea of the European attitude toward fast cars, fashion and sex. In a bold commercial move, he also sold exotic sexual devices, which were bought in bulk from the manufacturers and advertised in the magazine under the genteel brand name "Evelyn Rainbird."

I was asked to give legal approval to every new gadget. The collection contained gadgets you sat on and tools to reach hard-to-get-at places. Most of the items were so weird it was hard to tell how they were used. Guccione's sister ran the "sex toy" department, which I thought detracted from the upscale image of the magazine. But she steadfastly disagreed.

"I have the best rubber and metal people in the world making these things," she insisted. And the amazing part was that she did.

We both decided I was not the one to get involved in this area of merchandising, so I limited my legal services to First Amendment and commercial problems.

As circulation increased, Guccione's next move was to go after

Playboy's advertisers, some of whom had already begun to defect on their own, attracted by *Penthouse*'s impressive circulation figures. *Playboy* struck back with a letter to some of its advertising customers falsely claiming that *Penthouse* had inflated its sales numbers. This was the challenge Guccione had been waiting for, and in 1974 he sued Hefner for $40 million in damages in a commercial libel suit.

Suddenly the corporate war between *Penthouse* and *Playboy* took on a legal dimension. It was like Chrysler suing Ford, only in this case the companies did not produce sex symbols, they produced sex magazines. Both sides used pre-trial discovery to spy on each other: Guccione to gauge the extent of Hefner's panic, which was extreme, and Hefner to rifle Guccione's business records, which were a mess.

Guccione ran his empire like an Italian grocery store. He conducted all of his business at home, attentively listening to matters that interested him and ignoring the rest. He was an artist, and as such he "visualized." He did not deal in facts, a bad habit that complicated the *Playboy* case considerably.

Hefner's lawyers tried everything to have the case dismissed. They even accused the judge, Thomas P. Griesa, of being unfair to them because he and I were social acquaintances. I had attended a judicial conference as his guest and had once let him drive my Rolls-Royce. *Playboy* also claimed *Penthouse* had failed to produce certain corporate records. Griesa, who is known to get testy in matters of alleged discovery abuse—he had blocked the massive Westway project in New York City in favor of the striped bass because of a "doctored engineer's report" and had once held the attorney general of the United States in contempt for failure to turn over FBI secrets—bent over backwards to help *Playboy*.

The charge was a desperation move by *Playboy*, but with Griesa it had the desired effect. As the proceedings dragged on, attorneys for *Playboy* requested more and more discovery from *Penthouse*, information that had little or nothing to do with the suit. Griesa ordered it turned over anyway. When I finally found one batch of documents in a warehouse that contained projections that Guccione's accounting staff had repeatedly denied existed, I dutifully turned the documents over to the *Playboy* lawyers. As a reward, Griesa denounced the *Penthouse* representatives as liars, excoriated me from the bench and abruptly threw the case out of court.

Guccione may have lost his showdown with *Playboy*, but not before he let it be known he was ready to take on any foe in sight. His next project proved he was not kidding.

A year after the *Playboy* suit began, *Penthouse* published an investigative article on the La Costa Country Club in San Diego, charging, among other things, that the state-of-the-art resort was built and controlled by friends of organized-crime figures. After years of selling soft-focus crotch shots, Guccione wanted to do something more important, something Hugh Hefner would never try. If the *Washington Post* could bring down Richard Nixon, he would go after something even bigger. The two young writers of the piece, Jeff Gerth and Lowell Bergman, were Guccione's Woodward and Bernstein. His target was the mob.

The impact of the story was immediate. Not only did it infuriate crime bosses and the resort owners, the legal problems it created showed how their influence riddled California's judicial system and the rest of the country.

"The primary founders of La Costa were syndicate 'bluebloods,' " wrote Gerth and Bergman. "The bulk of the financing . . . since its inception ten years ago has come from friends in the scandal-ridden Teamsters Central States Pension Fund. . . . La Costa has been controlled by the Moe Dalitz mob—which includes Dalitz, Allard Roen, Merv Adelson and Irwin Molasky. . . . It was Dalitz who persuaded then-president of the Teamsters Union James Riddle Hoffa to finance Las Vegas casinos, starting with [Dalitz's] Desert Inn and related properties, with Teamsters retirement cash."

La Costa, the writers concluded, was a place where hoodlums from around the nation gathered to do everything from playing golf to planning murders.

It was the hardest-hitting article ever to appear in *Penthouse*. Yet it was not exactly news. La Costa had been written about many times before in the press. The *New York Times* had raised questions about its financing, calling it a "rest and relaxation" spot for the underworld; the papers in neighboring San Diego regularly reported on the comings and goings of its shady clientele. The $87 million spa was even mentioned during the Watergate hearings when witnesses revealed that Nixon administration conspirators met there to plot their cover-up.

This time, however, the people named in the story decided to fight back with a $630 million lawsuit. At roughly $100,000 a word, it was the biggest libel award ever asked for in an American court.

In 1974, shortly before the article appeared, quite by chance I had visited La Costa. A vast complex of white motel buildings and a golf course that looked like a semi-arid cemetery, it reminded me of Las Vegas. There were fountains, doormen who looked like ex-boxers and many peculiar guests. I realized how peculiar when the tennis pro arranged a doubles match for me, and one member of the foursome was a recently convicted recipient of bribes, former New York state senator Burt Podell.

Around the same time the *Penthouse* story appeared, big changes were occurring in organized crime. The top figures in the mob were diversifying their business holdings, and like any corporate executives moving into areas where their trade was not welcome, they wanted only positive press. Suing *Penthouse* was a good way to begin. Any jury, they assumed, would automatically hate Guccione, and after an easy court victory against him, the rest of the media would get the message.

Dalitz, Roen, Adelson and Molasky were indignant at being linked to organized crime and they denounced *Penthouse* at a press conference kicking off their lawsuit. Known collectively as "DRAM," they hired the legendary Louis Nizer as their chief counsel. Close to eighty and nearly blind, Nizer still had his share of cunning. Ten months before the trial began, he reached a separate secret settlement with the two writers, who suddenly apologized for their story and withdrew from the case. In the beginning, they had been the zealots who wanted to take the fight to the Teamsters and the mob. Now, as the trial date drew near, they decided that backing down might be the wisest—and maybe the safest—thing to do.

In a letter of regret, they wrote, "New evidence has led us to give further consideration to the article and [La Costa's] claims of defamation." Their letter referred to the fact that Dalitz was given the Las Vegas Man of the Year award in 1978 and that he and Roen were involved in a number of community-improvement projects. It ended with the authors saying they were sorry for "any unwarranted harm [they caused] the plaintiffs."

In the 1950s, a special U.S. Senate Crime Committee headed by Senator Estes Kefauver had described Moe Dalitz somewhat differently. Although Dalitz had never been convicted of a crime, he was identified as a racketeer and a longtime associate of organized-crime figures. Roen, his partner in several Las Vegas casinos, had been found guilty during the 1960s in one of the biggest stock-fraud scandals in history.

I never learned the real story behind the departure of Gerth and Bergman. In any event, their leaving created a huge hole in the *Penthouse* defense. With the writers out of the picture, proving the truth of their article would be even more difficult. To make matters worse, Gerth and Bergman's lawyer, Gloria Steinem's former boyfriend Stanley Pottinger, whom they claimed to have hired for a second opinion but really used as a "go-between" to settle with Nizer, had undoubtedly picked up some valuable tips on our game plan. And it seemed likely he shared them with the other side. Anyone could see that Nizer was cutting corners in his attempt to win. I made a motion to remove him from the case for dealing with my clients without consulting the attorney of record. The motion was granted. Despite the fact that he had violated the canons of ethics, he appealed and was reinstated. The judge who removed him and who was assigned to try the case shortly thereafter removed himself from the case.

After a while such reversals became standard procedure. I made a total of thirty-seven appeals in the case, almost all of them handled by the same "randomly selected" panel of appellate judges, who invariably ruled against *Penthouse* on every issue of substance.

Roen and Dalitz dropped out as plaintiffs when it was decided they were public figures and could not prove malice against *Penthouse*. As for La Costa and Molasky and Adelson, the two founders of Lorimar Studios, makers of such hit TV shows as "Dallas" and "The Waltons," the appellate court said that their status as public or private figures and their libel claim would have to be determined by the jury that decided the truth of the La Costa story. It was a ruling that turned constitutional law on its head, but it was the law for this case.

During seven years of pre-trial hearings, the case traveled from state court to federal court and to the state supreme court, before finally ending up in a dingy superior-court room in Compton, a black suburb of Los Angeles. The neighborhood was right out of a Raymond Chandler novel, with pastel bungalows, palm trees and a murder rate that kept the local police busy twenty-four hours a day.

Trial judges are assigned cases in various ways. Some jurisdictions do it by computer; in others they're chosen by court administrators on a rotating basis. Since judges differ greatly in fairness and intelligence, savvy lawyers play the selection process like a game of draw poker. An attorney who knows the territory will often refile a case several times until he gets the judge he wants. For obvious reasons, the visiting side is at a disadvantage in an out-of-town court. Hiring a local co-counsel is one way to learn which judges to avoid, but not even that strategy helps when the judicial deck is stacked the way it was in Compton.

The judge we were dealt at the last moment before trial was a man named Kenneth W. Gale. We had less than an hour to look into his record and were told by a clerk before we started that if we passed on him, "the next one would be even worse." Not a good sign.

California publishes a book containing the pictures and legal biographies of each judge in the state. There was no entry for Gale. In the short time we had for a background check, we could not even determine where, or whether, he had gone to law school. As a judge, Gale was a complete mystery man. And with nothing to go on but the clerk's warning, we took him.

Judges are lawyers. Contrary to popular belief, they are not the best lawyers, but frequently they are the best-connected. Some come from prestigious law firms, but more often they are plucked from the second and third levels of talent by political parties to run for the job. Most judges are not well paid, nor were they successful attorneys when they practiced law, yet in their courtrooms they have ultimate authority, which gives even the worst of them more power than the president.

A gnomish man with wavy gray hair and missing several fingers on one hand, Gale made it clear from the opening day of the trial that *Penthouse* would have a hard time defending itself.

He would not allow the magazine to introduce research materials used in the preparation of the article. In spite of a federal court order, he withheld documents generated by the original grand jury investigation into La Costa. He also refused to let jurors see the March 1975 issue of *Penthouse* in which the story appeared, commenting that the publication would probably offend 60 percent of the American public. "The court's personal feeling," he said, "is [that] the magazine [doesn't have] a very high class of person [who] would be a regular reader."

Before meeting Gale, my strategy was simple: to prove that the story about La Costa was essentially true by establishing that Adelson, Molasky and company had built the resort using loans from the Mafia-friendly Teamsters Central States Pension Fund and that underworld figures regularly met there, as the writers claimed. The plan was to call as a key witness Jimmy "the Weasel" Fratianno. He was a former hit man turned government informant who could testify about mob meetings he had attended at La Costa and tell jurors how the teamsters' union pension fund was used by the Mafia like a bank to finance legitimate and illegitimate business projects. All very logical.

After seeing Gale, though, I soon realized that logic would not apply.

Nizer, who looked like a shrunken head in a three-piece suit, addressed the jury first. With his hair combed straight back, he gave the appearance of a dashing relic as he supported himself on the corner of the plaintiffs' table and read from notes his assistants gave him. His eyesight was so bad there were only a few words on a page and the letters had to be printed five inches high.

"Irwin Molasky and Merv Adelson [have been] men of impeccable character all of their lives," he proclaimed, seeming to chew each word as he spoke. "[There has] never been a semblance of any claim against them . . . that reflected upon their honor. And yet . . . they are berated as gangsters, hoodlums, the center of all evil. They were boys from poor but good families."

Lawyers are paid to make arguments sound like moral judgments. But Nizer was laying it on thick.

In my opening statement, I told the jury we would prove La Costa was built and maintained for the benefit of the mob. I explained how the resort was designed as a safe haven for criminals on working vacations. Since Mafia members prefer to conduct their business in person rather than over the telephone or by mail, La Costa, far from the cops and other cares of the world, was the perfect place to relax and make deals.

"People who are the heads of rackets not only go [to La Costa] but are given the run of the place," I said. And their gracious hosts, Adelson and Molasky, had to be aware of the clientele.

Merv Adelson was the first witness to take the stand. He said he was "mortified" by the *Penthouse* story, adding that "it [was] a blow to me that La Costa would be connected to any kind of manipulations or illicit operations by anyone." Adelson said his life was so "shattered" by the article that he became "reclusive," sold his house in Beverly

Hills and moved to "a place not in the center of things." He made it sound like he had become a monk.

When I asked him to tell the jury where he had exiled himself, he answered, "Malibu."

Every morning Adelson arrived at the courthouse in a black Mercedes. Every afternoon a Lorimar Winnebago would pull up outside and deliver a gourmet lunch to him, his fellow plaintiffs and whatever movie-star guests were joining them that day to eat under an umbrella. It was like a scene from a "Dallas" episode, with Adelson needing only a pair of lizard-skin boots to be J. R. Ewing, the Texas version of a feudal lord, crafty, mean and tasteless. That J.R. had become something of a cultural icon must have made Adelson and the rest of his business partners feel a certain pride. True, they owned the rights. But more than that, J.R. was good publicity. If people could like him, they could like them too.

Flanked by color blowups of the *Penthouse* article and the cover of the magazine, which showed a young woman inching her tank top over her right breast, Adelson described how he began working in a delicatessen. He characterized himself as a struggling Las Vegas developer when he first met Dalitz in the mid-1950s. He and Molasky, another developer whose specialty was building garages, got to know Dalitz, he claimed, when they purchased several lots adjoining the golf course at Dalitz's Desert Inn casino. Adelson said their initial business venture together came when he and Molasky joined a group of investors formed by Dalitz to extend a private Las Vegas hospital. The expansion project was financed by a loan from the teamsters' union pension fund. In 1961, they teamed up again to build the Stardust Country Club on the Las Vegas Strip. Four years later they built La Costa. As it turned out, they had been involved in over twenty deals together. DRAM was a very cozy little group with very big plans.

Adelson and Molasky's next venture was Lorimar, a word they coined by combining parts of their then-wives' first names.

In court, both Molasky and Adelson denied that Dalitz had opened the door to the teamsters' pension fund. The evidence showed otherwise. Since the two had begun a business relationship with Dalitz and Roen, the four-way partnership had been one of the pension fund's best customers, accounting for millions of dollars in loans and additional millions in equity deals. As part of its loan agreement with La

Costa, the teamsters bought 15 percent of the resort at a bargain price, and later sold the same shares for a profit of millions.

Not surprisingly, the teamsters' loan came with strings attached. The union demanded the right to appoint three members to the La Costa board of directors. One of them was teamsters' consultant Allen Dorfman, later indicted for accepting kickbacks. Adelson testified that all he really knew about Dorfman was that he was a decorated war veteran. Dorfman was murdered in Chicago in a gangland-style execution in 1983.

Adelson also claimed to have only limited knowledge about Moe Dalitz's background. But at eighty-two, Dalitz was one of the most illustrious figures in the annals of crime. Able to trace his mob ties back to such underworld icons as Lucky Luciano and Bugsy Siegel, he even had the distinction of having been chased out of Cleveland in the 1940s by the city's celebrated public safety director, Elliot Ness.

"My interpretation of organized crime may be different than yours," said Dalitz when I put him on the witness stand. "If a person makes money from gambling," he said, "he would be a gambler. If he made that money from bootlegging, he would be a bootlegger. I don't know what you mean when you say organized crime."

And Judge Gale agreed, declaring that everyone knows there's no such thing as organized crime in California.

I could tell by the jurors' skeptical expressions that the evidence, despite Nizer's many sustained objections, was sinking in.

A libel trial is designed to dredge up the past. Yet their pasts were exactly what Adelson and Molasky, with the help of their lawyers, wanted to disguise. Moe Dalitz knew it would not hurt his reputation to admit that he was once a member of the Purple Gang of the 1930s. Adelson and Molasky were different. They wanted to be thought of as worthy citizens. Before meeting Dalitz, they were resurfacing driveways. Afterwards they were entrepreneurs, building million-dollar resorts, producing TV shows, moving huge sums of money through friendly Sun Belt banks. They went very quickly from nothing to multimillionaires. And now, as I said in my opening address to the court, they were pretending to be honest, hardworking businessmen.

To prove it, La Costa's lawyers brought in an assortment of character witnesses. This part of a trial always reminds me of the after-dinner speeches at a retirement party. Nizer turned it into a TV special. Every day limousines would arrive with a new group of stars to testify about his clients' good qualities. They would be ushered down the aisle to first-row seats by attendants, as if they were being shown to their table at Ma Maison. The casting call included Mike Douglas, Linda Gray and Don Rickles. Sports figures Don Drysdale and Pancho Segura showed up. So did judges, politicians, priests and rabbis, each delivering the same message: that Merv Adelson and Irwin Molasky were honorable men of good reputation.

On the other hand, the guest list at La Costa, which read like a *Who's Who* of Mafia elite, told another story. The resort provided complimentary accommodations to mobsters of all persuasions, from Louis "the Tailor" Rosanova, whom Molasky said he only knew "as a fine golfer," to the legendary Meyer Lansky, who explained in a deposition that he had gone to La Costa only twice to take walks and visit a sick acquaintance.

Three months after the trial began, Gale complained that "the trouble with this case is that there are sixteen lawyers and only one judge." The real trouble, though, was Judge Gale, who seemed to be doing everything he could to help the other side. Gale had the most limited knowledge of the law, yet he contrived an apparatus by which lawyers would get hamstrung. First, he would say you were assuming facts that were not in evidence when you asked a question. Then, when you tried to establish the facts to make the evidence admissible, he would hold that they were irrelevant. Furthermore, you could never ask the same question twice, even in two different ways, without risking contempt. In this manner he prevented attorneys from introducing anything he didn't want to hear. Time and again he prevented the defense from questioning witnesses and introducing testimony that directly linked the La Costa owners to crime bosses—or in Moe Dalitz's case proved that he was one. And twice when I tried, he cited me for contempt.

At some points Gale seemed to be incompetent; at others he seemed to be part of a cover-up. In the morning the trial would make progress. After lunch, there would invariably be more roadblocks. It was almost as if Gale was getting his orders during the noon recess. But it wasn't until I brought Jimmy Fratianno to the stand that the real Judge Kenneth Gale emerged and I learned what I was really confronting.

Fratianno was an ex–Mafia killer and a marked man. Since joining the federal Witness Protection Program, he had given testimony in various cases that had been responsible for convicting dozens of organized-crime figures. I planned to use him as I would any other paid expert who testifies at a trial. His rate was $250 an hour, a steal considering what he knew. Fratianno could explain how the Mafia operates, how members are inducted, what's expected of them and how they profit from their connection to one another and to corrupt public officials. After a criminal career that involved gambling, bribery and many murders, he understood how mobsters worked. And he knew exactly how they worked at La Costa.

Gale first ruled that a criminal cannot qualify as an expert on crime. This was novel thinking. Who could be more knowledgeable? At the same time he ruled that Ralph Salerno, a former New York policeman and a lecturer to the Los Angeles Police Department on Mafia activities, was not qualified either. Fratianno, Gale determined, could only testify about events in which he had participated personally.

Then, when Fratianno tried to tell of a Mafia plan hatched at La Costa to kill entertainer and television producer Desi Arnaz, the other side objected and Gale instructed the jurors to disregard what little Fratianno had said. The story he would have told was how Chicago mob boss Sam Giancana, angered by the portrayal of mobsters in Arnaz's television series "The Untouchables," wanted to have him murdered. Fratianno met Giancana at La Costa in the 1960s to make the arrangements, but three attempts to kill Arnaz all failed. This was a Mafia event at the resort in which Jimmy was directly involved, but it was too remote, too speculative, too prejudicial, Gale ruled.

Judge Gale was not the only one helping the plaintiff's case. San Diego sheriff John Duffy, who had received campaign contributions from La Costa's owners and whose office failed to turn over evidence from a bartender informant proving that prostitution and gambling went on at the resort, was also doing all he could to assist.

"I personally know Merv Adelson, Allard Roen, Irwin Molasky . . . and others in the management of La Costa," Duffy said in a sworn affidavit given on behalf of the resort's owners. He added that "no evidence of criminal activity by La Costa or the management of La Costa . . . has ever been detected."

Just when it seemed that everybody connected with the case was on the take, something strange happened. I was contacted by a member of the San Diego grand jury that had been convened a few years earlier to look into organized crime. She offered to supply me with a copy of letters and other documents Duffy had signed then, including statements by him about organized crime at La Costa.

"I always thought we had a crooked sheriff," she said on the phone. "Now I think you have a crooked judge. I don't care if I go to jail, somebody has to see these things."

In addition to Duffy's grand jury material, there was a statement by Evelle Younger, the former California attorney general and now a name partner in the California law firm representing La Costa, Adelson and Molasky, in which he also said La Costa was a haven for mobsters.

The material made it abundantly clear that Duffy had lied in his most recent affidavit. According to what he had told the grand jury seven years earlier, he believed that "the decisions" of organized-crime figures meeting at La Costa "influence actions taken throughout the United States." He offered as an example the suspected killing of former teamster president Jimmy Hoffa by mobster Tony Provenzano, a regular guest at La Costa. "Investigations have disclosed that some of the principal suspects in this case were surreptitiously meeting at La Costa prior to [Hoffa's] disappearance," Duffy had said.

That testimony was all the proof we needed to show what kind of place La Costa was. Gale had to be aware that Duffy's two statements didn't match, since a federal judge had given him the grand jury material to review and release. But when I called Duffy to testify about the discrepancy, Gale cut off every one of my questions, threatening me with contempt if I continued.

From Judge Gale's actions it was obvious to me that he was involved in this case up to his neck.

What made Fratianno's appearance all the more significant was that when the *Penthouse* article about La Costa had first been published, he had sued the magazine too for suggesting that he was a "notorious hit man." Fratianno's case got to the deposition stage before it was dismissed, but how it originated had an important bearing on the La Costa trial.

Looking more like a Florida retiree than a former hoodlum, Fratianno entered the courtroom surrounded by marshals. When I put him on the stand I asked about his lawsuit.

QUESTION: Mr. Fratianno . . . this *Penthouse* article . . . called you an infamous hit man. Had you ever been called a hit man before?

MICHAEL SILVERBERG [Nizer's co-counsel]: Not relevant, Your Honor.

THE COURT: Sustained.

QUESTION: Who brought the *Penthouse* article to your attention?

SILVERBERG: Not relevant, Your Honor.

THE COURT: Sustained.

QUESTION: Did you sue *Penthouse* magazine?

SILVERBERG: Not relevant whether he sued, Your Honor.

QUESTION: I think it's highly relevant.

THE COURT: I will sustain the objection.

QUESTION: At or about the time that the March 1975 issue of *Penthouse* magazine appeared, did you have a conversation with Johnny Roselli?

Silverberg objected again. And again it was sustained.

I tried a different tack, and asked Fratianno if he had consulted anyone before suing *Penthouse.* I wanted to show that the suit was the mob's idea, and Roselli, who lived at La Costa, was the link. Before I could get my words out, Gale angrily cut in: "Mr. Grutman, I sustained an objection. You are in contempt of court."

Gale was not going to let Fratianno discuss anything about his *Penthouse* suit. And when court recessed that day, I found out why.

Fratianno was taken into a holding cell outside the courtroom. When I came in, he was smoking a big cigar and pacing back and forth.

"What the fuck is going on in there?" he demanded out of the corner of his mouth.

"I don't have any idea," I replied. "Is there something you're trying to tell me?"

"Yeah," he said. "That guy is supposed to be a friend of mine."

"What guy?" I asked.

"The judge."

"A friend of yours?"

"Yeah," said Fratianno. "I've known Gale for a long time. My wife knows him too. He was my lawyer. He helped me with my parole."

I could hardly believe what I was hearing.

Then Fratianno dropped a bombshell. After he had filed his suit against *Penthouse*, at the request of the late West Coast mobster Johnny Rosselli, he went to see *Kenneth Gale*, then a San Pedro lawyer, for legal advice about the case.

"Gale knew what I did for a living," said Fratianno. "And he told me I had an excellent case."

That's why Gale would not let me question Fratianno. He had been Jimmy's lawyer and obviously did not want this fact mentioned in court. Gale should never have been assigned to try this case. An impartial judge would have recused himself. He surely knew about his Fratianno connections when, at the very outset of the trial, he was made aware that Jimmy would be a key witness and that we needed special courtroom protections for his safety.

I immediately had an investigator look into Judge Gale, and what he uncovered was amazing. Not only had Gale interceded on Fratianno's behalf with a parole officer in 1971 while he practiced law in Las Vegas, he also represented one of that city's most notorious union racketeers. The pattern continued after he moved to California. When Gale was picked to be a judge, he was a labor lawyer in San Pedro, a mob-infested harbor town south of Los Angeles.

Gale's personal life was no less intriguing. When he was forty-one, he married a fifteen-year-old girl in Salt Lake City, where he owned a go-go bar. Several years after that marriage ended in divorce, he married a Soviet woman in Russia. Here was one judge who got around.

On the basis of his failure to disclose his relationship with Fratianno, I moved for a mistrial. Gale's past experience and associations, I said in the motion, showed he had good reason not to expose organized crime and political corruption and to favor "the Las Vegas interests represented by the plaintiffs."

If "the fix" was in, whoever the contractor was could not have picked a more dedicated workman than Gale. The evidence, as lawyers like to say, was clear. Nonetheless, Gale denied our mistrial motion, saying that he did not know Fratianno well and Fratianno was not an important witness. We then petitioned the California Supreme Court to have him removed from the case. Meanwhile, the trial continued for three more weeks with Gale still controlling the case from the bench.

The revelations about Gale appeared to take even Nizer by surprise, but he never skipped a beat in his summation to the jury. He asked them "to strike a blow for decency" by returning a guilty verdict against *Penthouse*. He spoke for the entire day.

When it was my turn, I took just as long. The case had lasted more than six months. Notwithstanding Gale's efforts to block our defenses, *Penthouse* had put in enough proof to show that La Costa was a mob hangout from day one and that the statements in the article about its owners were reasonably accurate.

I told the jurors there was no room for compromise as to the plaintiffs. "Don't think just because you sat here so long that you should give them something. Whatever you give them, you will be giving the country away."

Then turning toward Adelson and Molasky, I said, "Ladies and gentlemen, sitting in that front row is utterly unappeasable, unshakeable, unsatisfiable greed and avarice. They've got money. And now in this grotesque, monstrous case, they want something else. They want something from you that you must not give them. They want respectability."

Years of acrimony did not end with final arguments. After the jury left the courtroom, Adelson, the TV producer and movie mogul (and now husband of television newswoman Barbara Walters), called me over and snarled, "Mr. Grutman, if Lorimar ever does a movie about a fat scumbag lawyer, would you play the part?"

The scowl on his face told me we would win.

The jury deliberated for three weeks before returning a verdict in favor of *Penthouse*. Everything the *Penthouse* article had said about La Costa and the mob ties of its owners was, in the minds of the jury, if not true, at least reasonable. But in less than a month Gale overturned the decision as to Adelson and Molasky, calling it "a miscarriage of justice," and ordered a new trial.

He would not be presiding, however. The chief judge of the State Superior Court removed him from the case without explanation.

On December 5, 1985, as a second La Costa trial was about to begin, the opposing parties decided they had had enough. They agreed in a joint statement "to settle their differences by discontinuing further litigation." *Penthouse* had won a favorable verdict the first time around and would undoubtedly win again, but not even Bob Guccione could hope to outspend the other side.

Fourteen million dollars and seven years after it began, the case was closed.

La Costa and its proprietors sued *Penthouse* not to fight for the truth but to make sure the truth about organized crime would never be told. The jury, in its collective wisdom, did not believe them.

Years ago the criminal underworld was made up of thugs who ran illegal businesses out of basements and back rooms. Today it is hard to tell where the underworld ends and the business world begins.

The La Costa trial provided the most thorough examination of how the Mafia operates since the Senate hearings of the 1950s. More importantly, what it revealed to me was how much a part of everyday life organized crime has become. The *Penthouse* jurors denied Dalitz, Adelson, Molasky, Roen and La Costa the respectability they wanted. In the long run, though, that mattered less than something else they already had.

Money.

CHAPTER 9

BLAMING THE VICTIM

It was a hot summer day in 1984, and Brian Timms's grandmother decided to take three-year-old Brian for a swim at the Kerr Lake Country Club just outside of Raleigh, North Carolina. The club, which had two swimming pools, one for adults and one for children, was a tobacco-land oasis where semi-well-to-do families in the area came to relax and cool off. Brian loved to play in the wading pool, and on this particular day while he splashed with friends his grandmother sat nearby keeping an eye on him.

Every swimming pool has a filtration system that draws water through a drain, cleans it, then pumps it back into the pool again. For some reason, the system in the Kerr Lake pool was lacking an important safety feature. Rather than having the usual two drains (the second to relieve pressure in case the first becomes blocked), the Kerr Lake pool only had one. And when Brian sat on it, the pressure—which had built up to 900 pounds per square inch—sucked his intestines out.

Although doctors were able to save him, as a result of the accident Brian became what the medical profession calls a "bowel cripple," someone incapable of eating or digesting any food on his own. Brian must be fed nutrients through a tube attached to a hole in his chest and drink water in measured doses from an eye dropper. He will live like that for the rest of his life—all because of the way a swimming pool was constructed.

The way a North Carolina statute had been written made things even worse.

In order to be considered by the courts, a case has to be filed within a certain period of time after someone is injured. Until that period (called a statute of limitations) expires, anyone can be a target for a lawsuit. Miss a deadline, and no matter how just the cause, a case has absolutely no legal standing.

The Timms family asked me to represent them. As soon as I could, about thirty days after Brian was injured, I filed suit against the club, the swimming pool contractor and the drain manufacturer. To my amazement, the time limit for suing anybody connected with building the pool had already run out.

The reason, I soon discovered, was a law enacted several years earlier by the North Carolina legislature designed to protect insurance companies. It's called a "statute of repose," and similar statutes now exist in thirty-six other states.

Unlike a statute of limitations, the period of time defined by a statute of repose does not start running when someone gets hurt. It begins instead when the insured item is manufactured or sold. The law allows insurance companies to attach an arbitrary "life span" to insurable goods of all kinds. The time period is the same for a stair railing, an elevator cable or a plastic drain. When the theoretical life span of the item ends, so does responsibility for any damage it causes.

If a hundred-year-old house falls down, it would be hard to imagine that the builder is still responsible. On the other hand, if the same thing happens to a *five-year-old* house, it might be reasonable to assume just the opposite. Reasonable, unless the house is covered by a *four-year* statute of repose, in which case the builder's insurance company gets off without paying a cent in damages.

The statute of repose for the Kerr Lake swimming pool expired one month before Brian Timms's injury occurred. Like most people, the Timmses had never heard of a statute of repose and could not believe such an unjust rule would protect the people responsible for what happened to Brian.

Prevented from suing the company that constructed the pool, the Timms family sued the country club for negligence. They won that case. But because the club's liability coverage was limited to $100,000, the amount of money they recovered was only a small fraction of the sum needed to care for their son.

Having access to the courts is a fundamental guarantee under the U.S. Constitution—except in states where statutes of repose exist. There, the rights of insurance companies take precedence over the rights of individuals, and, like Brian Timms, people harmed by negligence can be foreclosed from suing before accidents ever occur. It's part of a long tradition of special treatment enjoyed by an industry that was exempted from federal antitrust laws in the late 1940s and has been raking in easy money ever since.

Insurance companies do not get rich by collecting policy premiums; they get rich by investing them in stocks, bonds and real estate. Just like banks, insurers are required by law to keep reserve funds available for paying claims. Those funds generally represent a small percentage of a carrier's overall worth. No matter how wealthy it may be, whenever a company wants more money to invest, it merely announces that claims are threatening its reserves and raises its rates, or looks for ways to limit its obligations to pay them.

Although increases need government approval, getting the okay from politicians is just a matter of asking. Whatever insurance companies want, they get, usually with little or no explanation.

If lawmakers are sympathetic to the needs of the industry, state insurance commissions are even more understanding. The commissions, which are supposed to oversee insurance company practices, are generally run by ex–insurance executives sent to work for the government the same way the Russians send KGB agents to work at the UN.

Despite rate rollbacks in California and calls elsewhere for better policing, the effort to control the insurance business remains a bureaucratic charade. Every year, for example, most commissions make random checks of company files to see how claims are paid, why people are rejected for policies, and whether regulations are being followed. Armed only with pencils and pocket calculators, commission investigators are no match for an industry that uses high-speed computers to measure its cash flow. A 1988 survey of insurance commissions by the National Association of Professional Insurance Agents reported that most commissions "lack the personnel and tools" to do their job and "lag behind the rising level of sophistication" in the companies they are monitoring.

Nowhere is the effect of that sophistication more apparent than in the skillful crisis-inflation techniques insurance companies use to publicize their need for more money. In 1975, the average malpractice premium for obstetricians was $5,000 a year. Today, it is nearly twenty times that much. The reason why, say the insurance companies, is not incompetent doctors but an epidemic of lawsuit-happy victims, a "crisis" that justifies rate increases for health-care providers and recipients.

A recent study of malpractice in New York State showed that of the tens of thousands of deaths and injuries tied to medical negligence every year, only a small fraction ever involve lawsuits. Researchers from Harvard University discovered that in the 36,195 cases reviewed, less than one percent of the victims actually filed claims. That hardly sounds like the crisis insurance companies say it is.

With every product-liability "crisis," insurance rates for manufacturers go up. With every school-safety "crisis," insurance rates for education facilities go up. If there is a business more unimpeded in its pursuit of profits than the legal profession, it's America's insurance industry.

Lawyers, at least, are accountable to the courts for their actions. They can be disciplined, disbarred, even jailed for violations of trust. Insurance companies, thanks to their astute political funding practices, are accountable to virtually no one. If a policyholder tries to defraud his carrier, he can go to jail. Company officials are rarely if ever prosecuted for doing the same thing to their customers.

Insurance companies *can* be sued. But try it and you will find out how powerful they really are. Shielded by laws and political deals, the industry has created a psychology of dependence that puts its method of doing business beyond question. With the right coverage, people are told, every accident can be repaired, every misfortune corrected. However, as the Timms case and thousands of others like it show, the only ones protected from misfortune are the insurance companies themselves.

Joseph Heller's novel *Catch-22*, whose title has become a synonym for no-win situations, has a character named Yossarian, someone any insurance agent would love to meet. The book is set in Europe during the Second World War, and Yossarian's greatest fear is that his luck is running out. Everything, he thinks, is trying to kill him. Not only are enemy bullets planning to blow his brains out, his own body is part of the plot; his heart, his lungs, his liver, every one of his vital organs is after him.

"That men would die," Yossarian decides, "was a matter of necessity." But how they die "was a matter of circumstances" beyond their control.

To Yossarian, life is a series of accidents waiting to happen. Any minute a combination of bad timing and natural attrition can spell doom. Insurance companies reap windfall profits by delivering the same panic-producing message. American consumers spend roughly thirteen cents out of every dollar they earn on insurance. What they are buying, they assume, is financial security. If they wreck their car, fall down the steps or have their patio furniture stolen, their agent will show up the next day with a check to cover the costs. That is another message insurance companies deliver.

But trying to get one of these great protectors to pay a claim—even when you happen to be a policyholder who has been faithfully sending in money for years—is no easy task. Contrary to what the TV commercials imply, damage awards are not automatic. And frequently the initial response from insurers is a flat refusal to pay anything. There are three standard ploys all of them use to deny or delay claims:

1. The most common tactic is to demand receipts for lost or damaged goods. If they have been misplaced, stolen or destroyed by fire, the company is under no obligation to honor the claim.

2. Next on the list of escape clauses come "acts of God," a phrase that appears in every policy. Insurance companies can sound like Old Testament prophets when they are talking about storms, floods and other natural disasters, whose damage they automatically blame on divine intervention, never their customers' negligence, which they would have to pay for.

3. When it's not God's fault, and the claim involves personal injury, insurers like to invoke the concept of "collateral sources." This happens when the insured party is covered by more than one carrier, and while lawyers spend years arguing over who's responsible for paying, the victim languishes.

The first judge of whether a claim will be paid and for how much is never the friendly agent who sold the policy but someone known as a claims adjuster. The job title tells you exactly what he does—adjust the claim, either by offering a lower amount than requested, or in some cases adjusting it down to nothing at all.

Claims adjusters are an insurance company's first line of defense against its customers and anyone else seeking damages. Their methods may vary, but their function never does: to save the company money any way they can. Their business is finding out what happened, and if they dislike what they find, they start manipulating the facts, the same way lawyers do, until they fit their company's payment policy.

"Whenever I'm working an accident, I always tell people to go first class," said an adjuster with a stingy Pennsylvania insurance agency. " 'Forget the health clinic,' I say. 'See a good doctor. And don't worry. We'll pay.' What's it gonna cost, a hundred bucks? That's nothing. It makes them like me, and when they like me they settle for less."

Another crafty claims adjuster, known to his colleagues as "Bonus Bob," has probably saved his New York company millions of dollars in settlement costs. Rather than accusing people of lying about their injury claims and making them mad, he takes a more subtle approach and plays on their guilt.

"I have a little speech I give a dozen different ways," Bob confided, requesting that his last name be kept secret for professional reasons. "I usually begin by saying that I meet lots of people in my line of work and most of them are honest. Right away that lets the person I'm talking with know I think he's honest too. Even if his claim is a total lie, that impresses him, and most of the time he'll try to do whatever he can to prove I'm right."

Once he has charged the atmosphere with morality, Bob begins phase two of his plan. If the claim involves an injury, he asks the person to move his arm, walk across the room or perform some other exercise so he can gauge the extent of the harm done. Bob watches in silence for five minutes or so as the guilt and confusion build. Then in a very soothing tone he makes his offer—$250—and shuts up again.

"Seven out of ten people accept it," he said. "Sometimes not saying anything is the best bullshit there is."

In the event an adjuster is unable to settle a claim on the spot, his job takes on a slightly more sinister aspect. He tries to trap his unsuspecting victim into making a statement that can be used against him later in court.

If someone's house is robbed, the adjuster will try to make him admit he left the door unlocked. If he's been hit by a car, the investigator may get him to say he wasn't watching where he was going.

Both are examples of something known as "contributory negligence," and good enough reasons all by themselves to make the plaintiff lose his case.

The best claims adjusters are gifted sympathizers, experts at soothing the emotional scars accidents cause. As you are describing a car wreck to someone who seems to care so much about your personal welfare, it's easy to forget he would be very happy to give you absolutely nothing for all your pain and suffering.

In most big cities, traffic mishaps are a common cause of insured injuries, but an adjuster who knows his business can destroy a five-figure pedestrian-knockdown claim in no time.

Ask most people who have been hit by a car what happened and they will invariably say, "I never saw it coming."

A car can flatten you like a pancake, or it can knock you into the next state. But if you want to collect any money, you had better see it coming. Otherwise it could be contributory negligence, and you are at fault.

Every year adjusters reject millions of dollars in honest claims, decisions that are often never challenged because most people are too frustrated by red tape to pursue matters any further.

If they do, they meet the insurance company's next line of defense. After the claims adjusters come the attorneys. When a case falls into their hands, the fight can become long and dirty. Insurance companies do not like to part with their money, and their lawyers are masters at making life miserable for anybody who pushes a claim too far. Creating paranoia is a trade specialty. Plaintiffs in insurance cases can expect to be spied on by private detectives, have their financial records turned inside out, their friends and employers harassed, and every embarrassing incident in their lives used against them.

The nerve center of the attack on any claimant's credibility is the Central Index Bureau, a Kafkaesque repository of injury records, with branch offices in all major cities. Every whiplash, every broken arm or leg ever claimed against a carrier is stored in the bureau's computer files. Only insurance companies and their attorneys have access to this information; nevertheless, a shrewd plaintiff's lawyer with the right connections can easily learn what data the industry has on his client, and whether he's dealing with a good case or a professional victim.

Attorneys who specialize in insurance claims like to compare themselves to gladiators. In a typical case a lone plaintiff's lawyer has to face defense teams of ten or twenty company lawyers and investigators. With odds like that, only the strong survive. A client should not be fooled by tough talk, or by promises of easy settlements. An insurance case is not just a gamble, it's a war of attrition, and any attorney who suggests otherwise should never be trusted.

Almost all negligence cases are handled on a contingency basis, a percentage arrangement that allows attorneys to receive up to one-third of the winnings. With that in mind, the insurance industry for years has been lobbying state legislatures to impose a cap on lawyers' fees. That only seems like consumer protection. The goal is to discourage attorneys from taking on cases. The economics are simple: If lawyers stop making money on cases, they will stop fighting claims in court, and if that happens, the public will be at the complete mercy of insurance companies.

A case I handled a few years ago in New Jersey shows what can happen. My client was a telephone company executive named Michael Mollo who liked to play softball on weekends. Mollo, a corporate jock in his mid-forties, was very competitive, and in a game one day, with his team ahead by nine runs, he decided to stretch a triple into a homer. The catcher tagged him out at the plate, but Mollo's momentum sent him flying headfirst into a steel backstop, and as a result he became a paraplegic.

New Jersey has a law that caps the lawyer's fee in negligence cases at 24 percent of the first $1 million in damages. For higher awards the attorney's share is decided by the judge.

Mollo's New Jersey lawyer had tried to interest a number of trial attorneys in taking the case. None was willing. The case was just too chancy. Not only would the suit be complicated by multiple defendants—a city government, a school board and the fence company that put up the backstop—the 24 percent maximum, assuming Mollo won, would hardly begin to cover the costs of the litigation.

If I represented him, Mollo said, he would ask the judge to waive the restriction and pay me the standard 33 percent of any amount over a million dollars. Half that amount would go to his New Jersey attorney. Even so, I thought the case had merit and I went to work on it.

I was right. After two years and over $400,000 in time and expenses, there was one piece of evidence the other side could not deny: the backstop had been built too close to home plate (twelve feet instead of the required twenty-four feet). But when insurance companies for the city and the fence contractor settled for $3 million, Mollo became greedy, as clients often do, and reneged on his bargain, keeping most of the settlement proceeds and all of an additional $2 million in collateral awards he would have forfeited if there had been a trial.

Although I had taken all of the risk, after deducting the other lawyer's cut I was left with less than $2,000 profit above my actual time charges and disbursements. I was also left with a firm determination never again to try an injury claim in New Jersey, which was precisely the effect the insurance industry was hoping for.

We live in a society where people sue one another for the fun of it, yet in the case of insurance companies, litigation, or the threat of litigation, is the only way the public can fight back.

If it can be proved that an insurance carrier acted in "bad faith" by denying someone payments he deserved, a court can tack on punitive damages to a claim and make a favorable verdict worth millions. That's why so many insurance cases that make it to trial are usually settled on the courthouse steps.

If there is any way to avoid it, no company wants to face a jury. It's well known among lawyers that jurors tend to favor the injured party in lawsuits. The problem, from the insurance companies' point of view, is that juries also like to play "tooth fairy" with damage awards. The elderly and disadvantaged who make up a large percentage of today's juries have few opportunities to get revenge on the system. In a negligence case, they can have the satisfaction of making an insurance company hand over millions of dollars.

What the industry would prefer to the present system is an expanded version of no-fault, flat-rate compensation for accidents and injuries that removes the element of blame and along with it the risk of six- and seven-figure settlements.

Disputes could be resolved without lawyers. However, the financial benefits would all go to the insurance companies, just as they do now in workmen's compensation cases. People injured on the job and covered by workmen's "comp" insurance are prohibited by law from suing their employers. Instead, they are awarded a fixed sum of money based on what the insurer decides their injury is worth: $5,000 for a missing finger, $8,000 for a lost eye, $12,000 for a severed limb. To anyone attached to his body parts, these amounts may seem alarmingly low, but imagine the savings they represent to insurance companies.

That there should be retribution paid for suffering is a concept that has been a part of Western culture from Greek tragedy to "The People's Court." Whether the offense is a parking-lot nick or a nuclear melt-down, there is a natural desire to see mistakes corrected and those who caused them make amends. That is precisely why there are doctors, lawyers and malpractice suits.

Everyone who has surgery is required to sign a medical consent form, an agreement acknowledging the normal risks involved in any operation. If read carefully, the first sentence can make even the most desperate candidate for surgery have second thoughts about going under the knife. "Medicine is an inexact science," it begins, and by the time patients get to the end, one of life's great myths is shattered.

Americans used to think of doctors as miracle workers. A generation ago, a malpractice suit was something only incompetent physicians had to worry about. The consumer revolution of the 1960s changed that by showing people how they were being butchered by the medical profession, and what they could do about it.

Twenty years later, there are few who would think twice about taking their doctor to court. Half the obstetricians in some cities have been sued for malpractice. In response to insurance-rate increases for all physicians, groups of doctors and wealthy hospitals like the Mayo Clinic have become their own insurance companies, stockpiling huge cash reserves to cover their members and fighting every malpractice suit to the limit of the law. The result has not been fewer surgical errors, just a greater reluctance to pay for them.

Rochester, Minnesota, is a company town unlike any other in the United States. It has been that way since 1907, when two doctors, William and Charles Mayo, the sons of a local physician, opened a group medical clinic there. From the beginning, the Mayo brothers set out to provide the best health care money could buy. Soon they were attracting famous specialists in every field and with them a select group of patients.

The clinic collects cases much like a law firm does. Rare diseases are of particular interest to Mayo doctors, and an elaborate computer network keeps them informed on potential clientele from around the world. The more arcane the affliction, the more eager they are to bring the afflicted to Rochester for closer study. Despite a reputation for treating rich patients, Mayo's real mission is research, which it conducts in two local hospitals, in its own medical college and in labs and examining offices all over town.

For most of its existence, Mayo has had almost no competition. But in recent years other medical facilities, many just as good, have sprung up in New York, California and elsewhere. Faced with a squeeze on its profits, Mayo officials decided the way to meet the challenge was to increase patient turnover, hoping that any losses in revenue would be offset by added volume. Doctors took on more cases, performed more operations, and consequently ran a greater risk of making mistakes.

What Lourdes is to faith healing the Mayo Clinic is to medicine, and after seventy-five years in business, until 1983, it could still say it had never been successfully sued for malpractice.

Malpractice exists when there is no other explanation for the catastrophic results of medical care. If someone goes to the hospital with a burst appendix and dies during the rush to the operating room, it's hard to fault the doctor. However, if someone is operated on for a foot infection and ends up in a coma, there might be good reason to suspect malpractice. In a malpractice case, the plaintiff's lawyer has to convince the jury that a physician deviated from "standard practice," and by doing so directly caused the plaintiff's injury.

Doctors accused of malpractice are uniformly reluctant to settle cases out of court, since that would be tantamount to an admission of guilt. But most doctors do not understand juries or the insurance business. Given a choice between a possible multimillion-dollar trial verdict and a settlement costing considerably less, an insurance company's preference is obvious. Some companies are unwilling to insure doctors for malpractice unless they give up the right to refuse settlement.

Hospital and physicians' self-insurance groups tend to be just the opposite. They never settle out of court. That was the attitude of the Mayo Clinic. And with their long string of victories, who could blame them?

In 1983, I represented Mrs. Joan Hutton, a grade school teacher from Yorktown, New York, in a malpractice case against Mayo. Mrs. Hutton had gone to the clinic several years before to be operated on for a neurological condition that impaired the movement of her arms. When she left, she was almost completely paralyzed.

Mrs. Hutton was the perfect Mayo patient. Recommended to the clinic by her brother, a priest who had dried out in its state-of-the-art alcohol treatment center, she was the victim of a rare neuromuscular disorder called *syringomyelia*. Her case was assigned to Dr. David Piepgras, one of the country's foremost neurosurgeons. Although his services were in great demand, Mrs. Hutton fascinated him; not only did she exhibit all the classic symptoms of the disease, her condition, he believed, was 100 percent correctable.

The operation Dr. Piepgras wanted to perform looks more like a medieval torture than a medical procedure. The patient is seated in a metal frame with his shaved head locked in a brace. Then holes are drilled through the skull, instruments are inserted and hours of delicate brain surgery follow.

If Mrs. Hutton decided to wait, another operation date might not have been available for months, and by then it could have been too late. Dr. Piepgras stressed the importance of acting fast, and after pondering her options for thirty minutes, she agreed to the surgery.

At that point, Mrs. Hutton became part of a daily operating schedule that rivaled a busy day at O'Hare Airport. The clinic has thirty-two operating rooms at its disposal, and bright and early every morning, patients are lined up in the corridors outside, each one waiting his turn to be operated on.

Mrs. Hutton's operation proceeded exactly as planned, until near the end, when an air bubble, known as an embolism, was spotted in her bloodstream. The outcome of such a phenomenon can be tragic, and in her case it was.

An embolism is one of the risks in any operation, a risk Mrs. Hutton accepted, whether she knew it or not, when she agreed to have surgery. The issue in her legal claim against the clinic was not how the embolism developed but how the team of doctors operating on her responded to it.

Whenever air is found in the bloodstream, standard procedure calls for laying the patient flat on his back. Just as turning a soda bottle on its side causes air at the top to move toward the middle, reclining the patient keeps the embolism away from his brain. This was not done with Mrs. Hutton, and the reason why was the basis for her malpractice suit against Mayo.

When it became clear that it had a major lawsuit on its hands, the clinic's lawyers began laying the groundwork for a defense. One of the doctors involved in the operation wrote a scholarly paper about Mrs. Hutton's case, suggesting that her problem was caused by a rare heart condition (that is to say, an act of God). Next, attorneys for Mayo refused to release the clinic's operating files, claiming that to do so would violate the privacy of the patient. Like the lawyer-client privilege, which prevents private conversations between an attorney and the person he represents from being used as evidence in court, the doctor-patient relationship protects a person's medical records. But in this instance it was not information about patients Mayo was protecting; it was information about doctors, specifically Dr. Piepgras's operating calendar for the day he performed surgery on Mrs. Hutton.

A judge granted our motion for the records, and what they revealed made it apparent that Mayo's commitment to volume business had backfired. At the same time he was operating on Mrs. Hutton, Dr. Piepgras was operating on several other patients.

People in Minnesota are proud of the Mayo Clinic, and convincing a local jury that one of its most renowned physicians was guilty of sloppy surgery would not be easy. To avoid having to try, I made a motion to get the case transferred to New York, where Mrs. Hutton was living when Mayo doctors first contacted her. The motion was denied. I had the operating files, but the clinic, which doesn't like to play "away" games, would be in its home court.

The trial took place in St. Paul, and on the first day the other side started sneaking the little advantages that come with knowing the territory. If there's an edge to be gained by sitting close to the jurors, the position goes to the plaintiff, who bears a heavier burden of proof than the defendant. By the time I arrived in the courtroom for opening arguments, the Mayo attorneys had already set up shop at the table next to the jury box where the plaintiff customarily sits. I took up the issue with the judge, and was informed that my opponents had gotten there first and that was that.

Mayo's game plan was a basic blame-the-victim defense. Its chief lawyer, James O'Hagan, argued that what had happened to Mrs. Hutton was "an unpredictable and unpreventable paradox." A few years later, O'Hagan, a former law partner of Walter Mondale, would be accused of misappropriating millions of dollars from Mayo in a bogus settlement scandal. On this occasion, though, he was determined to save the hospital as much as he could. Malpractice defenses often rely heavily on ambiguity, and Mayo's attorneys were pouring it on. One of their expert witnesses testified that Mrs. Hutton's stroke was caused by "micro-emboli," air bubbles so tiny no one could possibly detect them or be held responsible for any damage they may cause.

The "micro-emboli" theory seemed to impress the jury. Still, air bubbles alone weren't what the case was about. There was no disagreement that an embolism had caused Mrs. Hutton's paralysis. Her suit against Mayo was based on a contention that doctors had reacted too slowly to remedy the problem.

To support that claim, we put a nurse on the stand who testified that Dr. Piepgras was also engaged in another operation when Mrs. Hutton was stricken. Then, the attending anesthesiologist admitted that it took twenty minutes before Mrs. Hutton was given the proper emergency care. This testimony was supported by an expert witness I brought in from the Harvard Medical School. There are not many doctors who would testify against the Mayo Clinic, but Dr. John Ryan did, and what he said had a stunning impact on the jury. A grave mistake was made, he said, a mistake that could have been avoided if the surgeons involved had not been in such a hurry to see their next patients.

With Mrs. Hutton in no condition to appear at the trial, the clinic's lawyers had tried to make her the victim of a one-in-a-million freak accident. In fact, she was a casualty of "speed surgery." Even the most reluctant jurors could see that. Just as they could see that Dr. Piepgras and the other physicians on trial were protected by the resources of a gigantic corporation—one rich enough to insure itself—while Mrs. Hutton had nothing.

That was the theme of my final argument.

"The Creator did not anoint whoever comes under the name of Mayo with infallibility," I told the jury. Win or lose, the Mayo Clinic would still be in business, I said. But look what happened to Mrs. Hutton: Her husband had divorced her after she became paralyzed; she had lost her son, whom she could no longer care for; she lost her home, lost her happiness and her freedom. Assembly-line medicine had taken away everything except the little that was left of her life.

"What more can she lose?" I asked, pausing long enough to let the irreversible sadness of the woman's condition sink in.

"Here is a woman who lives in a dismal, bleak despondency. . . . But you can help remake Joan Hutton," I said, putting in a request for $5 million and adding, "What a pitiful price to pay for a human life."

Those who criticize negligence lawyers for playing on people's feelings overlook an important part of every personal injury trial. In this case attorneys for the Mayo Clinic had used scientific double talk to cover up their mistake and keep their money; I simply used plain talk to pry some loose.

During his summation, Mayo's lawyer compared what happened to Mrs. Hutton to a natural disaster, suggesting her paralysis was her fault. Then in a macabre twist of logic, he said that paying her anything would only "compound the tragedy."

But members of the jury saw things differently and awarded her $2.1 million. If they did not come up with the amount requested, they did give Mayo its worst legal defeat in history.

The effect, however, didn't last long. Like any business, the clinic got back its millions by passing the loss on to its patients. As for Dr. Piepgras, his reputation survived and soon the demand for his services was greater than ever. The only one to suffer permanent damage was Mrs. Hutton, and for her no amount of time or money could change the results of her stay at the Mayo Clinic.

Insurance companies say that payments to people like Brian Timms and Joan Hutton are draining them dry. Yet nothing can match the money carriers make by delaying or denying honest claims, or simply by sounding the crisis alarm and raising their rates.

Since the government seems unable to help, the only way to keep insurers honest is to take them to court, to fight their attorneys with yours. But insurance companies have been hard at work protecting themselves and their clients by lobbying politicians to lower damage awards, limit lawyers' fees, and generally make it harder for people to sue for malpractice. As a result, malpractice case filings in recent years are down by 70 percent. The benefits to carriers are obvious: The more people they can keep out of court, the more money they can keep in their pockets.

Malpractice and product liability are symptoms of the thoughtless pursuit of profits, and if the consequences are not always correctable, the causes should be. When manufacturers injure their customers, or doctors and lawyers fail to deliver the care and counsel they promise, the only useful remedy is to make them—and their insurance companies—pay. Take away the ability to collect damages and consumers become powerless, and much poorer, victims.

CHAPTER 10

FAMILY FEUDS

In the legal profession, divorce lawyers are known as "bombers" because of all the destruction they leave in their wake. If war is politics by other means, divorce is another name for mutual annihilation, and attorneys who deal in marital affairs are famous for their scorched-earth tactics.

One friend of mine in the field used to say that if his adversary's client was still solvent when he got through, he hadn't done his job.

The ground rules changed in the late 1960s, when most states adopted laws making divorces easier to obtain and, theoretically at least, less vicious. Before then, a divorce required fault. Moral issues were involved; there were good spouses and bad spouses. Now, with the exception of child-custody fights, getting divorced is almost always a financial negotiation, a matter as likely to involve accountants and real estate appraisers as it does lawyers.

Attorneys who handle nothing but divorce cases continue to see—and profit from—personal behavior at its worst, only today it comes in the form of hidden assets rather than motel snapshots.

In keeping with this change, divorce lawyers refer to what they do as "matrimonial" law, a pleasant-sounding term that describes how the scope of their work has expanded in recent years to cover every conceivable entrance and exit in a relationship, from prenuptial agreements to post-marital visitation rights.

With more than half the marriages in this country ending in divorce, the exit end of matrimonial law is big business. Divorce lawyers are America's highest-paid social mechanics. They are the pit crews that fix up romantic wrecks and get them back on the road. One of the big names in the fast-track end of the trade, Raoul Felder, even writes a monthly column in *Fame* magazine that keeps readers informed on the latest developments in love and the law. Taking up the subject of adultery, he recently observed, "There's only one thing left for the true adventurer: cheating on a spouse. For someone with a predilection for peril, cheating has it all—clandestine meetings, cryptic phone calls, coded messages, risk of discovery, and the possibility of physical danger. It's the very definition of life on the edge."

Not to mention life on the extended-payment plan. Felder, who has handled divorces for such notable wives as Mrs. Frank Gifford, Mrs. Carl Sagan, Mrs. Martin Scorsese and Mrs. Alan Jay Lerner, knows the kinds of mistakes that get husbands in trouble—and in debt.

Another divorce specialist, Marvin Mitchelson, who invented the legal concept of palimony, lost some of his star quality after several female clients sued him for rape. Just the same, his name is synonymous with high-stakes human affairs and with wronged wives, girlfriends and centerfolds. So prized was Mitchelson's wise counsel at one time that *Penthouse* publisher Bob Guccione used to award Pets of the Year an hour of free consultation with him.

"A woman is like a Stradivarius," Felder said of female clients. "The humidity has to be right to play it."

Playing their clients is exactly what divorce attorneys do. Most women come to them in a state of emotional and economic vulnerability, since it's usually the husband who controls the money and the wife who has to fight for her fair share. Whether she gets it depends on two factors: her lawyer, who may or may not have her best interests at heart; and what is euphemistically called the "mood of the court," where, in domestic relations cases, it is still a man's world.

To dispel any doubts to the contrary, consider what happened to Dr. Elizabeth Morgan, the Washington plastic surgeon who was locked up for two years during a post-marital dispute after refusing to tell a judge the whereabouts of her five-year-old daughter. She claimed to be protecting the child from her ex-husband, whom she accused of sexually molesting the girl. Morgan was cited with contempt, and it took an act of Congress to get her out of jail.

When fewer women had jobs, divorce lawyers often worked for wives on a deferred-payment basis, collecting their fees from husbands when the case was over. The arrangement made sense because most women were unable to pay in advance. But, then as now, the fix was usually in right from the start.

Despite going through the motions of haggling over support payments, it is common practice for the husband's lawyer to offer the wife's lawyer an extra-large bonus to settle for less. Since negotiations are conducted in private, the wife usually has no idea what's going on until the deal is struck and she's out of luck.

Although attorneys have not stopped selling out their clients, with more divorces involving working women, they generally ask for all or part of their fee up front. The exception is a big-money breakup where the husband is rich, the wife is totally innocent and a sizable support payment hangs in the balance, in which case a lawyer is likely to put off taking his cut until the end, when all the husband's assets are accounted for.

Even then, unforeseen obstacles can delay the disbursements. A tragic example occurred during the late 1970s in the notorious case of New York socialite Patty Starr and her South American playboy husband, Alfredo Cernadas. After a brief and rocky marriage, Patty decided to get a divorce. There was no prenuptial agreement, so Alfredo had good reason to be concerned. His previous wife, a wealthy Palm Beach heiress, had given him a big settlement when their marriage ended. Now he stood to be the financial loser. Alfredo begged Patty to reconsider, and when she refused, he shot her, then killed himself.

The murder-suicide made the divorce moot, but it only added to the complications surrounding Alfredo's sizable assets. Enter an attorney representing Patty's relatives, who argued that his clients were entitled to all of Alfredo's wealth. His theory was that Patty had outlived her husband by several minutes, making her his sole survivor, her heirs the indirect beneficiaries of his estate—and him the recipient of a sizable share in their profits as part of his legal fee.

Like all attorneys, a divorce lawyer's business depends on people's problems. Unlike other lawyers, his income rests entirely on the unpredictable nature of romantic affections. The main reason divorce attorneys like advance payments is their biggest fear—reconciliation.

There is nothing like the stress and strain of divorce proceedings to make a husband and wife realize that marriage may not be that bad after all. When this happens, lawyers for both sides can be adversely affected. Not only is paying off attorneys low on the agenda for a couple getting back together again, they may even start blaming their respective lawyers for making their troubles worse. And frequently they are right.

Even though some couples have spent their whole married life fighting, few wives feel comfortable or confident facing their husbands in court. Lawyers strengthen their resolve by keeping them mad at their former mates. Fanning the fires of anger is an art and, depending on the psychological needs of the woman involved, can mean office hate sessions or quiet evenings over dinner and drinks, both of which will appear later on the bill as services rendered.

Divorce lawyers are notorious for seducing their vulnerable clients, and clients are notorious for giving in. While the usual targets are women, female attorneys have been known to take advantage of male clients in need of emotional reinforcement. It would be rare to find a divorce attorney not motivated by money. But sex is an on-the-job perk many find hard to resist, especially when it serves the added purpose of helping the client end his or her marriage, thus improving the lawyer's chances of being paid.

One Los Angeles attorney, I'm told, keeps a "casting couch" in his office. His rule of thumb: If a would-be divorcée is not on it and under complete control by the second visit, he drops her case. A New York lawyer, who thought of himself as an expert in the area before he was disbarred, used to brag about seducing his female divorce clients, then bedding them down on his desk, covered for the occasion with copies of the *Law Journal*.

Marriage is a contract, and getting out of it with everything they think they have coming can be a rare achievement for both spouses. Some couples require a merciless fight over property and savings just to admit their marriage is finally over. Others are so fed up with one another, they will do anything to get away, although financially dependent wives generally learn to regret their haste.

Before she abruptly ended her two-year marriage, a well-known feminist writer, on the advice of her attorney, raided her joint checking account and removed three-fourths of the $25,000 it contained. Her husband, a prominent Boston lawyer, could easily have spared the money, which he regarded as loose change. What really got him mad was the economic manifesto she left behind as a good-bye note. To retaliate he instructed the couple's accountant not to pay his wife's taxes. He assumed she would be too busy having fun to pay them herself, and she was. Six months later, she had the divorce she wanted, but she also had the IRS after her, and that entanglement lasted longer than her marriage.

These days there are specialists who do nothing except give expert opinions on assets in matrimonial affairs. I asked one, Stanley Goodman, a New York attorney and CPA, how he could stand the continual battles over love and money. "Like anything else," he said, "you get used to it." He also commented that in all of the hundreds of cases he had handled only two involved spouses who had an amicable relationship after the divorce.

When a couple has children, a negotiated settlement can be particularly nasty. And when there's money at stake, reaching a satisfactory agreement on how much each party keeps can turn the children against their parents and each other.

Such antipathies arose in the first divorce case I ever handled. The divorce itself had taken place more than thirty years earlier, but the aftermath was still being felt in the mid-1950s, when the matter landed on my desk at Wellman & Smyth.

The case involved Mrs. Edith Prindeville, who was being short-changed by her children after her husband died. The Prindevilles had been divorced in the 1920s. Since then Mrs. Prindeville, who had never remarried, had been living handsomely on the alimony provided by her husband, Albert, who struck it rich on Wall Street.

After Mr. Prindeville's death, however, the payments to his wife stopped, and his children, who stood to inherit the bulk of their father's fortune, showed no inclination to support their mother in the grand style to which she was accustomed. Mrs. Prindeville was understandably concerned.

The Prindevilles had been divorced in Paris. After some digging, I learned that neither had actually been in that romantic city at the time. Their divorce had been arranged by Mr. Prindeville's lawyer, an underhanded rascal by the name of Dudley Field Malone, who conducted the whole affair with stand-ins.

In those days, foreign divorces were one way of circumventing strict state laws in America. It seemed to me a very strong argument could be made that the Paris court had no jurisdiction. That would make Mrs. Prindeville not her late husband's ex-wife but his widow, and under New York law automatically entitled to one-third of all his earthly possessions.

Instead of subjecting Mrs. Prindeville to a drawn-out money battle with her children, I came up with a plan that seemed fair to both sides, and might even bring the family together again. Under the terms I devised, Mrs. Prindeville (technically the widow Prindeville) would agree to sign a document promising to leave her children her one-third share of the family fortune when she died, and in exchange all they had to do was continue the support payments she had enjoyed for the past thirty years.

What could be kinder? Or more prudent, since setting aside Mrs. Prindeville's portion of the estate to pay for her upkeep would also be a way of avoiding taxes?

The Prindeville children were represented by Dunnington, Bartholow & Miller, a law firm every bit as WASPy as Wellman & Smyth. Here were all the makings of a favorable agreement. Not only were the two firms alike, their top partners Walter Dunnington and Herbert Smyth, my boss, were both members of the Quiet Birdmen, an elite corps of World War I pilots, honor bound to help one another through any crisis.

It was the sort of gentleman's agreement I had learned to respect.

The day I came to the firm, Wellman was in Scotland playing golf, and my first assignment was to prepare a case for trial involving the deaths of two sailors. The men had drowned in Lake Ontario returning to their ship after a night of drinking. Now their families were suing our client, the oil company that owned the ship. It was a grisly case. On a visit to upstate New York with Smyth, I studied pictures of the dead bodies, which had been pulled out of the water with grappling hooks. A surviving crewman claimed the ship's captain had made no attempt to rescue the men. The suit was eventually dismissed when it was proven the sailors would have drowned no matter what rescue efforts were made. Still, the macabre facts are not what I remember most about the case.

One evening, after taking depositions, Smyth and I met some lawyers he knew in a hotel bar for drinks. Smyth bought the first round of drinks, and I paid for the second. Later that night, Smyth came to my room enraged over what I had done.

"If I want to buy a round of drinks, I can," he said. "You may not do it, because you're not my equal."

That was how things worked at Wellman & Smyth.

As I explained our side's theory about the Prindevilles' flawed divorce and our proposal for assuring Mrs. Prindeville's welfare, I noticed Dunnington giving me the once-over. First he examined my shoes, then he studied the cut of my suit.

"And what do the children get?" he interrupted.

"That's what he's coming to," said Smyth, feebly sensing Dunnington's dissatisfaction with me and any solution I could come up with for Mrs. Prindeville's financial problem.

"That's all well and good," Dunnington said, fingering his gold Quiet Birdmen lapel pin. "But has it ever been done before?"

At this point, Smyth was becoming uneasy.

"No," I said. "But, after Columbus, anyone could find America if he tried. I think the plan will work."

"Well, I don't." Dunnington sneered.

"But she's their mother!" I said.

"That's not the issue," Dunnington concluded. "I think we'll pass."

With Smyth unwilling to take his esteemed colleague to court, Mrs. Prindeville's fate was sealed. And while her children later relented and gave her a token allowance, it was nowhere near the amount their lawyers helped them obtain, and all because Smyth was more loyal to his old chum than to his client.

I have seen some divorce cases where the opposing spouses totally ignore one another, and others where it takes marshals to keep them apart. No-fault eliminates much of the unpleasantness that used to accompany broken marriages, yet a peaceful parting of the ways is not for everybody.

That's something I learned representing the wife in a divorce case I will never forget. She and her husband had been screaming at each other so long they developed a whole language based entirely on insults. Separately the two were unbearable. Put them in the same room, and you had all the necessary ingredients for double premeditated murder. I have never seen two people who hated each other so much. Once during a pre-trial hearing, the judge threatened to gag both of them if they could not control their tempers. They fought in the hallway outside the courtroom, in the elevators, in the parking lot and in the Greek restaurant across the street. When their divorce was finally granted, I was never so happy to have ended a case in my life.

A month later I ran into the husband's lawyer, who felt the same way.

"Who do you suppose they're berating now?" I said.

"You haven't heard?" he replied. "They were remarried last week."

Some people are incapable of saying good-bye without a fight. And for a few especially strange couples, fights are so fulfilling, they can't say good-bye.

No legal action requires more complete personal disclosure than divorce. Financial records, work histories, psychological problems, sexual functions and malfunctions, are all laid out in a divorce trial. Which explains why most cases are settled before they ever get that far, and why those that do go to court usually turn into legal psychodramas.

Divorce attorneys are experts at destroying self-esteem, a handy talent when it comes to milking a case for everything it's worth. One of the up-and-comers at this loathsome practice is Richard Golub. As a litigator, Golub compares himself to a drill bit. His function, he says, is to bore into witnesses until whatever he's looking for comes gushing out.

He had the chance to display his skills on camera in 1989, when he represented Sandra Jennings, who claimed to be the common-law wife of actor William Hurt. Common-law marriages are recognized in thirteen states, including South Carolina, where Jennings and Hurt lived together for a month while he was filming *The Big Chill*. On that basis, Jennings, who had a son by Hurt, was suing him for half of his $10 million net worth.

Common-law marriages have not been recognized in New York, where the trial was held, since 1933. To make the case stick, Golub tried to show that Hurt regarded Jennings as his wife.

Step one was to get Hurt flustered.

With the actor's lawyer objecting to nearly every question his client was asked, Golub, who has made two music videos and thinks of himself as a rock star, complained, "He's interrupting my *rhythm!* And *rhythm* is everything."

At that point Hurt got into the act.

"You're amazing, putting on a show," he said from the witness stand. "Get your rhythm right."

Here was Golub's cue, and he let Hurt have it.

"You had yours right, pal, when you had Alex, didn't you?"

Hurt was stunned.

"You . . . can't permit that," he said to Judge Jacqueline Silbermann. "He's mucking around with the conception of my son, making a perverse, insulting little joke about it."

Hurt was wounded, and the judge, clearly moved by his plight, called an immediate recess.

Step two was to take advantage of the movie actor's well-known penchant for cosmic babble, which Golub accomplished when he got Hurt to admit that his "spiritual union" with Jennings meant more to him than a marriage.

If motive was the issue, Hurt's goose would have been cooked. But lacking a contract, his relationship with Jennings, no matter what it meant to either person, was on shaky legal footing.

"An agreement to marry cannot be inferred from the fact that the parties are living together," decided the judge, observing that usually "the contrary is true."

In a strange case of legal déjà vu, Silbermann was the very same judge who had presided over Golub's divorce from actress Marisa Berenson a year earlier. At the time, she had ruled that he could share in his wife's earnings if he could prove he had helped her career. Failing to do so, he came away empty-handed.

Golub's performance this time, however, was not entirely wasted. He put a lock on Jennings's $24,000 a year in child support and almost guaranteed her another try for more. Silbermann, he insisted, had fallen "madly in love" with Hurt, and when she interrupted Hurt's cross-examination for twenty minutes so the actor could compose himself, she gave the other side excellent grounds for appeal, and, thus, one more way to make the actor settle.

For couples ending their marriage by mutual consent, divorce can be as simple as drawing up a separation agreement, dividing their property and then, after a prescribed period living apart, having a judge sign the final papers.

But when a couple is fighting over money, particularly for large amounts, getting a divorce can be like playing jurisdictional hide-and-seek. In the precedent-setting Rosenstiel case, which bounced from Connecticut to New York to Mexico to Washington to Florida and back to New York again before it was finally resolved, jurisdiction became the crucial issue.

Lewis Solon Rosenstiel was the principal stockholder of Schenley Liquors, and in the early 1970s his disclosed worth was in the neighborhood of $450 million. Like most men of immense wealth, he was used to getting his own way. Fearing that his wife, Susan, whom he wanted to divorce, would extract a sizable chunk of his fortune, Mr. Rosenstiel went to elaborate lengths to dump her without losing money.

The couple had several addresses, one of which was in Connecticut, where laws were more congenial to Mr. Rosenstiel's plan. He hired the ten best law firms in the state. Instead of being relegated to the eleventh-best Connecticut firm, Mrs. Rosenstiel retained the services of Louis Nizer. He convinced a judge that the Rosenstiels only visited Connecticut on weekends and that their actual residence was located in New York. So the case was sent back to Manhattan, where they had a townhouse with fifteen servants.

Mr. Rosenstiel's lawyers struck back by charging that Mrs. Rosenstiel's Mexican divorce from her previous husband was invalid, which meant she had no claim to any part of their client's money, since her marriage to him was illegal.

Just to make sure, Mr. Rosenstiel arranged to have the attorney general of Chihuahua, Mexico, paid $400,000 to declare his wife's proxy divorce from her prior husband Felix, the president of the Romanian National Bank, null and void. When Nizer found out what had happened, he set out to invalidate the invalidation on the grounds that it had been obtained by a bribe. That case went all the way to the U.S. Supreme Court, which decided in favor of Mrs. Rosenstiel, upholding the validity of Mexican divorces where only one spouse was present, provided the absent spouse had executed a waiver of appearance. Not to have done so would have bastardized thousands of people born to parents who were also divorced by proxy in Mexico. Undaunted, Mr. Rosenstiel looked for another angle.

On the advice of his new lawyer, the late Roy Cohn, he moved to Florida, where he bought a small piece of property in Miami and went through all the mechanical steps of becoming a Florida resident. He opened a Florida bank account, got a Florida driver's license, registered to vote in Florida, subscribed to Florida newspapers. "Florida is my home," he declared in a letter to his wife, whom he invited to come down for an all-expense-paid vacation so they could be divorced.

It was obviously another trick. If Mrs. Rosenstiel took him up on his offer, a Florida court would have jurisdiction to strip her of her sizable New York separation allowance. Moving as fast as he could, Nizer went to a New York federal judge and got an injunction against Mr. Rosenstiel proceeding in a Florida court. He was too late. Three hours before the judge in New York signed the injunction, Mr. Rosenstiel not only got divorced, he got married again.

Susan Rosenstiel was allowed to keep only the money from her separation agreement; however, she had a pre-nuptial agreement that entitled her to a great deal more. The court in Florida had the power to dissolve the Rosenstiels' marriage; it did not have the authority to take away Mrs. Rosenstiel's pre-existing property rights, since neither she nor her lawyer had appeared at the hearing.

That had been the law since 1861, when women whose husbands disappeared during the Civil War could ask the courts to end their marriages but could not abrogate the property interests of their missing spouses.

As Susan Rosenstiel's new lawyer, I was of the opinion that the same law could be used to overturn the Florida decision. When a New York judge disagreed, there was nothing else I could do for Mrs. Rosenstiel. Finally, when Mr. Rosenstiel died several years later, her separation allowance ended. His children and his latest wife inherited his estate, and Mrs. Rosenstiel, the last I heard, had been arrested for shoplifting.

A divorce reveals husbands and wives in all their spitefulness and greed. The most common compulsion on both sides is the urge to destroy, and when spouses have finished with one another, it's not uncommon for one or both to turn on their lawyers.

The angriest clients I have ever represented have been in divorce cases. One of them was a woman named Lillian Goldman, who had hired and fired ten different attorneys before I came along.

Her late husband, Sol Goldman, had run a billion-dollar real estate empire, and at the time of his death in 1987 he was among New York's wealthiest landlords, with more than 600 parcels of property to his name. Mrs. Goldman was suing for half the estate. Their dispute did not just involve Lillian and her late husband; her children were suing her, and she was suing them too.

As family feuds go, the Goldman case stands as the biggest private lawsuit in New York history, and the prospect of earning several million dollars myself, assuming I could win the case or obtain a settlement, perhaps made me underestimate the plight of my ten predecessors. Mrs. Goldman was to attorneys what Bluebeard had been to his wives, although in the excitement of her many-faceted litigations, I failed to heed the obvious warning signals.

The Goldmans were married on Christmas Day 1941 just before Sol was to go into the Army. Using money he saved from his job in his father's grocery business and ignoring his mother's advice ("Never leave the store, Sol. It's a gold mine"), he started buying and selling Depression-era foreclosures. By the end of the war, he took on a partner, Alex Di Lorenzo, a pharmacist suspected of having ties to the underworld, and soon the two were buying up property all over town. Unlike other real estate tycoons, they did not syndicate their holdings. They owned everything themselves.

That made them rich. It also made them more vulnerable to fluctuations in the economy, and when the bottom dropped out of the real estate market in the early 1970s, Goldman and Di Lorenzo lost 40 percent of their properties. After the banks foreclosed on the Chrysler Building, Lillian and Sol's pride and joy, Sol went into a depression so severe he could barely sign checks.

At the height of his money troubles, Sol wanted to sell everything he owned for a few million dollars. Lillian, however, was adamantly opposed. Instead she hired a lawyer and, following Di Lorenzo's death, had their partnership dissolved, with Sol and Di Lorenzo's son each taking 50 percent of the business. Her adroit move saved the Goldman fortune.

Over the next ten years, the market made a miraculous comeback. Between 1974 and 1986, Sol's real estate holdings increased in value from a few million dollars to an amazing $1 billion. He lived to make deals, sometimes flipping the same piece of property within days. He owned the Plaza Hotel, the St. Regis and the land under the Olympic Towers. He owned several blocks on Park Avenue and the corners of Fifth Avenue and 57th Street, which he bought and sold in one weekend at a net profit of $11 million. Fat, bald and obsessed with making money, he was the embodiment of the Monopoly man.

One of the secrets of Sol's success was his total disregard for the normal rules of doing business. An agreement with him meant nothing. He never stopped negotiating. If he was selling, he insisted on more. If he was buying, he had to pay less, and even then it usually took a court order to get him to pay anything.

The more money he made, the more suspicious he became that someone was trying to take it. His principal suspect was Lillian. The two fought constantly. Sol accused her of stealing him blind; Lillian accused him of having adulterous relations with various women. During a particularly heated disagreement, Lillian claimed he dangled her out the window of their thirty-first-floor Waldorf Towers apartment. Sol, she insisted, was trying to kill her.

As tensions mounted, the whole family felt its effects. Three of the four children even signed sworn statements saying their mother should see a shrink.

These affidavits, Mrs. Goldman said, were part of a plot hatched by her husband's lawyer, Raoul Felder, to turn her children against her after she had hired Roy Cohn to help her get a divorce.

In 1983, Felder and Cohn had worked out a deal that would give Lillian $5 million "living expenses" and one third of Sol's estate outright when he died. All she had to do in exchange was drop the divorce action and waive her right to an equitable distribution of property. Lillian thought she could live with that, and under pressure from Cohn signed the waiver agreement. When she showed it to her former son-in-law, who was also a specialist in matrimonial law, he warned her not to make any settlement with Sol. If she did, she could be cutting herself out of $500 million.

Lillian had good reason to feel cheated, particularly after what happened next. While looking for theater tickets she thought were in Sol's coat pocket, she found a letter from her lawyer, Roy Cohn, to Felder. In it, Cohn complained that "after the job we did for the

Goldmans—including saving Sol's exposure of 3 or 4 hundred million dollars equitable distribution," he was "shocked" that Sol would only offer him $100,000 as a fee. "I put myself in your hands and his," Cohn protested. "I thought I was dealing with friends who would recognize what my friendship had meant."

This letter had all the telltale signs of a conspiracy between her lawyer and Sol's. Lillian promptly fired Cohn and slapped him with a $1.5 billion lawsuit. She also started legal action against Sol to have the property waiver declared invalid. When the case was finally ruled on in September 1987, she ended up a three-way loser. The agreement was upheld; Cohn had died before her suit against him could be decided; and Lillian was awarded alimony in the paltry sum, by Goldman standards, of $700,000 a year, still a state record.

For months before the decision, Sol's health had been failing. When he wasn't in the hospital for kidney dialysis, he was so weak he had to be driven in an ambulance to inspect his real estate projects.

In October 1987, less than three weeks after his court victory over his wife, Sol died. Since they were never divorced, Lillian, now his widow, was entitled to one third of his estate *outright*, as the waiver agreement stated. Sol's will on the other hand provided that her portion of the inheritance be held in trust, and she would receive income only during her lifetime.

Suddenly, a $700,000 yearly alimony payment turned into a windfall closer to $700 million. Lillian Goldman was on the verge of becoming one of the richest women in the world. Her loss was a gain and Sol's win a setback for the children. Sol's lawyers, Raoul Felder and the firm of Simpson, Thacher & Bartlett, wasted no time making an emergency U-turn. The same waiver agreement that they had argued was valid a month earlier, they now insisted was both void and unenforceable.

It was at this point in the proceedings that I got a call from Mrs. Goldman. My assignment, as lawyer number eleven, was to get her the money she was owed from her husband's estate, which meant getting it from her children, two of whom were firmly planted in the driver's seat because they had been named co-executors of the father's estate.

At Sol's funeral, Raoul Felder read a passage from Shakespeare's *King Lear*: "Why should a dog, a horse, a rat have life, and thou no breath at all?" It was an apt selection. Like Lear, whose will started a civil war among his daughters, the fight over Sol's fortune turned his wife and children into bloodthirsty enemies. Since Lillian had moved out on Sol, her children contended, she was no longer their father's wife when he died, and therefore not entitled to any part of his estate.

Her own family had turned on her. Here was raw, rancorous greed at its ugliest, and their mother struck back with vengeance. If the children wanted a fight, they would get one. Only this time, she was not only going to use law firms, she would also use law schools. Sensing the battle with her estranged children could go on for years, like the famous case of "Jarndyce v. Jarndyce" in Charles Dickens's *Bleak House*, Lillian proposed to give a percentage of her winnings to the law schools at Harvard and Yale if they would continue the struggle with the estate after she died. Yale expressed an immediate interest.

Until her case was decided, Mrs. Goldman demanded an advance of $2 million a year to cover her living expenses. Her children, who wanted all of Sol's estate for themselves, opposed her, saying she had enough money already—over $100,000 a year from a trust fund. Lillian Goldman could spend that much in an hour! The $100,000 her children were talking about might not even keep her in shoes. After all, she had been used to sables, caviar and the most expensive clothing. With over $1 billion of real property in the estate, why should she have to scrimp?

Marie Lambert, the judge in the Manhattan Surrogate's Court where Sol's will was being probated, consistently sided with the children and flatly refused to give Mrs. Goldman any advance funds. Meanwhile, in her generosity, she made ample funds available to Alan, Jane, Deedee and Amy, the Goldman children. Mrs. Goldman's plight called for a trip to the Appellate Division, where, after two reversals, the surrogate finally ruled that Mrs. Goldman was entitled to a $2 million advance each year, as well as her own jewelry, stocks and bonds totaling over another $1 million.

In return for these services, Mrs. Goldman, who had learned from Sol how *not* to pay bills, stopped paying mine. When I pressed her, she fired me and hired Milbank, Tweed, her twelfth legal representative in the case. They lasted ninety days and were followed by number thirteen in the parade, civil rights lawyer William Kunstler, who, Lillian believed, was a champion of women's rights and therefore the perfect man to handle her problems. He was promptly followed by yet another firm.

It was a relief to be rid of the burden the Goldman case had become. What had looked in the beginning like a relatively simple matter, since Lillian's position was so clearly correct, had turned into a quagmire of motions, hearings and delays. In addition, I had to contain Mrs. Goldman, who behaved on occasion like the tyrannical Red Queen in *Alice in Wonderland*.

Lillian Goldman, like many chronic litigants, became a creature of circumstances. When she realized how she had been betrayed by her husband and cheated by Roy Cohn, her world turned into an armed camp. No one, not even her children, could be trusted. Much of the credit for this belongs to Cohn, who epitomized the depths to which attorneys can sink once they put their minds to it. Cohn gained fame as a Communist hunter with Senator Joseph McCarthy in the 1950s and later was indicted three times on charges including bribery, perjury, obstructing justice, mail fraud and extortion. He was never convicted.

"If you need someone to get vicious toward an opponent, you get Roy," Donald Trump once remarked. "People will drop a suit just by getting a letter with Roy's name on the bottom."

Cohn was so feared that despite almost constant complaints against him, the Association of the Bar of the City of New York could only muster the nerve to disbar him when he was safely on his deathbed. It was Cohn who once tried to trick eighty-four-year-old Lewis Rosentiel, at the time being treated with Thorazine, into signing his name to a document that would make Cohn an executor of his multimillion-dollar estate. Cohn did it by suggesting the papers had something to do with his ex-wife, Susan. This was a lawyer as unscrupulous as they come, and when Mrs. Goldman put herself in his care, she walked into a one-man viper's nest.

I have represented some of America's richest people, and for most of them money is a kind of Midas curse. It does not bring happiness or peace of mind, but unappeasable suspicion, which Mrs. Goldman displayed by suing everyone in her path.

She reminded me of my own mother, whose lawsuits against her brother Harry over their father's estate turned into years' worth of frivolous litigation. First Harry forced their father, who had a fortune in real estate, to change his will, leaving everything to him. Then my mother sued Harry. Then Harry sued her. Next she and her mother sued Harry. Eventually, they tried to get me to take their case, but I refused. "All I want," my grandmother said to the judge in one of the trials, "is for there to be peace in the family." With everyone preoccupied with dragging each other to court and relishing it, tranquillity was out of the question.

Like my mother, now over eighty and still suing relatives, in-laws and anyone else she doesn't like, whenever Mrs. Goldman wanted to make someone's life miserable, she retained a lawyer to do the job and made his life and hers miserable in the process. Shortly after my departure, the appeals court granted the motion I had filed for her allowance. In addition to an immediate payment of $2 million, she would receive a $2 million advance every year until the issue of Sol's will was settled. That amount broke Mrs. Goldman's old New York record by $1.3 million a year.

I told one reporter covering the story that when Mrs. Goldman visits my grave I hope she will say, "He got it for me."

Just to make sure I am rewarded in this life, I sued her for my fee and a fair share of the wealth that I helped her obtain on a reduced-rate retainer because she was an "indigent" widow.

Divorce clients frequently complain about lawyers who lack proper sympathy for their cases. Mrs. Goldman really did not want sympathy, she wanted revenge—against her husband, her children and anyone who got in her way. Litigation became the only thing in her life that matters. Sol made deals, she makes court appearances. Her many lawsuits were the legal equivalent of total war, and when I left, the battle was still raging.

CHAPTER 11

THE LORD GIVETH

TV evangelist Jim Bakker sat at the defense table in a Charlotte, North Carolina, courtroom with tears in his eyes. Just released from a four-day mental evaluation after claiming that giant insects were trying to kill him, Bakker was the picture of dejection. Gone was the boyish twinkle that made "PTL Club" viewers glad to send him millions of dollars. Once someone larger than life, or at least larger than five-foot-six, he now looked too small for his suit.

Then, as his attorney began to cross-examine a key witness for the prosecution, something happened. Suddenly the old Jim Bakker, confident and telegenic, seemed to return. He cocked his head and listened intently. After weeks of legal pounding, here at last was a line of questioning that could actually get him off the hook.

"Do you believe in the Devil?" Bakker's eighty-two-year-old lawyer, George T. Davis, asked the witness on the stand.

"Yes," replied Aimee Cortese, who had served on the PTL board and carried hush money to Jessica Hahn, the church secretary/centerfold whose fifteen-minute blind date with Bakker led to his downfall.

"Do you believe in possession by the Devil?" Davis continued.

"Yes," Cortese said.

"Do you believe that demon possession [influences] the activities of mere men?" Davis inquired. Cortese thought for a second or two, then answered that she did.

"Do you believe [the Devil] can cause men to act in ways they can't explain?"

"Yes, I do."

"No more questions," Davis told the judge.

Jim Bakker turned toward the jury box. Slowly the corners of his mouth curled upward to form the same pleading puppet smile he used to raise money on television. It was a look that said, Help me . . . pay me; only now in the midst of Bakker's potentially career-ending trial on fraud and conspiracy charges, it was also a look that said, The Devil made me do it.

Here was a strategy tailor-made for true believers, a scenario that could only work in the Bible Belt. Maybe Jim Bakker sold God for a living, but his best shot at acquittal was the Prince of Darkness.

All fraud is based on misleading information, telling people things that are not true, first to gain their confidence and then their money. Some crimes rely on brute force; others need cooperation, and by tempting his victims with something they believe or want to believe, an expert at fraud makes them accomplices in their own swindle. According to the government's charges against him, that is exactly what Jim Bakker did.

His Devil defense used a similar technique. The idea was to cloud the facts in the case by appealing to the jurors' fundamentalist religious beliefs. If they bought the theory that Bakker was temporarily possessed and his crimes were directed by Hell, the argument might be made that he had diminished capacity, and therefore could not be held legally responsible for his actions.

Bakker himself continued the same theme when he took the stand in his own defense. Facts can be deceiving, he told the court. "Faith," he said, scanning the jury for friendly faces, "is the supplier of things hoped for, and the evidence of things not seen."

It was an odd admission for someone who worked in a visual medium.

Most religions teach that the kingdom of God is not of this world. Bakker claimed that the Lord told him to build a special version of Heaven on Earth and call it "Heritage USA." Jesus, he said, was the developer. But the financing was all his idea.

• • •

Jim Bakker was different from those broadcast ministers who read from the Bible and preached doom and gloom to their viewers. He did not rant and rave. He entertained. "The PTL Club"—part camp meeting, part talk show—was a friendly video get-together. There were songs, celebrity interviews and sales pitches. Unlike his competitors, Bakker not only pushed prayer books and salvation, he sold cut-rate vacations.

Sealed off from the outside world by a chain-link fence, Heritage USA, America's only divinely ordained theme park, was a planned community where the smallest detail repeated the same cheery message Jim and Tammy Bakker delivered on television. "Jesus Loves You— He Really Does" was the inscription embroidered on bathroom towels at the Heritage Grand Hotel.

Designed by church builder Roe Messner, using blueprints borrowed from Disney World, Heritage USA was a pentecostal Mecca where Bakker's followers could be with others just like themselves, people who had turned on their TV sets and answered the call. Everywhere, from the entrance road that circled past the wooden house where Billy Graham was born, to a swimming pool with piped-in church hymns, visitors were immersed in a full-service Christian ecosystem. There was a daily passion play in which an actor playing Christ was crucified and reborn, hourly prayer meetings and all-day seminars on Godliness, cleanliness and a hundred other related topics.

To PTL pilgrims, the resort was a preview of their final reward, visible proof that their otherwise unappreciated efforts in life could produce something of value. Sending money to Bakker was a contribution to their own salvation. They could watch their gifts add up every time they watched his show, and what's more, as paying PTL partners, they could go to Heritage USA and see the results for themselves.

What Jim and Tammy, who had met at a Minnesota Bible college, gave to their fans besides holiday packages was a chance to participate in a highly personal expression of love—but only vicariously as viewers who supplied funds for the Bakkers' building projects and shopping sprees.

When Tammy announced on the air one day that she was giving

her husband two giraffes for his birthday, the studio audience broke into spontaneous applause. Instead of feeling cheated by the Bakkers' wild spending habits, they were overjoyed. If wasting money made Jim and Tammy happy, their followers never complained, as long as they could watch them waste it.

Are preachers who promise spiritual rewards before they pass the collection plate committing fraud? If they are sincere and use the money for the purposes for which they solicit it, the courts say no. But when Bakker started a scam to sell free lodging for life in the Heritage Grand, he ran afoul of the law.

There may be many mansions in his Father's house, but Jim Bakker's high-rise hotel had limited occupancy, and that's why Heritage USA was a classic pyramid scheme. The number of people who paid $1,000 for hotel rooms was far greater than the number of available rooms. By offering three-day vacations rather than reserved places in heaven, Bakker had crossed the line between hope and deception.

Instead of using the money he collected to build more hotels, Bakker was charged by prosecutors with using most of the $158 million he raised between 1984 and 1987 to pay PTL's daily operating costs. He was also accused of diverting nearly $4 million to his personal use in the form of salary and bonuses as well as homes, luxury cars, plastic surgery and payoffs for Jessica Hahn.

I entered the PTL case in March of 1987, when I received a phone call from the Reverend Jerry Falwell, who was my client in the suit against *Hustler* magazine, then on appeal. I had also successfully defended his organization, the Moral Majority, in another libel case, so he was aware of my expertise in defamation suits. In some religious circles I was known as "Falwell's bulldog," and this time the TV evangelist wanted me to stop a newspaper from printing an exposé of the PTL ministry. The sex scandal that forced Jim and Tammy to give up PTL had not yet been made public, and Falwell, who was to learn later about the sordid details, wanted a peaceful weekend to attend a meeting Bakker had requested to arrange a transfer of power from the Bakkers to him.

At the same time, rival TV preacher Jimmy Swaggart seemed to be plotting an unfriendly takeover of PTL. He had asked Falwell to join him, but Falwell did not want to impair the image of evangelism with the kind of religious war Swaggart appeared to have in mind. If the Bakkers simply left PTL, then under the nominal authority of the Assemblies of God there was a distinct possibility that control of the multimillion-dollar ministry would shift to Swaggart, who, like Bakker, was an influential figure in that fundamentalist church group. At this point Swaggart's own sexual activity with New Orleans prostitutes had not yet made the news. But Falwell, a Baptist, was determined to "rescue" the crumbling PTL on his own and in his own way.

For several weeks he had been in touch with the Bakkers in Palm Springs, California, where Tammy was being treated for drug addiction at the Betty Ford Clinic. The *Charlotte Observer* had learned about Bakker's motel rendezvous with Jessica Hahn and the subsequent payment of church money to keep her quiet. Falwell wanted me to delay any negative press until he could assess the situation.

I offered the paper's editors an exclusive interview with Bakker the following week on the condition they hold up the story on Bakker's sex life. They agreed. With that damage temporarily under control, I met Falwell in Lynchburg, Virginia, and after a prayer before takeoff, we swiftly headed for Palm Springs in his private jet.

On the way, I learned that the PTL empire had been leaderless for months. Jim and Tammy were in hiding, and Richard Dortch, Bakker's somewhat inept secretary of state, was running the show.

While Swaggart was busy spreading stories of Jim Bakker's sexual orgies, other televangelists, eager to get their hands on Bakker's TV network, were also working overtime. When we landed at Palm Springs, Oral Roberts and Swaggart were already there. Falwell spotted their private jets parked side by side at the commuter terminal. Swaggart's Gulfstream had the cryptic inscription "I Will Go" painted on its tail. It was a church yard sale, and a host of media ministers would soon be there making bids for Bakker's prized broadcast facility.

From the outside, the evangelical movement may seem to be one big congregation. Inside it is really a gathering of many factions, some of which are led by preachers who despise one another. There is Falwell, supreme commander of the largest and most powerful Baptist church in America. There are charismatics, like Swaggart, affiliated with the Assemblies of God. And there are the Sunday morning miracle workers, like Oral Roberts, who claim to heal the sick and preach an updated brand of fire worship.

The history of Protestantism is the history of schisms and bitter theological disputes. But in PTL every manner of Christian, as far as Bakker was concerned, could praise—and pay—the Lord. In fact, he tossed Swaggart off his program once for denouncing Catholics. Bakker believed that money is money, no matter where it came from. And the moneymaking potential of PTL was so great that whoever ran it could be America's top preacher. Few contenders, not even Jerry Falwell, could envision the full extent of the organization's economic downside.

By taking over Bakker's ministry, Falwell saw himself as saving the movement by ridding the airwaves of sin. How much sin, though, remained to be seen.

With the possibility of a major religious power shift hovering in the background, we were escorted from the airport to a Palm Springs hotel by members of the PTL security force, a sort of gentile Jewish Defense League with .45 automatics. After a night's sleep and a prayer breakfast, we headed to see the Bakkers.

Jim Bakker greeted us at a prearranged hotel suite. Tammy was shopping. It was part of her outpatient therapy at the Betty Ford Clinic, Bakker said. His wife had become addicted to prescription drugs, and her treatment was in its final stages. Bakker flashed his famous surgically altered smile as everyone exchanged pleasantries. Then the two ministers retired to the bedroom to talk.

Bakker told Falwell about the sins he had committed with Jessica Hahn in a Florida motel, and they prayed. He also told him that without his help the PTL ministry would fold, and they prayed again. When they were finished, Falwell announced that Bakker was resigning and had requested him to assume the leadership of PTL.

Then, I went into the bedroom to work out the details of a public statement for PTL. That was when Bakker told me the X-rated version of his confession to Falwell. "I'm just a simple country preacher," he said. He was the one who was seduced. Everything was Jessica Hahn's fault, and the sex wasn't even that good.

"It was terrible," Bakker said. "Masturbation is better than that."

As we emerged with the paperwork, Tammy arrived in heavy

makeup. Jim Bakker saw her and they both began to cry. Having just given away PTL to his hand-picked successor, Bakker said he was happy that his work would be continued by someone as able and understanding as Jerry Falwell.

But the goodwill was temporary. The story of Bakker's sexual peccadillos came out in the *Charlotte Observer*, and within a matter of weeks he was accusing Falwell of stealing his church. What precipitated Bakker's attack was the discovery by me and Dr. Jerry Nims, Falwell's chief assistant, of horrendous financial misdeeds by Bakker that were later to form the basis for the government's fraud charges against him.

No wonder Bakker wanted his ministry back. However, PTL's problems, to say nothing of Bakker's role in causing them, made his return in any form highly doubtful. It did not take long to discover what the Bakkers had been doing. Millions of dollars in church funds had been diverted to their personal use, much of it going to pay for upkeep on their lavish lifestyle. In his first two months at PTL, Falwell collected some $14 million—a feat he marked by going down the water slide at the Heritage USA swimming pool with his clothes on—but even that amount was not enough to pay off more than a fraction of the ministry's debts.

The government had been watching PTL for years. Even as George Bush was trying to woo Bakker's support during the early days of the 1988 presidential campaign, IRS agents were examining PTL's tax status. By the time Falwell arrived, it was only a matter of weeks at the most before the Justice Department descended.

Falwell had hoped to make good on Bakker's promises and Bakker no doubt had hoped Falwell's political connections would protect PTL from a government probe. Indeed, the Bakkers surrendered PTL with every intention of taking it back once the Jessica Hahn story died down. As far as Jim and Tammy were concerned, Falwell was there on interim status to keep the cash flowing during their forty days in the desert. When their penance was over, they would return. Ironically, the forty days stretched into six months, and by then Jim Bakker was indicted for fraud and PTL was bankrupt.

Bankruptcy is a vehicle designed for the protection of financially troubled individuals and organizations. It permits deferring bills and temporarily escaping creditors' liens. Businesses use the bankruptcy courts all the time as an opportunity to regroup. Why shouldn't the same remedy be available to a church that was more like a family business than a church anyway?

PTL, in fact, employed the whole Bakker clan. Besides Jim and Tammy, there were aunts, uncles and cousins everywhere. Several Bakker relatives also ran a PTL-affiliated "kiddie farm" outside of Charlotte. The state paid them to take care of handicapped foster children, but being Bakkers, there was more to it than that. The kids were also trained as junior fund-raisers and regularly appeared on the PTL show to help bring in donations.

Jim and Tammy's favorite was a boy named Kevin, a severely deformed teenager who rode around in a motorized wheelchair that he operated by pushing the controls with a miniature pool cue held in his mouth. Jim Bakker decided that Kevin needed a home of his own, and brought him on the program to help collect the money to build it. The project, called "Kevin's House," became a priority second only to Heritage USA, and when it was completed, Kevin and Bakker's relatives moved in.

One of the tasks in any bankruptcy proceeding is to sell off certain assets in order to pay the bills. In this case Kevin's House was deemed expendable. On the day we asked for approval of the sale from Judge Rufus Reynolds, Kevin came to court in his wheelchair. (Meanwhile, I had found him another place to live, Heritage USA.) As Kevin pulled up next to me and parked, a hush fell over the courtroom. After a few formalities, Reynolds gave his permission to sell the house, and I turned to look at Kevin, who had been one of PTL's most effective fund-raisers.

"That's life," he said, sounding like someone who knew the party was over, and turned his wheelchair around and departed.

If Jim Bakker had quietly faded out of the picture, he could have lived quite well on the money he and Tammy had already taken from PTL. But he wanted more, and for that he needed the PTL Club. Rather than taking Falwell to court, his first step was to sue me for negligence. My offense, he claimed, was *allowing* him to resign.

Bakker hired international catastrophe specialist Melvin Belli to represent him. That he would put his fate in the hands of someone like Belli was the first indication of how desperate he was, and it didn't take long for the next sign to appear.

Twenty years ago, I helped a woman from Germany get through a problem she was having with the U.S. Immigration Service. We had been out of touch since then, until I received a letter from her shortly after Belli took Jim Bakker's case against me. She thanked me for everything I had done for her and said how much she wanted to help PTL. She enclosed a check made out to me personally for $1,000. The letter bore a California postmark that put its point of origin suspiciously near Belli headquarters in San Francisco.

Was it a trap? The thought did cross my mind. If I had cashed that check, I might have been expelled from the case—and probably disbarred—for accepting money on behalf of a client in bankruptcy. Not only would I have been in serious trouble, my client would have been defenseless. In both cases the advantage would go to Belli and Bakker.

I sent back the check with a nice thank-you note and never heard from the woman again. Not surprisingly, Bakker's suit against me was eventually voluntarily withdrawn, and now I am suing the Bakkers and their lawyers to recover the cost of defending myself in that frivolous action.

Without Jim and Tammy, PTL was just another born-again TV show. People paid their money to see the Bakkers. When they left, the ratings and the revenues would never be the same. In one last-ditch attempt to keep the enterprise breathing, Falwell's advisers brought in investment firms to refinance PTL's debt. Junk-bond genius Mike Milken even contacted Nims and Falwell with a plan to bail out the ministry. If Judge Rufus Reynolds had not thrown a roadblock in the way, PTL could have survived long enough to pay its bills. But Reynolds, a down-home good ol' boy and apparently a fan of Jim Bakker, ended any hopes of that by insisting that PTL's new board of directors have Bakker people on it.

At the time, Jim and Tammy were touring the South, telling reporters they were making a comeback. Putting their allies on the board of directors—James Watt, the beady-eyed former interior secretary, was one likely candidate—would only give them encouragement. The next thing you knew, the Bakkers would be showing up in a Rolls-Royce motorcade.

Falwell said he would not work with a board that contained any Bakker representatives. When the stubborn eighty-year-old judge called Falwell's bluff by sticking to his demand, I advised him to resign, and he did. That put an end to PTL, which will not be missed. At the same time it also denied thousands of duped viewers their only chance to be reimbursed for their lost vacations.

On the closing day of his trial, Jim Bakker sat impassively as he listened to himself called a Bible-thumping charlatan.

"That lie which is half truth is ever the blackest of lies," said the government prosecutor, quoting Alfred Lord Tennyson, to describe Bakker's deceptive fund-raising tactics. "That lie which is all a lie may be met and fought with outright," she continued, "but a lie which is part truth is a harder matter to fight."

Until the end, supporters continued to gather at the courthouse, cheering for Bakker when he arrived in the morning and left at night. Some prayed and a few, sounding like deranged chickens, spoke in tongues. If Dortch and Bakker's other top assistants had turned into government witnesses, part of his flock, at least, was still on its leader's side.

"He built Heritage USA for us," said one follower. "My faith isn't shaken in either Jim Bakker or Jesus Christ."

For a con man, that's the ultimate endorsement. Even after his fraud was exposed, his victims not only believed in him, they associated him with the highest standard of truth they could imagine.

Money and religion go hand in hand. The great cathedrals of the Middle Ages were built with contributions from people who probably believed they were buying their way into heaven. Whether they got their reward is debatable, but the cathedrals are still around. Today, rising out of the bushes like a fundamentalist Machu Picchu, Heritage USA is a vivid reminder to future generations not to believe everything they see on television.

Bakker was convicted of fraud not because of what he believed but because of how he used what others believed to steal from them. "Those of us who do have a religion are sick of being saps for money-grubbing preachers and priests," said Judge Robert Potter, dubbed "Maximum Bob" for his stiff sentences. He lived up to the nickname by giving Bakker forty-five years in jail. Judges often make examples of celebrity offenders, and that appears to be what Potter had in mind. The average sentence given to convicted murderers in the United States is eighteen years. The average time murderers actually spend in jail is eight years. Bakker will not be eligible for parole until 1999.

Of course, when he gets out will be up to his lawyers and an appeals court. The more immediate concern of Judge Potter and the Justice Department was not that Bakker should get what he deserved but that the American public should get the right message.

Jim Bakker's sentence was supposed to say the justice system is working. Is it? Should Bakker be punished more severely than a cold-blooded killer? Is fraud a worse crime than rape? Most people would say no. But murderers and rapists rarely commit their crimes on television. And that's where Bakker made a serious mistake. He flaunted his snake-oil scam in the most public fashion, and by so doing invited federal attention and intervention. In the electronic age, those whom the gods would destroy, they first make TV stars.

Corporations steal more money, organized crime hurts more people, and finally both do more harm to the nation and its welfare than Jim Bakker did. Even so, few Mafia bosses and fewer CEOs ever go to jail to pay for their misdeeds, and if they do, they are generally out in a hurry.

Jim Bakker was denied bail and led from the courthouse in chains not because he was a threat to society but because he was sufficiently powerless to be a perfect commercial for the legal process. Just as Bakker had used crippled children to raise money on his PTL show, he was being used by the judicial system to show what awful fate awaits anyone else who skims money from the Lord to build an air-conditioned doghouse.

Bakker shamelessly bilked thousands of people. However, despite the stiff punishment he received, restitution was not part of his penalty. Bakker's court-imposed fine goes straight to the U.S. Treasury. People who contributed to PTL will have to file suit and then wait in line to be reimbursed from the sale of the ministry's assets. With no Jim Bakker around to jack up the asking price, it's safe to assume that most of his fans will never see their money again.

Aside from all of its other economic implications, the PTL case raised a question about consumer protection that the trial never touched on: Should religious organizations be required to give a money-back guarantee?

The United States Supreme Court apparently favors a warranty for the faithful. The Court let stand a lower court decision that held that a Massachusetts church must return $5 million of the $6.5 million in donations it had received from one of its former members.

The case involved Betsy Dovydenas, an heir to the Dayton Hudson department store fortune. Her family, one of the wealthiest in America, revolutionized retail sales by inventing the shopping mall. When Betsy reached the age of twelve, her father opened a $25,000 checking account for her. By the time she was in her mid-twenties, her net worth was at least $19 million.

"We were Daytons," she once said in an interview. "There always was a sense that we were better, and I desperately wanted to be ordinary."

Like many children who grow up in rich families, she was embarrassed by her parents' wealth. She refused to attend private school, and after she graduated from the University of Minnesota, instead of joining the Junior League, she took up art and moved in with Jonas Dovydenas, a frequently unemployed Lithuanian photographer living in Chicago. Dovydenas, a run-of-the-mill talent, was fascinating to Betsy. They traveled together, discussed politics and religion, and when they got married in 1978 at a Reno, Nevada, wedding chapel, she happily shed her last name.

Two years later, the couple moved to a huge wooded estate in Lenox, Massachusetts, with its own mountain. Betsy busied herself with raising their children, while Jonas puttered around the mansion and drove his new tractor.

At the time, Lenox was also home to The Bible Speaks, a fundamentalist Christian sect that followed the teachings of its pastor, Dr. Carl Stevens. Stevens, a former truck driver from Maine with a limited education, found God and started a church based on a literal interpretation of the Bible. Compared to PTL, his church was like a Trappist monastery. Members lived on a former school campus in what amounted to welfare housing. They worked in menial jobs and contributed most of the money they made to church projects, one of which was smuggling Bibles into communist countries. Whereas PTL combined religion and show business, The Bible Speaks was a throwback to primitive Christianity, where the faithful lived in communes and converted the heathen in foreign lands.

Betsy Dovydenas had always wanted to belong to a church, but not the upper-class kind her family attended. Her grandfather, who she said looked like God, had been a Presbyterian minister with a very large and fashionable congregation in Minneapolis. Invited by her

cleaning lady to visit a Bible Speaks service in 1982, she was immediately attracted to what she saw. People were not just going through
the motions, they actually seemed to care about one another and the
work the church was doing. Here was the sort of ordinary pious life
she had always wanted.

She returned one Sunday with her husband, and when the collection plate passed by, she deposited a check for $600.

Her generosity did not go unnoticed. Stevens may have gotten his
divinity degree through the mail, but he was a very shrewd businessman. He befriended Betsy, as any clergyman would, sensed her religious needs and went about persuading her to join his flock. God, he
said, could use her money to do great things. This impressed Betsy.
So much so, that in December 1984 she made her first seven-figure
gift to The Bible Speaks. Although her husband was vehemently against
it, he acquiesced when she convinced him that God had directed her
to give the money to the church.

Stevens, the father of many children, some of whom served in his
church, was a widower. For several years he had dated a young former
model, Barbara Baum. Barbara and Betsy soon become friends and
Barbara became Stevens' fiancée. Barbara suffered from disabling,
chronic migraine headaches, and Betsy hoped that her $1 million
donation to the church would help cure them. When the headaches
appeared to have improved and Stevens and Barbara were married,
Betsy credited her latest check with miraculous powers. For the first
time in her life she felt good about being rich.

In January 1985, Betsy and Jonas made another contribution to
support a mission ship on which Bible Speaks adherents traveled to
Latin America to help the Miskito Indians. Jonas had gone with them
once to take pictures and thought another gift was a good idea. In
February, Betsy went to see her family in Minnesota. She also paid a
visit to her investment advisers and her attorney to discuss her financial
situation. When she returned to Lenox, she announced that her next
gift to the church would be $5 million.

Her family became very concerned. And when Jonas returned in
the fall from a photographic jaunt to Afghanistan, he decided something drastic had to be done. Betsy's father and sisters, with the help
of Jonas, who saw his own piece of the family's fortune in jeopardy,
tricked her into returning to Minnesota for a party where deprogram-
mers were waiting.

In a rented house in Wayzata in the middle of winter, Betsy was shown movies about Hitler and Jonestown, Mormons and Moonies. She heard lectures on mind control and "Scripture twisting." In the final phase of her treatment, she was sent to an Iowa facility called Unbound for people who have recently left cults.

Slowly Betsy began to change her religious views. She decided to leave the church, rewrite her will and avenge herself on Carl Stevens, who she now believed had duped her. At the urging of her father and Jonas, she wanted her money back, aware that getting it would mean destroying The Bible Speaks. Unlike Bakker, Stevens had spent virtually everything Betsy had given him on the church.

I represented The Bible Speaks in the case, and to me this was a classic First Amendment issue, not a matter of greed and fraud, as the other side claimed. It has been a fundamental principle of American law, embedded in our religious history and in our bill of rights, that courts cannot inquire into a person's spiritual beliefs, although they may be able to question his sincerity. And while the beliefs of Stevens and his followers may not have been the same as the Dayton family's or Betsy's after she was deprogrammed, they certainly passed the sincerity test.

People with college degrees had given up all their worldly belongings to follow Stevens and work for his church. What he offered was not three-day vacations but a form of long-term penance and self-denial similar to what certain orders in the Catholic Church practice. The problem was that Stevens had located his ministry in a part of the country that does not take well to offbeat fundamentalist religious leaders. Some Down-East Jeremiah with a bad toupee was not what most people in Massachusetts pictured when they thought of going to church on Sunday.

Just as there are community standards for sexual morality, there are also community standards for religion. Jim Bakker's lawyers were hoping those standards would work in their client's favor when they put on their Devil defense. In the predominantly Catholic city of Worcester, where the first Bible Speaks trial was held, community standards did not favor Dr. Carl Stevens.

After a few disastrous skirmishes in the hostile state courts, including one where the local judge refused to let me appear unless I took the Massachusetts bar examination, I decided to move the case into a federal bankruptcy court. And there we encountered Judge James

Queenan, a Holy Cross graduate who looked like an aging altar boy. If Betsy Dovydenas had given her money to the Catholic Church, which collects some $30 billion a year, and Stevens had been an Irish archbishop, everything would have seemed perfectly normal. Instead she gave her money to a Protestant evangelist, the sort of person who would have been burned at the stake in Salem, and that made all the difference to Judge Queenan.

Appointing himself the theological arbiter in the case, Queenan attacked Stevens for making statements to Betsy that were not "pursuant to sincerely held religious beliefs." Betsy had been hoodwinked, he said. Stevens had set her up and relentlessly preyed on her longing for spiritual fulfillment. She was a marionette at the end of a number of strings manipulated by Stevens.

In tones reminiscent of the Inquisition, the bankruptcy judge said the trial of Betsy's claims for restitution of her gifts "revealed an astonishing saga of clerical deceit, avarice and subjugation . . . unsurpassed in our jurisprudence in its variations . . ."

Predictably, The Bible Speaks lost on its religious claims and since the money Stevens had to give back was invested in the land and buildings the church occupied, its members were, in effect, ordered to work to repay Betsy her millions. Choosing not to remain in Lenox, virtual slaves of the court and the Dovydenases, almost the entire congregation left town and migrated to Maryland.

Like Moses leading his people out of Egypt, Stevens led his followers in a car caravan down Interstate 95 to the Promised Land outside of Baltimore.

Betsy protested to a reporter not long after Queenan's decision, "I'm no good at protecting myself. I'm shy, and was brought up to be too polite, made to want to please."

If that's true, had she been programmed by Stevens to give him her money? Or had she been reprogrammed by her family to want it back?

Athough the First Circuit Court of Appeals disagreed with Judge Queenan in some respects, it upheld Queenan's ruling that Stevens had taken advantage of Betsy's "susceptibility" and had used "undue influence." By refusing to hear the case, the Supreme Court agreed, and now all the tangible assets of the Bible Speaks church in Lenox belong entirely to Betsy Dovydenas.

In one sense, all religious influence is undue. Under the Constitution the freedom to follow any god is also the freedom to follow false gods, even if that means Jim Bakker and Carl Stevens. The problem is telling them apart, a task made more difficult by the role the courts are now playing.

Is religion a business or a state of mind?

If the latest legal decisions are any indication, that not only depends on how much money is involved but whose money it happens to be. When the rich lose faith, they get a full refund. When the poor get taken, it's buyer beware. Maybe in church the last shall be first, but in court it seems to be just the reverse.

CHAPTER 12

DO-IT-YOURSELF JUSTICE

FBI OUTFOXES KIDDIE KILLER! blared a *New York Post* headline on February 12, 1988. The story that followed described the capture of David James Roberts, who, until his escape from an Indiana prison, had been serving six life terms for rape, arson and five murders, including the brutal killing of two children.

But the FBI could not take all the credit for putting Roberts back behind bars. In fact, it hardly deserved any at all. "America's Most Wanted," television's first audience-participation crime show, ran his mug shot on its premiere broadcast, and within forty-eight hours TV viewers did something FBI agents had failed to accomplish in nearly two years of trying: They found David James Roberts.

At the time of his arrest, Roberts was working at a Staten Island homeless shelter, where residents who recognized his picture called a special 800 number and tipped off the feds.

"Not a bad beginning," boasted producer Michael Linder, who admits getting excited every time his show bags another felon, which happens at the rate of once every sixteen days.

On one wall of Linder's office at Fox Television studios in Washington, where the program originates, hangs a pistol target showing the life-size silhouette of a man with a bullet hole in his heart. On his desk is a sign that reads, "Watch Television. Catch Criminals."

"We started out as just a TV show," said Linder. "Now we're more like a prime-time police station."

Despite the praise it has gotten from law enforcement officials, the message that "America's Most Wanted" delivers is that its fans are better at nabbing crooks than the cops are. During the program's first year on the air, more than 150 crimes were re-enacted, everything from homicides and muggings to the case of a middle-aged aspirin addict responsible for stealing a half-million dollars in change from telephone coin boxes. Of the dozens of suspects featured, an amazing 44 percent were apprehended, more than twice the capture rate for the New York City Police Department during the same period. Television is supposed to promote passivity; in this case it has transformed millions of couch potatoes into a nationwide posse.

"Our viewers feel victimized by crime and by the failure of the court system," said the host, John Walsh, a Florida hotel developer until his son Adam was kidnapped and murdered in 1983. "We give them a chance to do something about it." Here's a show designed as pure revenge, a way for people to get even with the thugs who commit crimes and a warning to the incompetent judges, lazy police and slick lawyers who help them get away with it.

The program's most dramatic capture came in 1989, following the profile of mild-mannered accountant John E. List, a fugitive for eighteen years after he killed his mother, wife and three children in New Jersey in 1971. The problem of giving the audience something to visualize was solved by hiring a forensic sculptor to create a bust of List as he might look today. The likeness was uncanny, and a week after it was shown on the air, List was arrested in Richmond, Virginia. Several of his neighbors had seen the program and called the police. The *New York Times* was so impressed it ran the story on page one.

If "America's Most Wanted" and a half-dozen other shows like it are turning TV fans into video vigilantes, as critics claim, they also confirm something else: that criminals and escaped cons are not only beating the law—they're winning by default.

"There's no clear pattern as to why all these guys are out there," said Linder, sorting through a fresh batch of wanted posters on his desk. "But it's obvious they're too much for the authorities. In a way, I suppose, *we're* the court of last resort."

After considering the alternative, you can see why. Most people may not be familiar with how the criminal courts operate, but they do know enough about crime statistics to realize that the system is not working.

Some states, in a concession to the public's right to know, now televise courtroom proceedings, a step bar associations have resisted for years, and no wonder. If everyone could see what really happens—or more accurately, what does not happen—in court, there would be a mass outcry for reform. Judges would have to spend a full workday on the bench, prosecutors would have to prepare their cases, defense lawyers would have to show up with their clients, prisoners would have to be delivered on time for trials, and those found guilty would have to be punished sufficiently to show that law-abiding citizens were being protected. In other words, the entire legal process would have to be changed to run efficiently and effectively.

That has not happened. Televising court proceedings may have forced some judges and attorneys to clean up their acts. Yet a few courtroom highlights on the six o'clock news hardly present the whole picture. And that, if the legal profession can help it, will never be seen.

What goes on in criminal court—and in deals between lawyers before cases ever get there—is still one of the best-kept secrets in America. The effects are apparent everywhere, from trial dockets clogged with drug cases, to the gradual transformation of police departments into collection agencies for statistics on repeat offenders.

The tendency is to think of the justice system as a utility company. Turn a switch, and the lights go on. Assuming your bills are paid, the power is always there when you need it. The legal process is rarely, if ever, that simple or reliable.

The law, in theory, is a pattern of applied logic. In criminal courts, every day is Judgment Day. Cases are argued and pleas are bargained by lawyers supposedly trained to protect the innocent and punish the guilty. The underlying assumption is that most wrongdoers are reasonable individuals who carefully weigh the personal consequences of their behavior. Crime rates will go down, say some experts, when criminals realize what's in store for them.

In reality, prime offenders are no more deterred by the threat of punishment than they are by the idea of having a prison record on their resume. The most serious lawbreakers start their careers in grade school—like the seven-year-old boy in Ypsilanti, Michigan, who was recently ordered to stand trial on charges of raping a twelve-year-old girl—and only retire when they get too old to keep up with the competition. They are the real experts in the field, and the court system cannot even find most of them, let alone take them out of commission.

One out of every fifty-five adults in this country is under some type of court-ordered supervision, and that represents only a small percentage of all lawbreakers. The rest are out there using their skills, secure in the knowledge they will probably never be caught, and if they are, the odds are good that nothing will happen.

The most common crimes are crimes of opportunity, committed by people taking advantage of an easy target: houses with open windows and unlocked doors, cars with the keys left in the ignition. Anybody who wants to commit robbery, rape or even murder has an unlimited supply of victims to choose from, usually right in his own neighborhood.

In Florida, a new class of felons are role models for their counterparts elsewhere. Using everything from sophisticated communications equipment to police disguises, Miami criminals have honed their craft to a science. The "mob" is no longer the working metaphor for lawbreakers, it's the "cartel." Now even teenage drug gangs in the poorest areas of Harlem and East Los Angeles operate like Fortune 500 businesses, with management teams, accounting divisions and highly motivated sales departments.

Ideas are catching, and the "Rambos" and "Terminators," to say nothing of the Ivan Boeskys, have given rise to a whole new class of high-concept crimes. Criminals have become organization men. It's not hard to see why the courts, tied up in delays, confusion and red tape, are unable to put more than a dent in their population.

Plenty of legal help is available for anyone who wants to file a multimillion-dollar lawsuit. If you simply happen to be the victim of a crime, you are on your own. The reason is simple. If your problem is like most other criminal matters, there's no money in it. The legal business, wherever practiced, is driven by economic incentives, and with the exception of costly drug defenses, crime doesn't pay anyone, except the criminals who get away.

As "America's Most Wanted" so aptly suggests, seeing that justice is done is largely a do-it-yourself project. The criminal justice system is not designed to aid people victimized by crime but for the convenience of its employees and frequent users: judges, district attorneys and, of course, big-time criminal entrepreneurs who occasionally drop by with their defense lawyers.

A story I heard from a salesman I sat next to on a plane flight not long ago shows what the average person is up against. You do not have to be shot or beaten over the head to realize that public safety is a matter of luck. Everyone is a potential target for crime, and when it strikes, the victim soon discovers how blind justice can really be.

The man lived in Pittsburgh, and his house had been burglarized three times in the past five years. Each time the thief took the same things: cameras and clothes. On the last break-in, he jimmied open the back door and made off with his usual haul, plus a brand-new pair of sneakers.

After the first two robberies, policemen dusted for fingerprints and a detective took down a description of the stolen property. It was all very routine. And like thousands of similar crimes committed every day, nothing was recovered and no one was ever arrested.

Following the third robbery, the man decided if the police were not going to do anything, he was. He canvassed his neighborhood asking people if they had noticed any suspicious activity around his house on the day of the crime. After a few hours, his private investigation turned up two boys who had seen someone cutting grass that day.

"It was Joe Jackson," one boy said.

"Joe Jackson?" the man asked. "Does he live around here?"

"Yeah," the other boy replied. "Right down the street."

The man called the detective working on the case and told him that someone named Joe Jackson might have been involved. To his surprise, the detective informed him that Jackson had a long arrest record, and that burglarizing houses was his specialty. He would roam through neighborhoods knocking on doors, asking people if they wanted their grass cut. If a house was empty, he would break in, fill up a green plastic bag with whatever he wanted and casually walk away, pushing his lawn mower and carrying what looked like a big bag full of grass.

"That's probably what he did to me," the salesman said. "You should arrest him."

"Can't do that," said the detective. "We need a witness or you need to see him with something he took from you."

The man was furious, but more determined than ever. Whenever he had any spare time, he sat in his car outside of Joe Jackson's house. Days passed without any luck. Then he had an idea. If Jackson had stolen a brand-new pair of sneakers, it made sense that he would be wearing them.

Thinking more like a detective than the detective assigned to the case, he drove to the nearest playground. Sure enough, there were his sneakers running up and down the basketball court.

Here was all the evidence he needed. Jackson was arrested, indicted and, after several delays by his attorneys, pleaded guilty to a burglary charge.

The man felt justifiably proud that he had helped take a thief off the streets. The feeling ended fast. The next week, he heard the ominous sound of grass being cut next door, and he glanced out his window to see Joe Jackson pushing a lawn mower.

"I'm really sorry about that," said the detective. "A judge let him out of jail because of overcrowding."

The man could hardly believe it. The police had done virtually nothing to find the person who robbed him, and the court system had done even less to keep him out of circulation.

A few months later, there was a knock on the man's door.

It was a cop holding a baggie with something inside.

"Is this yours?" he inquired.

"Is *what* mine?" the man wanted to know. And with that the policeman pulled one of his stolen sneakers out of the bag.

The man shook his head in despair.

"You're a lawyer," he said to me. "Can you please explain what the hell's going on?"

Telling him he should put bars on his windows and doors sounded like shirking my professional responsibility. Yet that was the only good advice I could think of.

"I guess times have changed," he said. And I had to agree.

A courthouse used to be the hub of civic activity, the central point of reference in small towns and big cities. Courts were once seen as temples of justice, symbolizing the dominance of order over chaos and corruption. Today, with few exceptions, they are more like solid-waste treatment centers, where victims, defendants, witnesses and jurors are pumped in one end and out the other in a cycle repeated day after day, with no discernible improvement in the process or the by-product. Meanwhile, the lawyers and judges who are supposed to make the system function are either too exhausted or else too inept to do the job.

There is a criminal courthouse in the Kew Gardens section of Long Island that resembles courts in many large metropolitan areas. It's noisy, dirty and by eight-thirty every weekday morning crowded with patrons: people accused of crimes, people who saw crimes committed and people who have had crimes committed against them. In the lobby there is a larger-than-life mosaic mural that depicts the seven deadly sins, each one—avarice, envy and the rest—personified by a human figure acting out a particular evil. I have never seen a courthouse anywhere in the country that so vividly displays the reason courts exist in the first place.

But just as people have learned to live with the seven deadly sins, the courts now seem to treat wrongdoing as a necessary evil. If there are too many criminals on the loose it's because too often courts simply set them free. As a result, communities in cities all over America have become like extensions of jail, where good people live in fear and bad people get away with murder.

And even when the system appears to be working, it may be only a mirage. During a lengthy civil suit I was trying recently in Miami, the proceedings were broken up regularly while the judge and prosecutor disposed of criminal pleadings and sentencings. One day during such an interlude, as I sorted through my files, a case caught my attention.

The defendant, dressed in a pair of orange prison coveralls, was a small, thin Cuban man in his thirties. I could not see his face, but I could hear his story as he spoke through an interpreter. He had been in jail for five years, part of a fifteen-year sentence for failing to co-operate with local authorities in a drug investigation. He was in court without a lawyer, desperately trying to get his sentence reduced.

The man, on a single misguided occasion, had been a "mule," someone who carries drugs from one neighborhood to another. He did it as a last resort to support his family, he said. In Miami, he told the judge, he couldn't make a living any other way.

He had been arrested with a kilo of cocaine, and the prosecutor made a deal with him. If he cooperated with investigators, he would get off easy. The man signed a confession, giving up any right to a trial. However, when it came time to cooperate, he wished he had not agreed. He had told them about his own crimes, but the police wanted him to name more names, and when he refused he was ordered to spend a mandatory fifteen years in jail.

"I didn't know I would have to do this," he said.

If he informed, his family would be killed and he would be murdered in jail. In all likelihood, if he had been tried and convicted, he would be a free man by now. But since he had decided not to talk, he was still being punished. Keeping him locked up stopped making sense a long time ago.

Miami is the narcotics capital of America, and while far bigger criminals were plying their trade with relative ease, the prosecutor was determined to make the Cuban man pay for backing out of his deal. He had broken his word with the law, and now the law would break him.

"I am not a criminal," he pleaded. "I am a victim of the circumstances of life."

The judge and prosecutor talked to one another as if the man were invisible, and for all practical purposes he was. His case was like a hundred others that pass through the courts every day: cases where the victim loses, cases where the defendant loses, and cases that blend into one another until any distinction between victims and defendants completely disappears.

The basic issue here was not whether the man had committed a crime, but whether he had understood the implications of his bargain with the court.

No less than the salesman from Pittsburgh whose house was robbed, what happened to the man in Miami shows what is wrong with the criminal justice system and the plea bargaining process at the heart of it.

The same way most civil suits are settled out of court, most criminal charges are plea-bargained without ever going to trial. Cases are negotiated, often in bulk, not to achieve the fairest but the fastest results. And if sentences, whether they are too harsh or too lenient, do not suit the offense, too bad.

I remember a criminal defense lawyer in Detroit who was so eager to get rid of a client that he advocated a guilty plea for first-degree murder. The attorney was running for political office and did not want the case to become a campaign issue, so when the prosecutor refused to bargain, he simply waived a trial and told his client to plead guilty to murder one.

I watched as the Miami man was led to the courthouse holding cell. It was clear he would still be in jail at the turn of the century.

Was this a prudent use of prison space?

The man needed a shrewd lawyer not because he was being wrongly punished, although he was, but because without an attorney he was not equipped to play the legal game his situation required.

And a game is precisely what criminal law has become. The man's plight reminded me of a client I represented in Arizona in the early 1980s. His name was Ned Warren, and he was probably one of the most notorious real estate barons in the West.

Warren had been arrested in a highly publicized crackdown on land fraud. He was offered a deal by both state and federal prosecutors. In exchange for information on criminals and mobsters working in Arizona, he would get off with a suspended sentence. But when he could not supply the answers prosecutors were looking for, including information about who killed a reporter, they claimed he had breached a contract. A judge gave him six consecutive life sentences, totaling sixty years in jail.

Warren, who was in his sixties at the time, was sent to a nineteenth-century penitentiary in the middle of the desert. In effect the state had decided to torture him to death. Warren had a heart condition, and the state prison he was sent to had no means of caring for him.

I made a motion to have him moved to a federal facility in Missouri where he could receive proper medical attention, and a federal judge approved. Shortly after Warren's transfer, however, Arizona authorities took steps to redetain him in a game of legal Ping-Pong. Attorneys for Arizona convinced the Ninth Circuit Court that Warren had reneged on his plea bargain deal, and he was sent back to the state prison.

After Warren had spent two years seeking relief in Arizona courts, a sympathetic federal judge, Walter Craig, finally got to hear another plea to have him moved to Missouri. On the day of the hearing, Warren came to court handcuffed to a wheelchair. He was obviously in failing health, but prosecutors still demanded that he remain in Arizona. The judge said he would resolve the issue once and for all within a week. The following morning Warren died of lung cancer. The next day I received the court order that would have freed him.

What happened was a shame, the judge told me in a letter. Warren, he wrote, because of his notoriety, had been the victim of ambitious prosecutors.

Whenever I take a case like Ned Warren's, friends sometimes ask why I'm not representing the good guys. And I tell them any time a government, with all of its power and resources, takes unfair advantage of one of my clients, I *am* representing the good guys. Of course, not all attorneys would see it that way, but then, not many have seen what I have.

Moralists look at the world in terms of good and bad. Judges and attorneys look at it in terms of good and bad explanations: why one person should go to jail and another should not; why one should collect a multimillion-dollar damage award and another should have to pay. To the legal mind, all clients and all points of view are interchangeable; lawyers build cases by stirring up opinions and doubts, then rearranging them in whatever pattern serves their purpose. If that makes the world safe for corporate takeovers or just a more congenial place for small-time wheelers and dealers, that is what lawyers are paid to do.

And just because you hire one, no matter how compelling your case is, does not mean you will get your money's worth, much less any guarantee that he's even on your side.

A New York attorney I know has a reputation for handling dozens of cases at a time. He arrived in court early one morning to represent a hit-and-run victim, and as he unpacked his briefcase, he noticed he was not alone. A man he took to be opposing counsel was sitting in front of the bench reading a paper. The lawyer thought he looked familiar but could not remember his name.

"Excuse me, but haven't we met?" he said.

"We sure have," the man replied. "I'm your client."

INDEX

Brennan, William, 46
bribery:
   buying testimony vs., 89
   of paramedics, 53
   of police, 53, 57
Brilmayer, Lea, 34
Bruce, Lenny, 48
build-ups, 23
Burger, Warren, 34, 35
burglary, 127–28, 208
Burt, Dan, 107
Bush, George, 194

Cadwalader, John Lambert, 69–70, 74
Cadwalader, Wickersham & Taft, 69–70
Caligula, 130, 139
Capasso, Carl, 116
capitalism, 61, 81
car crashes, 57
Cardone, Daniel, 56–57
Carey, Hugh, 29, 74, 81
Carson, Johnny, 104
Carswell, G. Harrold, 134
cartels, 207
Carter, Jimmy, 39
cases:
   analyzing risk in, 106–7
   civil, *see* civil cases
   "crowd," 92–93
   delaying of, 49, 52, 104, 110
   judges assigned to, 143–44
   little details in, 85–86
   money supplied by, 71
   preparations of, 51, 100, 206
   profit and principle in, 65
   settlement of, 19, 22–23, 110–11, 165, 211
   see also trials
Catch-22 (Heller), 158–59
CBS, 37
Cement Renegotiation Commission, 96
Central Index Bureau, 161
Central Intelligence Agency (CIA), 100
Cernadas, Alfredo, 173
challenges, in jury selection, 123
Chambers, Whittaker, 106
Charlotte Observer, 192, 194
chemical pollution, 58
Chesley, Stanley, 92–93
child custody, 171
Chowder and Marching Society, 121
CIA (Central Intelligence Agency), 100

civil cases:
   delays in, 110
   evidence shared in, 91
   expert witnesses in, 128–31
   settlement of, 211
   typical pattern of, 77–78
Claiborne, Harry, 133
claims adjusters, 159–61
clients:
   accepting of, 28, 58
   corporate, 70
   as creatures of habit, 72
   determination of, 110–11
   as hostages, 30
   hunt for, 77
   imagined complaints of, 66
   lawyers' bond to, 53, 64, 137, 167
   as lawyers' enemies, 71
   money supplied by, 71
   payment denied by, 64–65
   seduction of, 174
   toughening of, 51
   trial as ordeal for, 100, 112
   as witnesses, 113
Cohn, Roy, 181, 183–84, 186
Coke, Sir Edward, 20
Collins, Jackie, 38
con artists, 25, 197
concurrent cause, 132
Con Edison, 45
conflicts of interest, 115, 123
Congress, U.S., 31, 34, 74, 172
Connally, John, 99
Constitution, U.S., 41, 47, 202–3
construction cave-ins, 57
contingency-fee system, 58
continuances, 110
continuing cause, 132
contributory negligence, 160
Cooley, Denton, 111
corporations:
   as clients, 70
   detectives hired by, 90–91
Cortese, Aimee, 188–89
Costello, Frank, 99
courtrooms, 45
   seating in, 167
   as temples, 46, 209
   as theater, 98–101, 112–16
courts, 57
   access to, 157
   bargaining with, 210–11

human nature:
  blind faith in, 132
  unpredictability of, 21
Hurt, William, 178–79
Hustler, 34–35, 39–50, 191
Hutton, Joan, 165–69
Hylan, John F., 49

IBM, 117, 123
Icahn, Carl, 60, 61, 62
Immigration Service, U.S., 196
injury and accident victims, 18–25
  faking by, 24–25, 51–52
  insurance companies bilked by, 22–
    25, 51
  insurance companies' blaming of,
    157
insurance commissions, 157–58
insurance companies, 75, 155–70
  bilking of, 22–25, 51
  government and, 157, 169
  individuals vs., 157
  investments of, 157
  lawyers for, 161–62
  "life spans" assigned by, 156
  ploys used by, 159–61
  rates charged by, 158
  victims blamed by, 157
investigative lawyers, 90–91
IRS (Internal Revenue Service), 64, 92,
  175, 194
Isaacman, Alan, 43, 45–46

Jackson, Joe, 208–9
Janoff, Bob, 21, 85, 87
Japan, number of lawyers in, 68
Jennings, Sandra, 178–79
Jews, Orthodox, 56
Johnson, Lyndon, 99
Johnson, Pete, 126–27
judges, 133–54, 206, 208, 213
  appointing of, 135
  cases assigned to, 143–44
  connections of, 144
  as law, 133
  misconduct by, 133, 144–53
  as politicians, 134–35
  power of, 136
  questions asked by, 50
  verdicts reversed by, 132, 153
Judicial Code of Ethics, 134
juries, 44, 117–32
  convincing of, 54–57, 115, 126

entertaining of, 118
excuse from, 120
grand, 121
hardships endured by, 119–20
intelligence of, 117–18, 122
lawyers' physical appearance and, 43
lawyers trusted by, 43, 54–57, 126–
  127
personality of, 125
researching of, 125
selection of 120, 121–26
sleeping by, 118–19
social status of, 124–25
susceptibility of, 55
trust of, 131–32
women on, 124
justice:
  do-it-yourself, 52, 207–9
  for sale, 134
Justice Department, U.S., 194, 198

Kassewitz, Jack, 84–84
Katz, Herb, 55
Katz, Manny, 54–55
Keeton, Kathy, 34–35
Kefauver, Estes, 142
Kennedy, John F., 89
Kevin's House, 195
King Lear, (Shakespeare), 184–85
Kissinger, Henry, 101–4
Koppel, Ted, 109
Kraft Foods, 79
Krassner, Paul, 39
Kreisell & Powell, 19, 28
Kumble, Steven, 71–76
  financial dealings of, 75
Kunstler, William, 186

La Costa Country Club, 141–49
  Penthouse story on, 136–37, 141–54
Lake, James, 76
Lansky, Meyer, 148
Lanza, Isobel, 138
law:
  appearance vs. reality in, 135
  as applied logic, 206
  belief in, 52
  as capital-intensive, 81
  civilization as product of, 20
  economics of, 50, 52–53
  examples set in, 198
  foundation of, 49
  intellectual income provided by, 76